Discipled by **Jesus**

HAL AND DEBBI
PERKINS

outskirtspress
DENVER, COLORADO

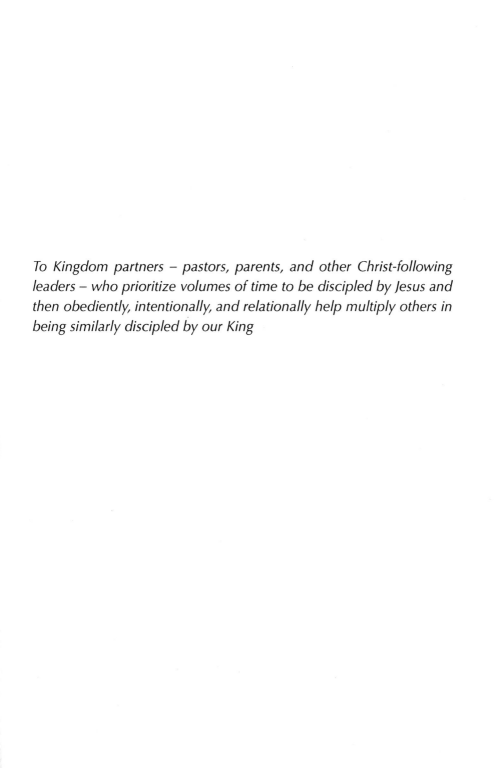

To Kingdom partners – pastors, parents, and other Christ-following leaders – who prioritize volumes of time to be discipled by Jesus and then obediently, intentionally, and relationally help multiply others in being similarly discipled by our King

Contents

Acknowledgments

In grateful honor and thankfulness to Ruth Todd for learning, loving, and living the contents of this writing. Her years of voluntarily and sacrificially serving her King to multiply the book's message will impact eternity significantly.

Barry and Darlene Franks, your partnership in being and making disciples, plus your invitation to live in your home for the eight weeks of this writing, are gratefully acknowledged.

All the pastors who have entrusted your congregations to us with our message and discipling processes are sincerely thanked.

Debbi, once again, this book would never have been written without your strong encouragement. Further, it would have been as colorless as a math text without your repeatedly persuading me to "add the stories, put in Little king Will, this is too complicated," etc. Thank you for your heart partnership and many helpful hours of wrestling through the editing process.

Commendation

"I simply will never be the same again…I've met Jesus! A real Person who loves me, cares for me and desires relationship with me. I can hear from Him and respond to Him as I would a beloved father, only closer still. I've been equipped to daily meet with Jesus on my own and with others. All this I have learned sitting around a table utilizing the teachings of Pastor Hal Perkins, which are clearly presented in this book. Truly life changing!"

Tanya Weron, M.A.

Have you ever heard a Christian say, "I've never been discipled!" Hal Perkins clearly demonstrates why and how this need not be the case in his new work, "Discipled By Jesus."

In his warm and personal style, Hal powerfully portrays how every follower of Jesus can be discipled, coached and mentored by Jesus' Spirit, His Word and His Body. Solid Biblical foundations are carefully laid and thoroughly explored in this inspirational work that profoundly addresses the deepest longings of the authentic Christ follower. Oh, to be like Him in our daily lives. Hal's personal life and walk with Jesus spills out of his writings and helps us grow in understanding how God is at work in us. This work provides us a powerful model of what it looks and feels like to commune with the Master in the intimacy the Father has with the Son and the Son with God's dearly loved children. This book is a blessing and a significant extension of Hal Perkins' ministry through the printed page. You will not be disappointed.

Dr. Woodie Stevens
General Director Sunday School
and Discipleship Ministries International
Church of the Nazarene

Introduction

An awakening is happening. Coming out of hibernation is an army, the army of Christ. Perhaps the most significant component of this army is multitudes of newer, younger soldiers. In unprecedented ways, tens of thousands of them gather for days at a time for nothing but praise, preaching, and prayer ... and fasting.

Almost every new generation of Christ-followers has its idealists. They desire to rise above the real and perceived mediocrity, apathy, and dumbing down of the discipleship of previous generations. Their challenge: they are not yet battle-tested.

Included in this awakening are many battle-tested Kingdom soldiers. They are too noble to compromise, and too loyal to abandon the battle or the army or even their particular tribe. Like the young, they still want to grow in being authentic disciples of Jesus. They passionately long to win the battle for the heart of every infinitely valuable person on the planet. But they have learned this lesson: to reach the multitudes – quantity – requires godly, holy soldiers and leaders of soldiers – quality.

The question is this: will the battle-tested, battle-weary older but uncompromising fathers have the grace, the wisdom and the skill to adopt and disciple these young warrior-zealots? Or will the young, without the coaching that Jesus' commanded for His future generals,[1] have to yet again wage this holy war as "undiscipled disciples" against a cunning enemy in an increasingly depraved culture? Without the kind of discipling Jesus provided for Peter, James, and John, the new generation, like previous generations, will see most of their comrades drift into the hated nominality, or worse, give up in despair. There exists a zealous cry in the hearts of many: Undiscipled disciples no more!

But how? How do we better make disciples to make better disciples? Does something need to be changed in our discipling processes? If so, what?

We preach, we teach, we go through curriculums, and that is good. Yet our "disciples" struggle as "doers of the Word" to "obey everything Jesus commanded."[2] They are often confused about what it looks like to "seek FIRST His Kingdom."[3] They struggle even more to articulate their relationship with Jesus and His Kingdom essentials.[4] Precious few have been sufficiently discipled that they intentionally adopt others to disciple until their disciples are also obeying everything Jesus taught, which includes making disciples of Jesus.[5] Many struggle with the first commandment, having whole-hearted passion for Jesus. Why?

Could it be that discipling must be much more about listening than we have understood? To be sure, our message must be accurately proclaimed. But how do we find out if our disciples have the message and are living it out? We can "tell" tens of thousands at a time; and we must. But we can only listen to one at a time. Jesus could teach thousands at a time, but He chose twelve "to be with Him."[6] By creating

---

1   Matthew 28:20
2   Matthew 28:20
3   Matthew 6:33
4   1 Peter 3:15
5   Matthew 28:20
6   Mark 3:14

a very small and tight-knit group, Jesus was able to accomplish many "relational tasks," including listening to His disciples' answers to His searching questions. Then came dialogue which led to understanding, conviction, and action.

In general, we have not _listened_ to find out if our disciples understood or could articulate the Truth, nor have we _listened_ to their Word and Spirit-guided plan to implement the Truth, nor have we _listened_ to their reports of how they implemented God's Truth.

Of greater concern, we have not _listened_ to their conversations with Jesus, thus failing to coach them in how to _listen_ to Him, their ever-present Discipler.

But who _listened_ to us? And who coached us to _listen_ to Jesus so He could disciple us?

DISCIPLING STRATEGY

Over 35 years ago I discovered that one of Jesus' significant discipling strategies was to ask questions. Chapters 7-16, the "how to" of this book, are based on questions Jesus asked His disciples and questions He might ask us.

"When Jesus looked up and saw a great crowd coming toward him, He said to Philip, 'Where shall we buy bread for these people to eat?' _He asked this only to test him,_ for He already had in mind what He was going to do."[7]

Imagine a little band of Jesus' contemporary disciples gathered to answer His questions. The focus of study and discussion is Jesus Himself. The questions are those Jesus might ask, and the questions are all about Jesus. The questions probe and test the group members' awareness of who Jesus is, what He is currently doing, what He is

---

7   John 6:5-6

thinking and saying, what He wants in the immediate future, and what He will do to empower what He wants.

1. The nature of Jesus: Do You Know Who I am?[8]

2. The activity of Jesus: Do you understand what I have done this week?[9]

3. The mind of Jesus: Are you listening to Me?[10]

4. The desires of Jesus: Do you truly love Me?[11]

5. The power of Jesus: Do you believe Me?[12]

UNIQUENESS

The uniqueness of this book is its focus on Jesus' real presence to disciple us by His Spirit – the Holy Spirit.

Christians rightly believe they are indwelled by God's Holy Spirit. Far too many assume the Holy Spirit works mostly independent of their conscious participation with Him. They believe that He unilaterally and independently empowers whatever He determines to do. And, of course, He is doing precisely what His perfect love and infinite wisdom know to be the highest good for the most. But how?

A less recognized provision for the release of the Holy Spirit's tangible power is tied to His voice, what He is saying. In the matters of salvation, holiness, right relationships – all arenas of eternal significance – much, maybe most, of what the Holy Spirit does is _speak_.[13] It is in

---

8   From Matthew 16:15
9   From John 13:12
10   From Matthew 17:5
11   From John 21:15
12   From John 11:26
13   John 14:15-18, 25-26, 15:26, 16:7-15

our listening, the recognizing and responding to what He says, that His visible, tangible power is released. When Christians listen to His voice, believe, and obey, then His power is "materialized." The Word actually becomes flesh, again. When Christians hear His invitation to exit their boat and walk on water, then through their obedient faith He empowers what otherwise would not be.

But when Christians do not recognize His voice, He is greatly grieved and His intended process to act in power through Christ's Body is greatly quenched.

Thus, this book dares to carefully encourage and coach the recognizing of the voice of the Holy Spirit. This includes believing that He, the Holy Spirit, will speak directly to the mind of authentic Christ-followers. The Spirit also speaks directly through the Word of God when the Scripture is not ignored or embellished. Further, Jesus, by His Spirit, fully intends to speak today through His Body.

The faith assumption is that what Jesus said about the Holy Spirit is true,[14] and that under careful coaching, we can all learn to better walk and speak by the Spirit instead of being governed by our flesh.[15] Thus, we can increasingly approximate walking as Jesus did,[16] talking as Jesus talked,[17] being holy as Jesus was holy,[18] and doing what Jesus did.[19] In short, we can and must be better discipled to better be the actual Body of Christ.

The book is divided into two sections. Chapters 1-6 focus on why we desperately need to move from being discipled by forces other than Jesus to being discipled by Him. Chapters 7 -16 describe and model strategies for being discipled by Jesus, drawn primarily from how Jesus Himself discipled His twelve.

---

14   John 16:7
15   Romans 8:1-14, Galatians 5:16-25
16   1 John 2:6
17   Colossians 3:16-17
18   1 Peter 1:15
19   John 14:12

How helpful it would be if I could capture in print what Debbi and I have observed morning after morning … night after night … all over our country. Little bands of "hungry-for-God" Christ-followers gather. They love learning to listen to their Lord speak through His written Word. They delight in learning to listen for and to the Holy Spirit, Who is often recognized as He speaks through His Word and even through Christ's Body. They are consciously determined to improve in recognizing and responding to His voice, as He speaks into their minds directly, and through the Scriptures, and even through each other, for they are the Body of Christ. In humility they tentatively share what they think Holy Spirit may be speaking to them. The group, equally humble and tentative, confirms or questions what has been shared.

It is normal for many to realize that they have just been encountered by the presence of their Living Lord. They recognize His voice. Jesus is present, coaching and discipling them.

Just as Jesus discipled Peter, James, and John long ago, He can disciple us, His 21st century disciples. His Spirit, His Word and His Body are present to reveal Him, and to coach us. To be sure, the means are different, but potentially and provisionally, just as authentic.

This writing attempts to catch the spirit, and "the Spirit," behind this "being discipled by Jesus now." If in fact we can be discipled by Jesus' Spirit, Word, and Body through a relatively simple process, we can then facilitate others being similarly discipled. If we then coach them in facilitating others, we can in fact make disciples who are increasingly Christlike, including that they make disciples who are increasingly Christlike, who also make disciples … and the multiplication of Christlike disciplemakers goes on. The authentic Christlikeness of these "little Christs" observably and exponentially impacts their worlds as He intended.

Section A:
Jesus' Intention and Invitation
to Personally Disciple His Followers

CHAPTER 1

Jesus Disciples Little King Will in Coming to Him

Jesus, the Word of God who became flesh,[20] desires and intends to disciple His 21st century followers every bit as much as He discipled Peter, James, and John thousands of years ago. To validate this truth biblically, and how Jesus intends to disciple His followers today, is the focus of this book.

To set the stage for understanding how Jesus intends to disciple His 21st century followers, we start with a parable.

A PARABLE

Think with me about the legend of Camelot with King Arthur and his knights of the round table. Picture the pomp and dignity as each member enters and places his sword at precisely the right position on the round table. Every member of the round table gave input to King Arthur about governing the kingdom, but once a decision was agreed to, it was King Arthur's responsibility as king to assign responsibility for implementing decisions to his knights, and to hold each accountable for implementation of their responsibilities.

What follows will surprise some Christ-followers. There is a "kingdom" in your heart, and a component, a "little king," that functions like

---

20   John 1:14

King Arthur did. Above all else, this component or "little king" is to guard your heart.[21]

The component? Your will. Let me name your will "Little king Will." You may invite King Jesus to come into your life, to capture your heart, and to govern and rule and reign. He will graciously serve and help you, even in ways totally unknown to you. But He will very, very seldom overpower and control your will, even though you ask Him to control you. King Jesus will not take away your will. You, through the set of your will to cooperate with the indwelling King Jesus, are responsible to see that His grace and truth are received and implemented. The indwelling Christ desires to strengthen your heart and transform your life, but usually does this with your willful, intentional, relational participation.

Imagine with me a crisis conversation that occurred in your heart one day involving all your internal heart-advisors, including your will.

Little king Will: "Welcome, my friends and advisors. It is time to start the meeting in our heart to determine the government of our little kingdom, our life. I am sure you have much to bring to the table for our consideration and determination. You all look a bit sheepish tonight, even apprehensive. What is up?"

Advisor 1: "Little king Will, we actually had a conversation in preparation for our meeting with you. We are very, very concerned about the condition of our life."

Little king Will: "You had a meeting without me? That could be seen as treasonous!"

Advisor 2: "We beg your forgiveness. We were actually just hanging out together one day and openly discussed that our life has gone from bad to worse, and that something was desperately wrong."

---

21   Proverb 4:23

Advisor 3: "We were not trying to cause trouble, little king. We were honestly trying to fulfill our task of wisely advising you in governing the kingdom of our life."

Advisor 1: "We truly honor you, little king Will. And we do not want to hurt you. We have considered all of our options. Of all of our options, it seems that that the very best thing for us to have our life be saved is to actually change kings." (Advisor 1 was prepared for little king Will to fly off the handle in rage. Instead of responding in anger, little king Will's head dropped and his eyes stared down at the table.)

Little king Will: "You are so right. I have tried not to admit it, but our life IS a mess, and I am ultimately responsible. I must be doing a terrible job of helping us come to the right decisions, or of enforcing the decisions we make. So, I need your advice. In your conversation without me, did you come up with any ideas that would solve the problems I am having in governing our life?"

Advisor 3: "Oh, yes, little king. We have heard that there is another King who is very strong."

Advisor 2: "And He is smart. We heard that He knows absolutely everything!"

Advisor 1: "Yes, and you are not going to believe this, king Will, but we have heard that this King is, at the very core of His being, absolutely good. He is not self-serving or cruel. He truly cares about all in His Kingdom. He is gentle, kind, even humble."

Little king Will laughed right out loud, right in the face of his advisors.

Little king Will: "You've got to be kidding. A king who is all powerful, and knows everything, who can do anything he wants, and is not self-serving? Humble and gentle? There's never been a king like that and there never will be. I think you, my trusted advisors, have been totally duped."

Advisor 1: "All we know is that everyone who has ever actually invited this King into their heart, and truly honored Him as their King, tells that He has saved their lives by changing their hearts."

Little king Will: "Really? Who is this king? What is his name?"

All of little king Will's advisors: "King Jesus!"

Little king Will: "Oh, I've heard of Him. Well, we've got nothing to lose. Our life is a mess. What do we need to do?"

Advisor 2: "We've heard that we must invite Him to enter our heart, and to let Him sit at our table, and help us run our life."

So, little king Will decided to talk with King Jesus about inviting Jesus into his heart as his new King.

Little king Will: "King Jesus, I have heard that You will come into my heart and that You can save my life. Is that true?"

King Jesus: "Yes, I can and I will, if you trust Me."

Little king Will: "Wow! That sure gives me hope because I have made an absolute mess of my life."

King Jesus: "I know."

Little king Will: "You know?"

King Jesus: "Oh, yes. I have been right here all the time. I've been watching you, and so wanting to help. In fact, I have been talking to you, but you were so caught up in being the little king of your own life that you paid no attention to Me."

Little king Will: "Really? You were there all along to help me?"

King Jesus: "Oh, yes. But you kept deciding to do everything your own way."

Little king Will: "And was that ever a boatload of bad decisions. Well, I have decided that I don't want to be king anymore. I actually hate being king. It is not at all what it is cracked up to be. Whoever is king is responsible, and when things don't go well, everyone blames the king. And things haven't gone well, and I am sick of being king. So, since You are a King, I have made a decision. I am going to take off my king hat – my crown – and give it to You, King Jesus. Here, You have it. I don't want to be king anymore. I want to make You King. Here, I give You my crown!"

Little king Will stood from the table, walked over to where King Jesus was sitting, handed Him the crown, and bowed before King Jesus.

King Jesus waited a moment, then put His finger under little king Will's chin, and lifted his chin until the two were making eye contact. King Jesus warmly smiled at little king Will, and then He winked, and spoke.

King Jesus: "Oh, little king Will. You don't know Me very well yet. I appreciate your intentions, but I do not need your little crown to make me King. I have My own crown. I have always been King. I am now the King of all the little kings, whether they recognize it or not. I always will be King of kings. One day, every knee will recognize Me as their King and bow before Me. But I don't force people to enter My Kingdom or – at this time – force them to submit to My government. I rule primarily by love and truth … for now."

Little king Will: "Really? A King with all power who rules primarily by love and with truth?"

King Jesus: "Yes. I have complete power to do anything I want. But the reason I made you is for real relationship, a mutually caring relationship that matures and partners by truth. Caring relationships do not force or coerce or dominate or intimidate. Please know that I care for you like you have never experienced from anyone. I really do. In fact, I care so much that I gave My life to save you from every sort of evil, now and eternally. I will save you through your having enough faith in Me to listen to Me, and to follow what I say. This will be a complete change of mind about who governs your life; it is called repentance.[22] You will have repented, little king Will, when you have changed your mind from doing your will and you set your will to do My Will. If you know Me well enough to put your faith in Me, You are able to make Me King of your life, and commit to doing My will. Is this what you had in mind when you offered me your crown?"

Little king Will: "I think so. And I can commit to this because I have faith that You really do care about me and know what is best for me."

King Jesus: "Perfect. You have figured out what many miss: faith in Me inevitably leads to committing to doing whatever I call you to do.

"But realize this, little king Will. I made you in My image. I made you a person, for an authentic personal relationship with Me. I made you with a heart much like Mine, including a will. This requires that I not take your freedom or your will-power from you. That's why I refuse to take your crown from you. I made you with the ability, the freedom, thus the responsibility to relate to Me and partner with Me."

Little king Will: "Partner with You?"

---

22   The change of mind needed to become a Christian: repentance

King Jesus: "Yes. I intend that someday you reign and rule with Me.[23] I create galaxies easily. I have the power to do anything My love and wisdom deem best. For all those reasons and more, I refuse to take your crown from you. I refuse to turn you into a robot. Here is your crown. Put it back on. I have sovereignly determined that you have no choice ... but to make choices. And if you truly want Me to save you, you must partner with Me in choosing, over and over and over, to find out and do what I tell you is best. You have not ruled well because you did not know nor defer to Me. But that can all change now that you are considering making Me your King. You will retain your own will, little king Will, with the very real responsibility to find and establish My will. You must grow in strength to make sure that nothing rules but Me."

Little king Will somewhat reluctantly put his crown back on. Then he spoke again.

Little king Will: "So King Jesus, will you really take the mess I have made of my life and save me?"

King Jesus: "It all depends upon how much you trust Me."

Little king Will: "Oh, that will be easy."

King Jesus: "Are you sure?"

Little king Will: "Well, all I have to do is let go and let You handle it, right? Isn't that what trust looks like?"

King Jesus: "Not so fast. There are untold numbers of people who say they have faith in Me but in truth they do not. In part they are confused because they think I will overpower their will and run their life without their partnering with Me. They think it is entirely up to

---

23   Revelation 22:5

Me to save them. They are only partly right. They think I mostly save them through My coercing or manipulating My will over and in and through them. They do not understand that I accomplish My will – and thus save them – mostly through coaching and discipling them … guiding them into all truth. They say that they have faith in Me, but they hardly ever seek Me. They do not learn how to listen to Me, and in so doing, they do not set their will to follow what I say, at any cost. If they do not listen to Me and seek to do what I say, they in fact do not have faith in Me. Little king Will, I can and will save you if you have authentic faith in Me, which means you will listen to Me and give yourself to believing and doing what I say. Do you believe Me? Do you truly have faith in Me?"

Little king Will: "I truly want to have faith in You."

King Jesus: "That is perfect. It is the beginning point. I see the desire of your heart. Little king Will, do what I made you to do: set your will to believe Me. Commit to believing Me. Just be careful to not be deceived into believing that you have faith in Me if you do not give yourself to being My disciple, to listening to what I say and seeking to do it. There are many, many who say they have faith in Me, but they pay very little attention to Me, doing mostly what they think and want, and end up ruining their lives. Then they blame Me, when in fact, they did not trust Me enough to even listen to Me.

Do you trust Me enough to pay attention to Me and let My will be your will? Before inviting Me into your heart, you need to count the cost of having a new King."

Little king Will: "Yes, King Jesus. I choose to listen to You and do whatever You say because I no longer trust myself. I trust You."

King Jesus: "Wonderful. Welcome to My Kingdom. I promise to save you now and eternally so long as you keep your will set to find and do

My will. And with My help, you can do that. No question. However, this will be a whole new way of living for you, for you have a lifetime of not seeking Me or My will. But I will help you get better and better. You are no longer alone, nor do you decide independently of Me. I will now dwell in you, and because you have faith in Me, you will learn to consult Me before allowing other forces to rule your life."

Before we observe King Jesus discipling little king Will in his new life with Jesus, there are some important concepts we need to consider about the human heart.

For now, put the parable of little king Will on hold. Return to our real life experience with Jesus. Christ in you, the Holy Spirit, truly desires and intends to disciple us.

But you say, "Are you kidding? Me? Discipled by Jesus?"

You probably have never sat around and wondered if Jesus Himself might want to disciple you. Or have you? Maybe, like me, you secretly wished you could hang out with Jesus around campfires or watch Him calm storms on the sea, like Peter and John did.

Have you ever wondered what it would be like to actually have Jesus disciple you? About how He might do it? You are probably thinking, "You are skipping reality. Being discipled by Jesus was reserved for historical guys like Peter, James, and John."

Maybe.

Many Christians think of Jesus' disciples as only twelve men, including Peter, James, and John, and they have never considered themselves to be disciples of Jesus, or that being His disciple is even an option. They would argue that it is ludicrous to think that they themselves could actually be discipled _BY_ Jesus Himself.

We need to biblically address and answer these questions:

- "Is being a disciple of Jesus *optional* or *necessary* for Christians?"[24]

- "Can a Christian be a disciple of Jesus unless that Christian is being discipled *by* Jesus?"

- "Can anyone in the 21st century actually be discipled *by* Jesus?"

- "If it is possible to be discipled by Jesus now, how does He do it?"[25]

Are all Christians to be disciples of Jesus? If so, how *does* Jesus disciple them? Without their knowing about it? Does it happen "on the run?" Does Jesus do everything automatically without their help? Or, do His disciples have anything to do with being discipled by Jesus? If so, how much? When? Where?

If contemporary Christians are to be discipled *by* Jesus, why have we not heard much about it? Good question, which we will respond to later!

Jesus certainly *can* disciple us now,[26] and there are many reasons why He wants to disciple us now.[27] Let's start by examining His primary process to disciple us: His Holy Spirit in our hearts.

THE HOLY SPIRIT IN OUR HEARTS
Jesus' first and primary way of discipling us is by pouring out His

---

24   Chapters 1-5
25   Chapters 6-15
26   Matthew 19:26
27   His reasons will be articulated throughout the first two chapters

Holy Spirit into our hearts.[28] Note Jesus' words to His disciples as a significant beginning point.

> *"I tell you the truth: It is for your good that I am going away. Unless I go away, the Counselor will not come to you; but if I go, I will send Him to you."*[29]

At the core of this book is the deeply held conviction that far too many Christians are tragically ignorant of or _undiscipled_ in how to walk by the Spirit. This includes many who argue vehemently that they are "born of the Spirit," even "Spirit-filled."

Jesus really meant exactly what He said. He said that it is better that He – by His Holy Spirit – be in us _spiritually_ rather than next to us _physically_ like He was with Peter, James, and John. (In all that follows, please remember that Jesus is in us _spiritually_.[30] In this book, I often refer to the indwelling Holy Spirit as "Jesus.")

THREE WAYS JESUS DISCIPLES HIS FOLLOWERS TODAY

1. Through His Word
   Because Jesus _is_ in us by His Spirit, King Jesus Himself can speak to us as we read the Book He inspired long ago. We can hear Him today as He speaks through His Word!

2. By His Spirit
   Because King Jesus indwells all those who have truly repented and turned to Him, He speaks _directly_ to His followers, personally guiding, reminding, and inspiring every bit as much as He did for Peter long ago.[31]

---

28   Romans 5:5, 8:9
29   John 16:7
30   Note the Spirit of God, the Spirit of Jesus, and the Spirit of Christ are one and the same Spirit: Acts 16:7, Romans 8:9-10, Colossians 1:27,
31   This reality will be clearly demonstrated from John 14-16 subsequently.

3. Through His Body
   Because of His indwelling presence in true believers, every time a member of the true church of King Jesus acts or speaks, it _might_ be that they are responding to the Holy Spirit. In that case, what we see and hear are the words of Jesus Himself becoming flesh in and through His church. Jesus speaks and acts (including making disciples) through His post-Pentecost Body. Jesus literally speaking and acting through His Body is intended to be normal.[32]

Jesus is present in His authentic followers by His Spirit, speaking through His Word, and living through His Body, to disciple whosoever is willing to be discipled by Him.

Let's further examining the presence and work of the Holy Spirit.

JESUS: "I DISCIPLE YOU BY MY SPIRIT"

Jesus' disciples must have been shocked when He said, "But I tell you the truth: It is for your good that I am going away."[33] I can imagine them thinking, maybe even murmuring to each other, "How can it be good for Jesus to leave us? What will we do? We left everything to follow Him, and now He is leaving us? This is terrible, not good."

And then Jesus went on. "Unless I go away, the Counselor will not come to you; but if I go, I will send Him to you."[34]

I personally have thought many times, "Jesus, I know You are right, but it is _very_ hard for me to believe that it is better to have Your Spirit in me than to have You next to me. If You were here, I could see You. I could hear You. I could ask You questions and not have to wonder if I was hearing You accurately. I could watch You and learn from You.

---

32 This concept is developed in Chapter 4
33 John 16:7a
34 John 16:7b

Why did You say it was better for You to give us Your Spirit than for You to be with us tangibly, incarnationally?"[35]

To help put in perspective Jesus' affirmation that it is better for Him to be "in Peter" (or you or me) by His Spirit than physically next to him, we need to consider the "composition" of both the Holy Spirit and our "hearts," where the Holy Spirit dwells and works.

Neither the Holy Spirit nor our "hearts" are "material," yet both truly "matter." Both are truly _real_ and truly _important_.

MATERIAL AND IMMATERIAL

Western culture is probably the most materialistic culture in all of history. What our culture values, what matters to our culture, is material … stuff. In other words, what matters most to our culture is matter! Matter matters.

By way of contrast, notice what we in western culture mean when we use the word, "immaterial." In this culture "immaterial" means unimportant. If something is "immaterial," it does not matter. If a good employee has a glaring weakness – a blind spot – and the boss says, "It's immaterial," that means the weakness is not that important. It does not matter.

But the truth is that it is the immaterial that matters _most_. You have a thought. It is immaterial … that is, it is not stuff …it is not matter. You could not open up your head, grab your thought, put it in a box, and take it under a microscope to examine it. But it is real, very real, and very important. It is your thoughts, and other "immaterial" components of your heart or soul that will live forever. It is your

---

35 Obviously, Jesus could not personally be with every Christian, everywhere, in a material body. One reason that it is better that He sent His Spirit is that He actually can now be en-fleshed millions of times over through His Body, the Church, as she is literally transformed into His likeness. His leaving to send His Spirit to indwell us is better on that count alone. 1 John 2:3-6, 1 Peter 1:14-16, John 14:12, etc.

"immaterial" mind, emotions, desires, and will that determine most of your present life. It is not so much your natural abilities, or what happens to you, that determines your life, but how you respond to all you experience. Your response is determined by the _immaterial_ component in you the Bible calls your "heart."

THE IMPORTANCE OF OUR HEART

The point: it is your heart, the immaterial component of "you," that determines both your eternal destiny and your present experience. Your immaterial world is more real than your material world, and infinitely more important. It is in your "immaterial" world – your heart – where the "immaterial" Holy Spirit dwells and disciples you.

God so loves every person in the world that He gave His only Son that whoever believes in Him would not have to perish but have eternal life.[36] But the majority are perishing. Why? Because God's love and/or plan are insufficient? No. People are perishing because the condition of their heart keeps them from responding to God's invitations to relationship. Do you realize how important your heart is?

God does not want anyone to perish; one person perishing is against His will.[37] But most have and/or are perishing. Why? Not because of God; He has done everything to make it possible that none should perish. It is because of the condition of their heart that people do not recognize or respond to what God makes possible, and thus perish. How important is our heart?

God sends His Holy Spirit to convict every one of sin and righteousness and judgment. Everyone! But most do not respond to the Holy Spirit. Is the Holy Spirit failing? No! Why do so many fail to respond to the Holy Spirit? The condition of their heart!

---

36   John 3:16
37   2 Peter 3:9

THE IMPORTANCE OF OUR HEART FOR EVEN THIS LIFE

The condition of our hearts even determines the quality of life we experience now. Life happens, both good and bad. Some respond with faith and love, which results in goodness, joy, peace, and great blessing. More respond with fear, anger, and hate, all of which leads to mental, emotional, and social pain and conflict. Why the differing responses to life? The condition of the heart. How important is our heart?

These eternal and temporal consequences based on the _condition_ of our heart are the reasons that we are admonished, above all else, to guard our hearts.[38] We must not be deceived. There is a high stakes battle for every heart. It is a moment-by-moment battle. It is a battle for the attentions and the affections of the heart. My heart. Your heart. Everyone's heart. Jesus died, in great part, for the privilege to enter our heart, "sit at the table of our heart," and disciple our hearts by His Spirit. Why? So we can be more than conquerors in this battle, both now and eternally.

Listening and being influenced by Jesus in our "immaterial" hearts is a moment-by-moment battle, for our hearts are seldom inactive. To the degree that our hearts are discipled by Jesus to be like His heart, our lives will be like His life, and we will be genuine disciples of Jesus. Result: Jesus will save us, both eternally and temporally. Further, Jesus will bless and save others by living His life through us.

For both our eternal and temporal benefit, we are incredibly foolish if we do not give ourselves to being discipled by Jesus. Being discipled by Jesus is all about how He, Jesus, speaks into our hearts by His Spirit, Word, and Body to transform what is in _our_ heart to what is in _His_ heart. It is about listening to and being influenced by Jesus far more than all the other voices that penetrate and influence our hearts. This is illustrated in the next chapter as little king Will wrestles with the "other voices" of his heart.

---

38   Proverb 4:23

CHAPTER 2

Jesus Disciples Little King Will in Governing His Heart

We started our journey by affirming that Jesus, the Word of God who became flesh,[39] desires and intends to disciple His 21st century followers every bit as much as He discipled Peter, James, and John thousands of years ago.

In Chapter 1, we met little king Will and some of his advisors who live with him in the heart. These advisors advised that he secure a new King. Through Little king Will's subsequent conversation with King Jesus, Little king Will repented, changing his mind and setting his will to trust Jesus to save him. He "changed kings" and entered the Kingdom of God. We now continue on with little king Will's new life with King Jesus joining him and his other advisors in his heart.

King Jesus: "Let's get started in My work of saving you. First, your problems are not primarily outside of you. They come from your own heart. To be sure, I could easily fix everything that has already happened, and stop all bad things from happening in the future. Or, I could make only good things happen, but to do all that I would have to force My will on everyone and everything else, which I seldom do … right now. To save you, little king Will, we must start to work on your inner being … in your heart … with the very advisors I gave you

---

39   John 1:14

from the beginning. I must help you to realize your role, and theirs, and help you get strong enough to fulfill your role. Shall we begin?"

Little king Will: "Sure."

King Jesus: "Let's start with the advisor sitting right next to you. From very early in your life, you have listened to him. He always comes to your meetings, and he talks … and talks … and talks … and talks. He hardly ever quits talking. In fact, when you try to sleep at night, he just keeps talking, often keeping you awake most of the night. Do you know who he is?"

Little king Will: "I don't have a clue. Who are You talking about?"

MIND
King Jesus: "Your mind. We'll call him Mind. I made him. He is an unspeakably wonderful helper for you. He is one of My greatest gifts to you. But because I was not in your life from the beginning, Mind was unenlightened; he had no light. All that he thought came from darkness, and was therefore partially or entirely deceived. He left Me out of his thinking because he was ignorant of Me. But he could not stop thinking, or telling you what he was thinking. This became a serious problem for you, because you listened to Mind, who was not listening to Me. Whatever he told you did not include My thoughts, for Mind was ignorant of Me and My ways.

"Mind was not only ignorant; he was arrogant, assuming he was right. His independence and pride was actually evil, for he left Me out and in the process naively but terribly deceived (and was in the process of destroying) you.

"And you knew no better than to listen to him and take his advice. You did whatever he said, for it was your Mind and it made perfect sense to you. Mind spoke, and you said, 'OK.' Thus, Mind, as one of your primary advisors, usually ruled your life, because what he recommended you approved of. It made sense to you. Without Me and My Truth in your Mind, everything Mind thought and recommended left Me out, and therefore was distorted at best, and usually dead wrong, and thus deadly. He never gave you My perspective; only his.

"I remind you, the worst thing about Mind is this: he is very arrogant, and he does not realize it. He always thinks he is right. Of course, you believed him. You put your faith in Mind.

"Do you want to know how you can tell how much you trusted Mind? Here is how you can tell. How many thousands of times have I heard you say, 'Well, I think …' Each of those times you were influenced, and then governed, by Mind. You did exactly what Mind recommended. In essence, you let Mind boss you around. How did it work for you?"

Little king Will: "Well, what Mind said made perfect sense back then, but now I see a lot of tragic errors in his advice. In fact, my life is pretty much a mess. That's why my advisors and I agreed to invite You into our heart."

King Jesus: "Remember, I did not and do not take your 'will-power' from you. I actually want you, Will, to get strong in relating and responding to Me. Here is what you must do. You must set yourself to not let Mind get his way any longer. Just as I won't take your will from you, neither will I take Mind away, as darkened and confused as he is. Even into old age, Mind will continue to sit at your table and pressure you by what he thinks.

"However, I have very good news with regard to Mind. Now that I am in your heart, and you are determined to listen to Me, I will be speaking directly and persistently to Mind. What I say will be so different from what he thinks that he will seldom recognize it as Me, at least to start with. In fact, Mind will often ignore Me because what

I say will be so totally different from what he has come to think. But over time, he will more and more be responsive Me. What I whisper will start to make sense to him, and he will more easily agree with Me. Thus, over time, he will increasingly tell you something very close to what I think and what I have whispered to him. Down the road, he will actually become a wonderful help to you by speaking to you the very things I have spoken to him. In fact, you will be transformed because Mind is being renewed.[40] But right now, he will continue to mostly tell you what he thinks, not the Truth I am telling him. So you must build some muscle, little king Will."

Little king Will: "Muscle? What? How?"

King Jesus: "Because Mind will not quit talking, you have to get strong enough to not let him rule you. In the past, he has. Unless you stop him from ruling you, he will, for all practical purposes, be the king, for you are doing what he advises."

Little king Will: "How do I stop Mind from ruling my life?"

King Jesus: "When he speaks, and he constantly does, you must slow him down. Be nice to him. He truly intends to be your helper. Slow him down by holding up your hand, and gently but determinedly, say, 'Shhhhhh …' to him. Then, take whatever Mind was saying, actually grab the idea, and bring that thought – every thought – to Me. It will be so hard that you will probably need both hands. Your goal is to grab and capture _every thought_ to make it obedient to Me.[41] You must work very hard in order to learn to trust Me with _all_ your heart, and to NOT lean on your own understanding. In all your ways, you must learn to acknowledge Me, that is, find out what I think and come into agreement with Me, and seek to do what I tell you. And I promise you this: I _will_ direct your paths by guiding and empowering your faith and obedience.[42]

40   Romans 12:1-2
41   2 Corinthians 10:5
42   Proverb 3:5-6

"So, before you just let Mind govern you, get strong enough to put on the brakes, grab whatever Mind says, and bring what Mind said to Me to find out what I think and want. That is putting your faith in Me into practice. Then live by your faith in Me by setting your will to think and do whatever I say.

Little king Will: "That sounds almost impossible."

King Jesus: "By yourself it is. But I am with you, and I will remind you and help you.[43] With Me, all things are possible.[44]

"Because this is all so new to you, you will often forget to bring what Mind says to Me before you let him have his way. When Mind realizes that you took his advice and that neither of you remembered to check with Me first, he might make an even bigger error: he might tell you that both you and he are failures. He might tell you to be very impatient with yourself, or maybe compromise, or make excuses for yourself, or blame others. Or, he might even suggest that you give up on your walk with Me and quit. We will later talk about where he might be getting those ideas.

"For now, you must learn to bring those self-rejecting or negative thoughts from Mind to Me, for, once again, Mind is talking without first listening to Me. I will not be the slightest bit surprised by your immaturity, and will not be the least bit impatient with you or Mind … for now. I perfectly understand how difficult is this new life with the battle to test all your thoughts with Me. Sooner or later, Mind will come to realize that I am not disappointed or angry about being in your heart, but rather am thrilled to be partnering in saving you, in spite of your old heart habits of listening to his naïve, godless advice.

---

43   John 16:7-13
44   Mark 10:27

"Do you believe all that, especially about learning to not lean on your own understanding about yourself when you mess up?"

Little king Will: "I hope so. It is all so new to me."

King Jesus: "Of course it is. You are, in fact, a brand new creation, for I am a totally new presence in your heart, and you have decided that you are responsible to let Me govern all of your heart and life. It is a totally new way of living.[45] Remember, together, we can do this. You must be patient with yourself, but doggedly persistent. I am, and will be. You must learn to always think what I am thinking about you, usually not what Mind tells you to think about yourself. Never forget, I am so thrilled with you and your heart commitment to know and follow Me, and I am not the least bit surprised by how difficult it is for you to learn to bring Mind to Me before acting."

"Are you ready to move on and talk about some of your other heart advisers?"

Little king Will: "I think so. Will the others be as difficult to deal with as Mind?"

King Jesus: "I will let you decide. The next advisor we must talk about is almost a Siamese twin to Mind, but not quite. But they are closely connected. Mind talks and talks. Your next advisor does not talk; he SCREAMS. At meetings, he pounds the table. He is LOUD. If you let Mind _influence_ you, you let this advisor _dominate_ you. He screams and hollers and pounds the table. You have let him boss you around and get his way. You are going to have to get strong, little king Will, because this advisor at your table is ruling (and often ruining) your life."

Little king Will: "That bad? Who is he? What is his name?"

---

45   2 Corinthians 5:17

EMOTION

King Jesus: "His name is Emotion. Just like Mind, I made him and he is good … when he is functioning as I intend him to function. He is in fact your most honest and open advisor. Mind sometimes thinks things that he does not tell you. But he is so close to Emotion that Emotion always knows what Mind is thinking. And Emotion cannot keep the secret. Whatever Mind thinks, Emotion feels. And those feelings come gurgling or screaming to the forefront.

"Emotion has almost ruined you because you gave in to his pressure. He is very, very loud and persistent. And over and over you let him have his way! Just think how many times he has ruled you. He got angry and you did things you've been sorry for ever since. He was afraid and you did some of the most ridiculous things for the wrong reasons. Are you aware how much Emotion dominates you?"

Little king Will: "I suppose I am not. How can I recognize him?"

King Jesus: "For starters, notice a phrase that I hear you saying, over and over and over. 'I feel …' is constantly on your lips. It comes straight from Emotion. Every time you say, 'Well, I feel …' you are probably about to let Emotion rule you.

"Here is what you must learn about Emotion. He has never had an original thought in his life. But, of course. He is not Mind, and he does not think. He feels. He is Emotion. Every time he is emotional it is because he has been listening to Mind. Whenever Mind has a thought, he leans over and tells Emotion. And Emotion feels – deeply and often loudly – everything that Mind tells him. If Mind tells Emotion of some danger, Emotion screams with fear. If Mind whispers to Emotion of some injustice, Emotion gets angry and hollers. If Mind tells Emotion of a loss in the family, Emotion grieves deeply. In short, whatever Mind thinks, Emotion hears and feels. Since so much of what Mind thought before I came into your heart was not accurate (for he left Me out of his thoughts), Emotion has felt and given great energy to Mind's erroneous perspectives. Do you know what you did with Emotion's wild anger and fears?"

Little king Will: "No. What did I do?"

King Jesus: "You let him boss you around. Think how often you say, 'I feel …' and then you do the craziest things just because 'you feel.' You were not strong like you needed to be. Emotion screamed, and you let him rule you. He got angry, and you let his anger govern you and get you in a massive mess."

Little king Will: "What am I supposed to do?"

King Jesus: "Well, just like you must get strong enough to not let Mind rule you, neither can you let Emotion govern what you do. When Emotion screams (and he will), you are responsible to understand what is going on. Mind has been talking to Emotion, as always. Don't let Emotion get his way. Hold up your hand to Emotion, and tell him, 'Shhhhhh …' Quiet him down in the best way possible, as soon as possible. Don't do anything until you get Emotion to quiet down. Then, turn to Mind, and ask him, 'What have you been telling Emotion?' Get Mind to tell you what he told Emotion. Then, bring whatever Mind tells you to Me. Again, you have to learn to bring every thought captive into obedience to Me. In this way, Emotion actually becomes a very healthy and helpful "tattle-tale," for most of your painful emotions quickly make you aware that your Mind has been thinking something different from what I think and want. Just like I gave your body physical pain to show you when something is physically wrong, so I gave you Emotion's pain and other manifestations to cause you to go to Mind and find out what he is thinking that is not the way I think.

"Here is the very good news. As I work in Mind to have him more and more think the way I think, Mind will be telling Emotion My perspective and truth, and Emotion will more and more feel peace, joy, and love. If you guard Mind and keep bringing what He says to Me, Emotion will soon help empower you with wonderful, strong positive feelings that I have always intended you to routinely experience. That is part of what I mean when I say that 'the Truth will set you free.'"

Little king Will: "This is starting to get exciting. Who else has been advising me?"

King Jesus: "Well, this next guy in your heart is really something. You can tell when you are letting Mind rule when you hear yourself saying, 'I think.' You can tell when Emotion is tugging to get his way when you say, 'I feel.' But there is another phrase you use regularly that reveals how much this next heart-member rules your life."

Little king Will: "It sounds rather ominous ..."

King Jesus: "Actually, you will be glad when you realize this next "ruler" in your life. Think back to how often you use this phrase: 'I want.' I have heard you say 'I want' many, many, times. Almost uncountable times. In fact, those two words - 'I want' – were some of your very first words. They were certainly your most often used words. They come from another of your advisors that I gave you: Desire. He has dominated you like none other since the day you were born."

DESIRE

Little king Will: "Desire? He _IS_ strong. Sooo strong. I suppose You have watched him rule me a lot?"

King Jesus: "You tell Me. How often do you say, 'I want!'?"

Little king Will: "Uhh ... probably a lot more than a lot?"

King Jesus: "How has that worked for you?"

Little king Will: "Oh, he probably was … uhhh … is my biggest problem. Let me guess. I need to get real strong and not let Desire run my life."

King Jesus: "You are figuring out what it is to trust Me. How are you going to deal with Desire when he screams what he wants?"

Little king Will: "Well, I am going to hold up my hand, and say 'Shhhhhh …' to him. I must be very sure to be kind to him because You gave him to me, and I will have Desire in my heart all my life, be he immature or mature, selfish or selfless. But I must not let him rule, else he becomes king. I must firmly tell him he cannot have his way until I bring the particular desire to You to find out what You think."

King Jesus: "Fabulous! What do you think will happen to Desire after I have been included in the conversations of your heart for a while?"

Little king Will: "Well, I know he will get to know You. I wonder if, as he gets to know You better, he might start to desire what You want?"

King Jesus: "I think you are getting help from Mind, who has been listening to us. You are exactly correct. The more that Desire sees and knows Me, the more he will value, even love Me, for I am the Desired of all Nations.[46] What do you think will happen when Desire really gets to know Me?"

Little king Will: "Well, let me ask Mind. I'm sure he has an idea."

Mind: "Well, little king Will; you can be sure that when Desire really gets to know King Jesus, he will turn into one of your most powerful helpers in finding out what King Jesus wants."

King Jesus: "Interesting. Can you tell us why you think that, Mind?"

---

46   Haggai 2:7

Mind: "When Desire really knows You, King Jesus, He will love and honor you so much that he will _want_ whatever you want. In your heart, little king Will, you will have Desire who wants what King Jesus wants, and that will be a powerful help to you."

King Jesus: "Mind, you are thinking clearly. You are becoming a very great help to little king Will. Anything else?"

Mind: "Yes … Desire always had great appetites for things and temporal pleasures and money and his own way.[47] He wanted to be secure, certain of being cared for, even popular and powerful. I can see all of that decreasing. As his love for You increases, King Jesus, it will influence him to want what You want … which includes saving every person on this planet through a healthy, holy church. Is that true?"

King Jesus: "Way to go, Mind. You are thinking My thoughts. Little king Will, did you notice that Mind brought his thoughts to Me to test them before telling you? He's getting it."

Little king Will: "Yes, and I noticed that You are now asking us all kinds of questions to test if we know what You think and want. You are helping us figure out if we are 'getting it.'"

King Jesus: "Asking you questions is one of My best ways to disciple your heart. By testing to see if you know and are practically committed to doing My will, you grow into My likeness better and quicker.

"Let Me add a bit to what Mind did not say about Desire. After Desire gets to know Me better, he will actually want what lasts for eternity. In fact, after I have worked with all your advisors, they will become your greatest allies in trusting Me. Mind will more and more bring you My thoughts, and in the process Emotion will be a positive support.

---

47   2 Timothy 3:1-5

Desire will actually so want what I want that it will be much easier for you, little king Will, to govern your heart entirely for Me. He will give you tremendous help, even energy, to seek and find My will.

"In fact, the more and longer and better you do your job of seeing to it that no one rules your heart other than Me, the more each of your advisors will actually partner with Me in purifying you. And then, through My work in your heart, you can actually become pure … trusting and loving Me with all your heart. Then you will be far, far stronger in guarding your heart in order to find and do what I think and want in every part of your life. You will, in very practical terms, be very much set apart for Me and make progress in fulfilling My holy purposes.

"But for now, as you have figured out, you must not let Desire rule. You must be strong in bringing what he wants to Me. If you do this, seeking first My Kingdom and My righteousness, then I promise to take care of all these other things that your advisors – right now – are very concerned about.[48] And the more you intentionally include Me in all your decisions, the more Mind and Desire will see Me for who I am, and trust and love Me, and become for you the true heart advisors I want them to be.

"Never forget, little king Will, whoever rules your decisions is the functioning king in that moment. Lost people who have not invited Me to be their King do whatever they think, and feel, and want. That is simply their natural, independent- of-Me, way of living. That is what I mean in My Word when I speak of 'walking by the flesh.'[49] When you allow yourself to live by your flesh, that is 'I think,' 'I feel,' and 'I want,' which is not yet transformed by My presence, you are, in each specific case, living in exactly the same way that lost people live. Yes, that is exactly how the lost live life. But I know you, little king Will. You are determined to know and follow Me instead of walking by

---

48   Matthew 6:33
49   Romans 8:5-13

your flesh, and I am delighted. Because you truly have faith in Me, you will work very hard to find what I think and want before you act, and more and more you will live as I did. And as you grow in love for Me, you will increasingly want what I want, and hate what I hate, and thus increasingly do My will."

Little king Will: "Thank You, King Jesus. This is all so encouraging."

King Jesus: "You are making quick and wonderful progress in walking by faith in Me, Little king Will. I know I am giving you much information, but I am about done with this basic lesson. Let Me mention a few more 'advisors' who come to your heart-meetings. You cannot keep them away. It is your responsibility to not let them govern by getting their way as if they were the king."

BODY

"Right across from you, looking you in the eye all the time, is Body. When he is young, he serves your decisions quite well, at least to the extent that he has been trained. As he gets older, he will increasingly start screaming during meetings. Many times you will be about to make a difficult but good decision when Body suddenly gets the picture and sounds like a rebel. If he thinks that the decision will be too hard or painful for him, he'll even throw a tantrum. He influences Desire very much. You'll often see them talking between meetings. For example, you will sometimes hear Body, through Desire, saying something like, 'I am too tired. I don't want to get up.' Again, just say, 'Shhhh …' to Body. Don't let him be king. Turn to Me and say, 'King Jesus, my Body is saying to stay in bed. I don't want Body to rule. Do You think I need more rest or should I get up?' Check with Me very carefully to see if Body's complaints are legitimate. You have to listen to Body, but he is not to rule.

PEOPLE

"There is a guy named People who almost always 'speaks into' your heart meetings. He "talks" almost equally to Mind, Emotion, and

Desire, and then through them to you. He has all kinds of opinions, especially about you. You may or may not have invited him to the table of your kingdom. Somehow he always seems to get in. Mind usually invites him without asking your permission. Desire and Emotion often invite him as well. They do not intend People to mess up the meeting. Since they can't seem to help inviting him, you may as well get used to him being at your table. You can recognize their presence at your meetings when you hear yourself saying, 'They think!' or 'They want.'

"Much of your new life will be spent with People who are not My people. They have not yet responded to My invitation to be their king. Don't be the slightest bit surprised that they do not think, or feel, or want what you are learning from Me. They legitimately might think you are strange.[50] You must learn like never before to truly care for them, even listen to them in order to better serve them, but do not let what they think and want rule you until you have brought the issue to Me to be sure it is what I want.

"There are some People I want you to very intentionally invite to your table. They are My People. You desperately need some of My People who are more mature than you in following Me as King to help you disciple your heart. However, you had better very carefully ask Me (and probably one of the most mature of My People you know) about which of My People to invite to help coach and disciple you in relating to Me, and serving Me. People can be your spouse, parents, or prayer partner. (By reading this book, you are inviting the author to sit at your table.) Even when you carefully choose to invite My People, remember that he has a round table in his heart and he brings his own set of advisors to your table. I have actually commanded[51] My People to see that some of them sit at your table with you. They should have been well discipled by My People in guarding their own hearts so they can coach you well at your table. I want you to

---

50   1 Peter 2:11, 4:4
51   Matthew 28:20

assemble regularly with My People,[52] and to diligently search for one or two who are suited to sit at your heart-table with you and Me for discipling purposes.

"My People can help you in ways that your heart advisors can't or won't. Still, don't let them control you because he is not your king.[53] When People talks, even My People, turn to Me and ask, 'My King, do You agree?'"

EVIL POWERS

King Jesus: "There is one more reality I must warn you about your heart. It is hard truth, but because I care, I must tell you.

"There exists a terrible, wretched, evil, vile being who hates Me. Because you are so precious and valuable to Me, this terrible enemy wants to get at Me by hurting or even destroying you.

"If he can't just come out and persuade you to leave Me, he tries to deceive you or seduce you in order to destroy you. He can do great damage at your table.

"He tries to seduce you, usually through Desire. He is also a master at deceiving Mind, who is then sure that he, Mind, is right, even though terribly wrong. He cunningly tries to get you, through Mind, to think and come to conclusions without checking with Me. This is the core way he tempts you.

"If none of this works, he will seek to cause direct problems for you, like attacking Body with pain or Mind with accusations or—watch this one—compliments. Attacking you with problems or pain is a dangerous last resort for him, for he knows these might drive you more fervently to Me.

---

52   Hebrews 10:25, 3:12-13, 2 Timothy 2:2, Matthew 28:20
53   Galatians 1:10

"Finally, if he can't kill your trust in and your love for Me, he'll put lies in the mind of other people around you so that he can kill your influence with them.

"This heinous enemy has access to your table to devour and destroy you.[54] He even showed up at My table regularly.[55] He seldom comes to your table personally; he commissions his evil spirits with fiery darts to attack Mind, Emotion, Desire, Body, or People.[56] He can get at you in many ways. He wants to seduce you into forgetting that I am your King. All he has to do is somehow get you to act like the king, making decisions without securing your King's will. He thus seduces you into living exactly like the worldlings, for that is precisely how they live … doing what they think, and feel, and want … living independently of Me, not dependently on Me.

"Sometimes representatives of your enemy boldly show up without much cover, screaming at you through Desire, Mind, or Emotion. They have many aliases, like Lust, Shame, Rejection, Unloved, Unimportant, Success, Appetite, Wealth, Beauty, and Power. Some of what they say sounds like truth, so you are tempted to agree. There are many more liars waiting to infiltrate your table. Watch for them.[57] These enemies attack through the darkness of any at your table. Like their father the devil, they are cunning and evil.

"I am sitting next to you by your invitation to save, coach and disciple every part of our new life together. If our enemy can keep you independently and habitually determining to say your own words and do your own actions, he can keep your new life mostly like your old life – full of inner and outer turmoil. He can disrupt your healing and holiness and happiness. With sinister intent, he seeks to destroy—if possible—your relationship with Me. If he cannot destroy you, with

54   John 10:10, 1 Peter 5:8
55   Hebrews 4:15, Matthew 4:1-11
56   Ephesians 6:10-18
57   1 Peter 5:8

rage he seeks to minimize your effectiveness in My purposes. One way or another, He is determined to create havoc in your loyalty and service to Me, your new King.

"Remember this: you cannot have two functional kings. Sooner or later a house divided will fall.[58] Every action comes from a decision, and there can be only one decision per action. Whoever makes the decision is the functional king. Every time you seek My will regarding any particular decision, you are putting your commitment to have faith in Me into practice. It is then that you are actually living by faith in Me."

WILL

"Finally, let Me remind you again that you, little king Will, are responsible for the discussions around the table of your heart. At your invitation, I sit at the table to serve you, but you still have to decide to whom, of all your counselors, you will give the last word. You will. In fact, that is your name—Will. Others have named you Spirit. Some include you in a group called Soul. I just like to call you Will.

As little king, your single role in governing is to make sure that I, King Jesus, am actually governing. You are not as strong as some say you are. Some tell you to not be ruled by Mind or Emotion. The fact is that Mind and Emotion are so powerful that, unless I influence and help them change, they will often get their way and make the decision. Without realizing it, you easily give in to Emotion, who feels deeply what Mind assumes to be true. You must make Mind find out the truth from Me. I am the Truth. If you don't, Mind will be influenced by others. What Mind thinks, Emotion feels. You will have a hard time overcoming Mind and Emotion. On the upside, when they get their way and things don't go well, and I convict them, they at least tell you they are sorry. At that reflective moment, you are strong enough to tell Mind to learn from Me, your Master Teacher. One reason why Mind

---

58   Matthew 12:25

recommended inviting Me to the table in the first place is that Mind responded to My truth, recognized that I was absolutely necessary to save you and your life, and recommended repenting. You must be strong enough to constantly send Mind to Me so that Mind has the habit of being sensitive to Me in everything.

"You made the best choice possible of your government and for your little kingdom when you chose Me to be your King. Remember, I am The King of all the little kings, even when they do not recognize Me. Someday they all will.

"As you listen to all your counselors and try to discern the deceivers, you need to make Mind, Desire, Emotion, Body, and even People submit their counsel to Me. Ask them: 'Did you ask our King?'

As little king, your single role in governing is to make sure that King Jesus alone is governing.

Do not tell your counselors, family, friends, and even Me that you have faith in Me and that I am your King if you, Will, are willing to let someone else rule. It is your job, Will, to see that I am included in the discussions and that all your table-advisors ultimately agree, or at least submit, to My thoughts and My desires.

REVIEWING MY HEART

The purpose of this lengthy parable was to dramatize how all our hearts work. Do you see the absolute necessity of guarding your heart? How much help will you need? How much help do other soldiers need, especially the young idealists who are ready and willing to fight this good fight for their heart?

Biblically, my heart is comprised of thoughts, emotions, desires, and much more. A cursory study of the Bible reveals the heart functioning in dozens of "*immaterial*" ways. In our hearts we think, meditate, receive reminders, trust, fear, experience contriteness, hold grudges, forgive, seek, desire, laugh, ache, cherish, hate, seek, love, worship, and on and on.

Ultimately, in our hearts we have a will. In our heart, we are able to make commitments, that is, to set our will. All of our heart activities inform and influence the heart of our heart, the will. As persons made in the image of God, we have the capacity to gather information, to identify our preferred future, and to set our will to achieve what has been conceived in our hearts. This is why we must with utmost care guard our heart, for from it we live or perish, both temporarily and eternally.[59]

Most do not carefully guard their hearts, or even realize the need to do so. Every one of our hearts has already been discipled – by all the influences we have experienced. Our hearts will continue to be discipled – by someone or something.

When a lost person truly repents, that person is "born of the Spirit." Jesus, by His Spirit, literally comes into the repentant person's heart. This is not a fairy tale. The parable of little king Will illustrated this very real, God-given provision for life transformation. "Am I listening and responding to King Jesus?" Or in the language of Paul, "Am I walking by the Spirit?"

Jesus will not force and unilaterally rule the entirety of our life. He did not create us to control us. He IS THE King, and certainly can overpower us when love and infinite wisdom call for control, but He seldom will do that. Jesus intends that you relate to Him as your King. But at the table of your heart, He takes off His crown. When you invited Him into your heart, He wrapped a towel around His waist. He is present to serve you, the little king, by sitting on your advisory board. In your mind, and by your will, you must see and relate to Him

---

59   Proverb 4:23

in truth: He is King of kings and Lord of lords. But from His side, He will guide and empower, but not make you His robot. He intends that you relate to Him as absolute King without His imposing His Kingship and Kingdom on you.

The meeting in your heart occurs continually. Contrary to much contemporary and very popular theology, you, the little king, are seated at your heart's table with *ultimate responsibility* for all decisions that are made.

> *God, in making us in His Own image for an authentic love relationship, has sovereignly determined that we have no choice but to make choices that determine our destiny.*

When you became a Christian, King Jesus came to sit at the table in your heart, joining a host of other "advisors." You became a Christ-follower because sometime in your past King Jesus, by His Spirit, usually through His Body, made you aware that you were naively or arrogantly ignoring Him. He spoke into your heart, revealing that you had and would continue to suffer heart and life damage for not trusting Him to lead you. Further, you would suffer severe eternal consequences for ignoring Him through perpetuating the independence from Him into which you were born. You came to realize His shocking love for you, and His offer to enter and help you with your heart. Jesus influenced you (by His Spirit, Word, and Body) to see and desire a whole new direction. You chose dependence on Him instead of independence from Him. He made it possible for you to welcome Him into your heart as your new King. You responded by setting your will to follow Him as your King. You changed Kings and entered His Kingdom. This is called repentance and faith. In repenting and believing Jesus, you made the ONE choice that trumps all other choices in determining what is best for you now and eternally.

Learning to say no to what we think, what we feel, and what we want is very difficult, but possible. [60] Learning to listen and respond to King Jesus is also difficult, but possible. King Jesus in us – the Holy Spirit – makes listening for and hearing Him possible. King Jesus speaks through His Word, making listening and responding to Him so possible. To be sure, the Word and the Spirit have in no way failed. Yet many Christians – so many – flounder and even fail as authentic disciples of Jesus. What is often missing and desperately needed is personal, intentional, strategic relational coaching in listening to and following Jesus. Jesus called this "making disciples," and commanded that every baptized person be thus coached. "Undiscipled disciples" is not acceptable. To help every Christ-follower be better discipled by King Jesus and better disciplers of King Jesus is my prayer for this book. Thank you for continuing on …

---

60   Titus 2:11-12

CHAPTER 3

I Want to Disciple You by My Spirit

Many years ago I was a teacher, and teachers love to review. As a strategic introduction to this all important chapter, will you indulge me with a bit of review?

King Jesus comes into your heart – literally – to lovingly serve rather than arbitrarily control you, though at any time He can and might unilaterally govern. He is the King and Lord and Master and God of the universe!

However, He normally relates to us by His Spirit's speaking and coaching, especially through His written Word. Jesus is the King and He intends you to relate to Him as your King. But at your table, He takes off His crown. When you invited Him into your heart, He wrapped a towel around His waist. He is present to serve you, the little king, by sitting on your advisory board. You must see and own Him for Who He is – King of kings and your God, but realize that, as God, He has determined to not unilaterally force His will on, in, or through you in most cases. Jesus has sovereignly determined that you have no choice but to make choices. You are made in His image. You have personality, dignity, and potential. He very seldom strips any of us of these qualities. He wants to prepare you for an eternity of love relationship with Him and for reigning in His Kingdom.

Loving relationships by nature require freedom. Jesus treats you with dignity as a free, sovereign, independent little king. He could easily overpower you and get His way in your heart, or shout so loud that you have no choice but to hear Him. But that's not how He normally relates. He, King Jesus, has come into your life at your invitation and He is seated next to you at your round table. King Jesus normally whispers in the midst of all the noise and shouting at the table. You have a very hard time hearing Him unless you tell everyone else to be very quiet. Often, the others are so unruly and unaccustomed to being disciplined that it is a battle to quiet them. The Spirit of King Jesus lovingly, patiently, and persistently keeps serving you, whether you recognize His voice or not.

This and the next chapter will establish how it is that Jesus disciples us by His personal presence, His Holy Spirit. We refer back to the discussion of material and immaterial from Chapter 1, that is, what is truly "real" and what truly "matters."

THE HOLY SPIRIT: IMMATERIAL

The most important component of the observations from Chapter 1 regarding matter, material and immaterial is this: Jesus is no longer material, but He IS here by His Spirit. His Spirit is immaterial, which was demonstrated to mean of infinite importance. The Holy Spirit is every bit as real as your thoughts, your desires, your emotions, and your will. Jesus TRULY comes into our heart by His Spirit, and His Spirit is more real than anything material and infinitely more impor-tant than anything material. Matter does not matter in contrast with the immaterial, which is eternal.

The Holy Spirit is identified as the Spirit of Jesus:

> "… After they came to Mysis, they were trying to go into Bithynia, and the Spirit of Jesus did not permit them … "[61]

---

61 Acts 16:7

Jesus, by His Spirit, was present in the lives of His first apostles, as He promised. This same Jesus, in the same way, is with us now. The Spirit of Jesus was and is as real as any mind on the planet. It is the minds of this planet that cause what happens to happen, including Jesus' mind. His infinitely genius Mind is constantly involved in the work on the planet. He is, among other things, whispering to every mind.[62] Most are not listening; some are, and those listening are following what they hear.[63] They are His disciples. They are not disciples of their own thinking, or of their culture, or necessarily of the religious traditions of their culture. To the degree that Jesus Himself is recognized and heeded, He restores and saves the world.

This very Mind, the Spirit of Christ, dwells in every truly repentant, born-again, born of the Spirit person.[64]

> *"And if anyone does not have the Spirit of Christ, he does not belong to Christ."*[65]

To be sure, the Spirit of Christ is real though immaterial. To be sure, He infinitely matters.

A major purpose of this book is to help Christ-followers secure the help they need to recognize and respond to this "Mind" who is a Person, the very Spirit of Jesus. Christ in us is the _hope_ of glory[66] Christ in us is the _provision_ for the manifest presence of God (glory) but not the guarantee. As we come into agreement with the Holy Spirit, our lives increasingly reveal and glorify our God. To the degree that we are insensitive to the Holy Spirit, we quench God's provision for our lives to glorify Him.

---

62   John 16:7-13
63   John 10:27
64   1 Corinthians 2:16, Philippians 2:5-9, Galatians 4:6, Romans 15:5, John 15:15
65   Romans 8:9
66   Colossians 1:27

Observe some of the things Jesus proclaimed He would do by His Spirit in His followers:

- The Holy Spirit counsels and brings truth:

    "And I will ask the Father, and He will give you another Counselor to be with you forever— the Spirit of truth. The world cannot accept Him, because it neither sees Him nor knows Him. But you know Him, for He lives with you and will be in you. I will not leave you as orphans; I will come to you."[67]

- The Holy Spirit teaches *all* things and remind of *everything* Jesus said:

    "But the Counselor, the Holy Spirit, whom the Father will send in My name, will teach you all things and will remind you of everything I have said to you."[68]

- The Holy Spirit testifies about Jesus:

    "When the Counselor comes, whom I will send to you from the Father, the Spirit of truth who goes out from the Father, He will testify about me. And you also must testify, for you have been with Me from the beginning."[69]

- The Holy Spirit convicts of guilt in regard to sin, righteousness, and judgment:

    "But I tell you the truth: It is for your good that I am going away. Unless I go away, the Counselor will not come to you; but if I go, I will send Him to you. When He comes, He will convict

---

67 John 14:16-18
68 John 14:26
69 John 15:26-27

the world of guilt in regard to sin and righteousness and judg-ment: in regard to sin, because men do not believe in Me; in regard to righteousness, because I am going to the Father, where you can see Me no longer; and in regard to judgment, because the prince of this world now stands condemned."[70]

- The Holy Spirit guides into all truth and tells what is to come:

"But when He, the Spirit of truth, comes, He will guide you into all the truth; for He will not speak on His own initiative, but whatever He hears, He will speak; and He will disclose to you what is to come."[71]

- The Holy Spirit brings glory to Jesus by taking from what is of Jesus and making it know to us:

"He will bring glory to Me by taking from what is Mine and making it known to you. All that belongs to the Father is Mine. That is why I said the Spirit will take from what is Mine and make it known to you."[72]

- The Holy Spirit speaks:

"My sheep listen to My voice; I know them, and they follow Me."[73]

"Everyone who is of the truth hears My voice."[74]

Because of the presence of the Holy Spirit in the life of Jesus' true followers, Jesus Himself is always present to guide, mentor, coach,

---

70 John 16:7-11
71 John 16:13
72 John 16:14-15
73 John 10:27
74 John 18:37

parent, lead, etc. That is, He is always present to *disciple* His followers. To be able to be discipled by Jesus, but not recognize it or know how to receive His discipling, is very sad. It is worse than sad. It is tragic.

Since the Spirit of Jesus indwells His true followers to disciple them, what kind of coaching is needed to be able to recognize and respond to the Holy Spirit? How much would that coaching be worth?

To begin to answer the above question, we need to understand what is perhaps the most under emphasized work of the Holy Spirit.

What is the work of the Spirit that is under emphasized? This is it: His work in Jesus!

> *Everything that Jesus Himself did in His incarnate Presence, He did by the presence and power of this same Holy Spirit.*

It was the Holy Spirit who filled, led, and empowered Jesus to do what He did.

- *"Now when all the people were baptized, Jesus was also baptized, and while He was praying, heaven was opened, and the Holy Spirit descended upon Him in bodily form like a dove ..."*[75]

- *"Jesus, full of the Holy Spirit, left the Jordan and was led by the Spirit into the wilderness ..."*[76]

- *"Jesus returned to Galilee in the power of the Spirit, and news about Him spread through the whole countryside."*[77]

---

75   Luke 3:21-22
76   Luke 4:2
77   Luke 4:14

- *"At that time Jesus, full of joy <u>through</u> the <u>Holy Spirit</u>, said, "I praise you, Father, Lord of heaven and earth ..."[78]*

- *"But if I cast out demons <u>by the Spirit of God</u>, then the kingdom of God has come upon you."[79]*

- *"... until the day He was taken up to heaven, after giving instructions <u>through the Holy Spirit</u> to the apostles He had chosen."[80]*

- *"You know of Jesus of Nazareth, how God <u>anointed Him with the Holy Spirit</u> and with power, and how He went about doing good and healing all who were oppressed by the devil, for <u>God was with Him</u>."[81]*

The very same Person and power that enabled Jesus to do what He did has been given to, birthed in, all true believers.

"Jesus answered, 'Truly, truly, I say to you, unless one is born of water and the Spirit he cannot enter into the kingdom of God.'"[82]

"However, you are not in the flesh but in the Spirit, if indeed the Spirit of God dwells in you."[83]

"But you will receive power when the Holy Spirit comes on you ..."[84]

"All of them were filled with the Holy Spirit and began to speak in other tongues as the Spirit enabled them."[85]

---

78   Luke 10:21
79   Matthew 12:28
80   Acts 1:2
81   Acts 10:38
82   John 3:5
83   Romans 8:9
84   Acts 1:8
85   Acts 2:4

"After they prayed, the place where they were meeting was shaken. And they were all filled with the Holy Spirit and spoke the word of God boldly."[86]

"Brothers, choose seven men from among you who are known to be full of the Spirit and wisdom. We will turn this responsibility over to them."[87]

"But Stephen, full of the Holy Spirit, looked up to heaven and saw the glory of God, and Jesus standing at the right hand of God."[88]

"And the disciples were filled with joy and with the Holy Spirit."[89]

Some Christians say to me, "I never hear God!" That is not accurate. They do hear His voice, almost always as thoughts coming into their mind. They would not have become Christians apart from "hearing" the call of the Holy Spirit.[90] Their problem is that they may never have been taught to test their thoughts to see if they might be "God-thoughts."[91] Or perhaps they actually assumed that the Holy Spirit would not speak to them in thoughts. They have true and good thoughts, not realizing the possibility, even probability that these "true and good" thoughts might be from the Spirit of Jesus.[92] They thus hear Jesus speak to them, but they simply do not recognize the thought to be from Jesus via His Holy Spirit. They have thoughts come into their mind, but because they have not learned to evaluate their thoughts to discern if they are from the Holy Spirit, they unintentionally "ignore" the presence and potential power of God.

---

86 Acts 4:31
87 Acts 6:3
88 Acts 7:55
89 Acts 13:52
90 John 6:44, 16:7-11
91 James 1:19, 1 John 4:1, 1 Thessalonians 5:19-22
92 Some Christians err on the other extreme, assuming that because they are "Spirit-filled" that whatever they think or feel or want is from the Holy Spirit.

HEARING AND LISTENING TO THE SPIRIT OF JESUS

Jesus' willing but untrained disciples very often "hear" the Holy Spirit but do not recognize the thought to be from Him. He whispers, and His whisper is recorded in our thoughts, but we do not realize it was God. When Jesus' disciples vaguely "hear" the Holy Spirit but do not sufficiently recognize the thought to have come from Him to respond, they say things like, "I know I shouldn't say this, but ..." We knew _what_ the message is, but we don't sufficiently realize _Who_ the message is from to obediently respond.

To listen biblically means to hear, to recognize, _and_ to obediently respond to the Holy Spirit. To hear and heed the Holy Spirit normally requires discipling in the ways of the Spirit. How to do this is described later in this book.

INDEPENDENT VERSES DEPENDENT

Jesus did nothing, said nothing, and even concluded nothing apart from consulting and coming into agreement with His Father.[93] This union of divinity[94] and humanity,[95] of Word and flesh,[96] was made possible in His incarnate state by the indwelling presence of the Holy Spirit, who led and empowered Jesus.[97]

Most need to be discipled in recognizing the Holy Spirit in order to live with this kind of sensitivity to the indwelling Holy Spirit. As we develop the discipline to bring more and more thoughts captive into conversation with Christ, we will come to better recognize and obey our King who indwells us.[98]

I want to think with Jesus, be sensitive to Jesus, and ask questions of Jesus ...

---

93   John 5:19, 30, 8:28-29, 12:49-50
94   John 1:1-3
95   Philippians 2:5-9, Hebrews 2:17, 4:15
96   John 1:14
97   See all above references to Jesus doing what He did by the power of the Holy Spirit
98   2 Corinthians 10:5

- as if He is important (which, of course, He is)

- as if He were present, literally with me (which, of course, He is)

- as if He speaks (which, of course, He does)

- as if He is My Lord and King and Master and God (which, of course, He is)

- as if He is worth including (which, of course, He is)

- as if He is trustworthy (which, of course, He is)

- as if He might like to be included in the conversation and the decision (which He does)

- as if I actually trust Him (which I say I do, but when I run ahead of Him, in practice I do not)

- as if Jesus is important to me (which I say He is, but if I do not consult Him, my practice mocks my statements)

- as if I actually love and care about Him and what He cares about (which I say I do, but when I fail to consult Him, in practice I am caring about me and what I want above what Jesus wants ... a functional denial that I love Him more than myself)

He who was entirely dependent on His Father calls us to come to Him, and to learn of Him, that we too might learn to walk by His Spirit and not by our flesh.

Committing to greater sensitivity to the Spirit of Jesus is usually not enough to make significant progress. Most of us need to be very accountable to an intensive and informed discipling process for progress in listening for the Lord before we act, talk, and decide. To learn to walk this sensitively to and dependently on Jesus (instead of independently) is a primary function of the discipling group activities that will be described later in this book.

After Jesus ascended and poured out His Spirit on all who would receive Him, the Spirit of Jesus led and coached Jesus' disciples in a variety of ways.

- *"'In the last days, God says, I will pour out My Spirit on all people. Your sons and daughters will <u>prophesy</u>, your young men will see <u>visions</u>, your old men will <u>dream</u> dreams.⁹⁹* [99]

- *"But Stephen, full of the Holy Spirit, looked up to heaven and <u>saw the glory of God</u>, and <u>Jesus</u> standing at the right hand of God."¹⁰⁰* [100]

- *"While Peter was still thinking about the vision, the Spirit <u>said</u> to him, "Simon, three men are looking for you."¹⁰¹* [101]

The Holy Spirit spoke to and directed the ministry activities of the early church:

- *"The Spirit <u>told</u> Philip, "Go to that chariot and stay near it."¹⁰²* [102]

- *"The Spirit <u>told</u> me to have no hesitation about going with them. These six brothers also went with me, and we entered the man's house."¹⁰³* [103]

---

99   Acts 2:17
100 Acts 7:55
101 Acts 10:19
102 Acts 8:29
103 Acts 11:12

- *"While they were worshiping the Lord and fasting, the Holy Spirit said, "Set apart for me Barnabas and Saul for the work to which I have called them."*[104]

- *"The two of them, sent on their way by the Holy Spirit, went down to Seleucia and sailed from there to Cyprus."*[105]

- *"And now, compelled by the Spirit, I am going to Jerusalem, not knowing what will happen to me there."*[106]

- *"Keep watch over yourselves and all the flock of which the Holy Spirit has made you overseers. Be shepherds of the church of God, which He bought with His own blood."*[107]

Those filled with the Holy Spirit are able to speak the very words of God:

- *"After they prayed, the place where they were meeting was shaken. And they were all filled with the Holy Spirit and spoke the word of God boldly."*[108]

- *"Coming over to us, he took Paul's belt, tied his own hands and feet with it and said, "The Holy Spirit says, 'In this way the Jews of Jerusalem will bind the owner of this belt and will hand him over to the Gentiles.'"*[109]

- *"One of them, named Agabus, stood up and through the Spirit predicted that a severe famine would spread over the entire Roman world. (This happened during the reign of Claudius.)"*[110]

---

104 Acts 13:2
105 Acts 13:4
106 Acts 20:22
107 Acts 20:28
108 Acts 4:31
109 Acts 21:9-11
110 Acts 11:28

- *"Finding the disciples there, we stayed with them seven days. <u>Through the Spirit they urged Paul</u> not to go on to Jerusalem."[111]*

The Holy Spirit strengthened and aided the early church:

- *"Then the church throughout Judea, Galilee and Samaria enjoyed a time of peace. It was strengthened; and <u>encouraged</u> by the Holy Spirit, it grew in numbers, living in the fear of the Lord."[112]*

- *"It <u>seemed good</u> to the Holy Spirit and to us not to burden you with anything beyond the following requirements:"[113]*

- *"I only know that in every city the Holy Spirit <u>warns</u> me that prison and hardships are facing me."[114]*

The Holy Spirit re-directed or even prohibited some ministry activities:

- *"Paul and his companions traveled throughout the region of Phrygia and Galatia, having been <u>kept</u> by the Holy Spirit <u>from preaching</u> the word in the province of Asia."[115]*

- *" … after they came to Mysia, they were trying to go into Bithynia, and the Spirit of Jesus <u>did not permit them</u>;"[116]*

A primary way the Holy Spirit works is by speaking to and through His Body. When the Body of Christ recognizes and responds to the Holy Spirit, the work of God is accomplished and the power of God is tangibly manifested. The 21st century church has all the provision

---

111 Acts 21:4
112 Acts 9:31
113 Acts 15:28
114 Acts 20:23
115 Acts 16:6
116 Acts 16:7

for power as the 1st century church. Why? In us, mere jars of clay,[117] dwells the same Treasure …

- the Spirit of Jesus[118]

- the Spirit of Christ[119]

- Christ in us[120]

Oh, how real is our awareness that this amazing Treasure, this stunning gift of Christ in us, is housed in very weak, often broken jars of clay. That this Treasure comes to dwell in very earthen vessels is almost as hard to believe as the Word becoming flesh,[121] but we do believe!

We desperately need to be _discipled_ to be sensitive to this Treasure, even to listen for the very Spirit of Christ indwelling us. We need a place and time to "practice His Presence." The meetings described later are an example of a place and time to practice His presence in order to be "Discipled by Jesus."

Because we have the indwelling presence of the Holy Spirit, we are called and empowered to walk as Jesus walked.[122] Walking as Jesus walked includes sensitivity to our Father's presence by His Spirit.[123] It is paramount that we …

> "Do not put out the Spirit's fire; do not treat prophecies with contempt. Test everything. Hold on to the good. Avoid every kind of evil."[124]

---

117 2 Corinthians 4:7
118 Acts 16:7
119 Romans 8:9
120 Colossians 1:27
121 John 1:14
122 1 John 2:6
123 John 5:19,30, 8:28-29
124 1 Thessalonians 5:19-22

We put out the Spirit's fire by simply failing to recognize and respond to His presence. We fan the flame of the Spirit[125] by honoring His presence. The primary way to honor His indwelling presence is to examine our thoughts. "Is that You, Jesus?" Rightly interpreted biblical thoughts are clearly from Jesus. Thoughts that do not pass the biblical truth test are to be rejected. If thoughts do not pass the practical test of being true, noble, right, pure, lovely, and admirable, they are seldom from the Spirit of Jesus.[126] It is in carefully developed "discipling communities" that we best learn, normally by practice, to test everything and hold to the good thoughts and avoid every kind of evil thought.

CAUTIONS

Some preliminary cautions are in order at this time.

- Are there those who assume that every thought they think and every word they speak are from God? It seems like it. "God told me" is regularly on their lips. Like Jesus, His disciples desperately needs to hear and speak God's Word, but not to naively assume that because His Spirit indwells us that all or most of our words are His words. I beg us all to be like Jesus: humble.[127] We have many thoughts in our minds that are not from the Holy Spirit; we have to carefully learn to "test everything." *"Now we see but a poor reflection …"*[128] As we are seeking to be sensitive to and guided by the Holy Spirit, I beg us to humbly say, "I wonder if the Holy Spirit is saying …" or "It seems to me that the Lord might want …" I desperately want to make progress in being more aware of the Holy Spirit, more guided and governed by Him. I want to be a part of a people who truly honor the Holy Spirit. I do not want others' dogmatisms or foolishness to drive us to an opposite extreme

---

125 2 Timothy 1:6
126 Philippians 4:8
127 Matthew 11:28-29
128 1 Corinthians 13:12

so that we do not listen for or "hear our Shepherd's voice."

- Some dear saints are so determined to "walk by the Spirit" that they cannot make it through their shopping process because they cannot know for sure if Jesus wants them to buy beans or corn. I personally want to include Jesus in every decision, more for being sensitive to and honoring of Him, than because of the eternal issue of discerning what is best between "corn and beans." (Many of the "corn and beans" issues can easily be figured out by gathering data and thinking. Having said that, I still want to get "better and better" at including Jesus in my thinking process. I don't want to ever leave Him out. I am not alone; He is in me. It is no longer I who live, but "we," Jesus and me.) The key is that we do not live with guilt and condemnation when we "forget" to listen for Jesus. I am completely relaxed with knowing that Jesus knows I want to include Him, even though much of the time I forget to include Him. Of primary significance is that I listen for and respond to Jesus regarding "right and wrong" issues (principles and righteousness verses selfishness and unrighteousness), and better verses best issues, which often are related to temporal values verse eternal values, and fear verses faith issues.

Jesus deeply desires to disciple us by His indwelling Spirit. For those with ears to hear, the Spirit of Christ makes increasing Christlikeness possible.

Chapter 4 explores two more of the primary ways that Jesus disciples us: through His Word and through His Body.

I Want to Disciple You Through My Word and Body

A pastor was emotionally torn, not knowing what to do. He had invited Debbi and me to lead a discipling conference for the parents of the church he pastors. The meetings started on Sunday and extended into the weeknights.

What was "tearing him up" was that his son's baseball coach had made a special point to call the dad/pastor with the message that the son was going to be the starting pitcher for the game that night. Humanly, the dad/pastor would far rather go to the game than another night of a parenting conference. Responsibility wise, the pastor was not overly concerned that his congregation would misunderstand him or find fault with him if he went to the game. He was more concerned about what I might think if he did not attend "my" parenting conference. He was very concerned what it would say and mean to his son if "Dad" missed seeing the very first time his son pitched … in order to attend a parenting conference. His ultimate concern was if the Lord had a preference, and if so, would the Holy Spirit make clear what the dad/pastor should do.

Dad/pastor came to me with the dilemma. I assured him that it was no problem for me for him to miss the conference. I suggested that it might be a good teaching moment to include his son in the decision making process. It would honor the son; it would help the son learn to bring decision making to the Lord; it would help the son listen for God's guidance through the Word, the Spirit, and the Body.

The dad/pastor agreed, and invited his son to help him find God's guidance with a tricky decision. Surprisingly, it was a "no-brainer" for the son. "Dad, you should go to the church meeting. Your job is to help the people come to Jesus, and that is way more important than my game."

Perhaps the son's "no-brainer" response should not seem surprising. The son "had been with Jesus," just like those who turned the world upside down.[129] He and his dad had been meeting with Jesus most mornings for months. He was learning how to recognize the voice of Jesus as the Holy Spirit planted thoughts in his mind. He and his dad were listening to Jesus speak to them through His Word. He was being helped to consider if his dad's words might actually be Spirit-initiated words. Now the son was revealing the transformation that comes from having his mind renewed.[130] He was learning to think with and think like Jesus. (Would the son's answer be different had he and his dad not been meeting? Probably. Would the dad have invited his son into the conversation had they not been meeting? Probably not. Is it always Jesus' best for a dad/pastor to miss a son's game to attend a parenting conference? Not necessarily. Where the scripture is silent, does the Holy Spirit give Jesus' disciples unique guidance based on the unique circumstances? I believe so.)

Jesus discipled both the dad/pastor and the son by His Word, Spirit, and Body. In this chapter, we will continue our journey as we think about the three primary ways that Jesus desires to disciple His followers: His Spirit, His Word, His Body.

---

129 Acts 4:13
130 Romans 12:2

JESUS DESIRES AND INTENDS TO DISCIPLE US THROUGH HIS WORD

We experience Jesus' Words in our minds by His Holy Spirit. We also experience His Word through the Bible. He objectively speaks to us, revealing Himself and other truth He wants us to know through His Word.

Try to imagine how much Jesus cares for us. Add to that His knowing how ignorant we are of His Truth, and His watching us inadvertently stumble in the dark, often falling into terribly destructive pits. By marrying His love for us and His awareness of how we need His Truth, try to imagine how He aches to have us recognize and respond to His Truth revealed in Scripture.

When my wife Debbi sends me an e-mail, I carefully read it. As I do, I am filling my mind with her thoughts. I am doing far more than "reading my mail." I am listening to a very real person named Debbi speak to me. I am "hearing her," not audibly, but in actuality.

Similarly, when I read the Bible, I am allowing the very thoughts and ideas of Jesus to enter into my mind. (Remember … our mind is one of the "immaterial" components of our life.) If I do not add to or detract from or distort the biblical message, but accurately receive His message, then I am actually listening to Jesus speak to me, as surely as Peter, James, and John did. Because of His great love for us, Jesus dances with joy every time we open His Word to listen to Him speak to us through His Word, for He knows how much we need His truth.

Of foundational significance is this: the actual, true, and primary Word of God is a Person. His name is Jesus. Jesus is the Word of God. To know the Truth, watch Jesus.

- *"In the beginning was the Word; and the Word was with God, and the Word was God."*[131]

---

131 John 1:1

- *"And the Word became flesh, and dwelt among us, and we saw His glory, glory as of the only begotten from the Father, full of grace and truth."*[132]

- *For the Law was given through Moses; grace and truth were realized through Jesus Christ."*[133]

- *Jesus said to him, "I am the way, and the truth, and the life; no one comes to the Father but through Me.*[134]

- *"He is clothed with a robe dipped in blood, and His name is called The Word of God."*[135]

Jesus physically embodied the very thoughts of God. He spoke and demonstrated the ideas, the values, the wisdom, and the message of His Father. If we want to know the "Word" of God – His immaterial, eternal nature, including His thoughts, His values, His desires – stare at Jesus, and listen to Him speak through His Word. As noted earlier, Jesus "materializes" the true and the right that is the "immaterial" life of God.

Sitting on my bookshelves are hundreds of books. A few of them are almost verbatim the same. Their titles: Holy Bible, King James Version; Holy Bible, English Standard Version; Holy Bible, New International Version; New American Standard Bible; etc. These "almost verbatim the same" books, all of which include "Bible" in their title, are held by most of Christendom to be uniquely different than the thousands of other books on bookshelves. That uniqueness? We have good reasons to believe that the Bible is a unique miracle. We have come to believe the Bible to be a divinely inspired document. We believe that, when accurately interpreted, a reader/student of the Bible is

---

132 John 1:14
133 John 1:17
134 John 14:6
135 Revelation 19:13

actually experiencing the very message of the Living God for all those He created in His own image.

The Lord Himself inspired scripture's writers to proclaim the temporal and eternal benefits of knowing and responding to His Word:

• Approximately 150 times Psalm 119 affirms the importance and the benefits of heeding God's Word

• The "good life" – now and eternally – is the sanctified life. "Sanctify them in the truth; Your word is truth. For their sakes I sanctify Myself, that they themselves also may be sanctified in truth."[136]

- The Bible is the teaching of Jesus, and if we hold to His teaching, we will know the truth, and the truth will free us from destruction at every level. "So Jesus was saying to those Jews who had believed Him, 'If you continue in My word, then you are truly disciples of Mine; and you will know the truth, and the truth will make you free.'" .[137]

- Our Father in heaven wants all of us, His creatures made in His image, to know about Him, about us, about relationship with Him now and forever, about our relationships with each other, about His purposes and plans for life now and eternally. Therefore, He inspired some of His people to record His message for us:

"All Scripture is God-breathed and is useful for teaching, rebuking, correcting and training in righteousness, so that the man of God may be thoroughly equipped for every good work."[138]

---

136 John 17:17, 19
137 John 8;31-32
138 2 Timothy 3:16-17

We will talk in much more detail about how Jesus disciples us through His Word in chapters 11-12.

JESUS DESIRES AND INTENDS TO DISCIPLE US THROUGH HIS BODY

Jesus' "great commission" to His first disciples was to do for others what He did for them, that is, disciple them.[139] He then commanded them to wait until they had been filled with His Spirit, which they did.[140] Having been with Jesus,[141] and now being filled with Jesus, they were expected and empowered to be like Jesus. This included adopting a few to spiritually (and when best physically) care for and feed like Jesus had done for them.[142]

My wife Debbi is a Jesus-follower. She has repented. She is indwelled by the Holy Spirit, just as Jesus was and as Peter, James, and John were. She reads and studies the Bible regularly. It is very *possible* that when she speaks, she could be speaking the very words of Jesus. Why? The Word of Christ dwells in her richly.[143] The Spirit of Christ is guiding her into all truth.[144] She has many thoughts; some of them she received from Jesus' Word and Spirit. She is capable of speaking the Word of God and doing the acts of God.[145] When she speaks, it could be Jesus speaking through her. What she does could be the very activities of Jesus. When I listen to her and watch her, I could be hearing and seeing Jesus in His "new Body." She is a part of the Body of Christ.

> *"Do not put out the Spirit's fire; do not treat prophecies with contempt. Test everything. Hold on to the good. Avoid every kind of evil."*[146]

---

139 Matthew 28:19-20
140 Acts 1:8
141 Mark 3:14, Acts 4:13
142 John 21:15-17
143 Colossians 3:16
144 John 16:13
145 John 14:12
146 1 Thessalonians 5:19-22

Whenever a Christian acts or speaks, it could be "prophetic," that is, initiated by the Holy Spirit, and accurately responded to by a Spirit-sensitive Christ-follower. How wonderful it would be if everything we heard from "our church" was an accurate response to the Spirit, as opposed to non-Spirit initiated thoughts or desires from sincere but insensitive church attendees. Christ-followers are deeply determined to "walk by the Spirit, not the flesh,"[147] for among many reasons, we are to represent (re-present) Jesus to His Body and His lost world. We Christ followers are truly to grow in walking as Jesus walked.[148] This is part of the fruit of walking by the Spirit, as illustrated by little king Will in chapter two.

We Spirit-honoring persons long to be alert to Jesus' presence through His Body. We carefully listen and watch for the Holy Spirit through other Spirit-indwelt persons in order to "not put out the Spirit's fire" for us through Jesus' Body. This is not to judge them should we discern they are "walking by the flesh," but in fact to experience what Jesus "looks and sounds like," when they are in fact "walking by the Spirit."

We thus "do not treat prophecies with contempt," but we carefully "test everything." ("Everything" includes what you are reading in this book right now. Could it be from the Lord? Is it?) We learn to "hold on to the good" and to "avoid every kind of evil."

Debbi and I were facilitating a meeting in the Midwest. Forty people came out on a Tuesday afternoon to be "Discipled by Jesus." It was the first time we had met as a group, and so I was carefully explaining each part of the meeting as we went along.

We came to the "Discipled by Jesus' Word" section. I asked us to open our Bibles and very painstakingly requested that we not add or detract from the plain meaning of the text. Having read the text, I

---

147 John 6:63, Romans 8:5-13, Galatians 5:16-17, 6:8
148 1 John 2:6

asked if we understood or if there were any questions. There were no questions. I then asked if anyone was willing to simply put the plain meaning into words from Jesus to us. "What exactly is Jesus saying to us through His Word?"

A woman who gave the impression of having been in the church for a long time responded. She probably did not understand my comments or question. She launched into a lengthy proclamation which was filled with wonderful, biblical perspective. The problem was that it had absolutely nothing, zero, zip, nada to do with the passage of scripture we were studying.

As she continued on, I became increasingly concerned, and frustrated, even judgmental. I finally interrupted her. "Thank you so much for all you are saying. What you are saying is very important truth. But I can't see how any of it comes from …" As I was fumbling for words attempting to graciously "rein her in," I heard weeping from the other side of the room. I looked over, and there was a most disheveled appearing lady imaginable. Her weeping diminished as she realized we were all noticing her. Then she spoke. "No one here knows me. I just got out of prison two days ago, and heard about this meeting. I came because I have so much pain, and so many questions. Everything that woman just said was an answer to some of my biggest questions." And she went on.

The point is this: Though this story is unusual, it clearly validates that the Holy Spirit is not only able, but normally desires to ministry profoundly into the deep needs of people as we gather to be discipled by Jesus. By every way of "testing," the long-time church attendee had been given healing, restoring, and even saving words by the Holy Spirit for the battered soul of a woman just out of prison.

How desperately we need a "safe" place to practice the presence of the Holy Spirit in and through His Word and Body. This is the meeting with Jesus and His Body proposed later in this book to practice being "Discipled by Jesus."

Whenever I am with any true follower of Jesus, or a group of His followers, it is possible that I might see and hear Jesus. Tragically, it is true that many of the "church's" words and acts are not of the Holy Spirit. That reality is precisely the passion motivating this writing that Jesus' Body be discipled, not by our flesh, the world, and the devil, but by the Word and the Spirit. Those being sanctified by the truth[149] must be discipled to wrap less mature Christ-followers under their arm and coach them in being discipled by the Word and the Spirit.

We celebrate all these Word-knowing, Spirit-sensitive, "aiming for perfection"[150] Jesus' lovers[151] who are committed to obeying _everything_ He commanded, including making disciples.[152] Because this quality of disciple can be present in Jesus' Body – His Church, it is possible for us to be discipled by Jesus through His church.

To be sure, I must take great responsibility to look and listen for Jesus through His Body. The extremes are obvious: we dare not assume all the church does to be of Jesus, because the church itself is greatly governed by thoughts, emotions, desires, motives, attitudes, etc. that are not yet transformed into Christlikeness. However, there is another extreme, and that is to fail to realize that the church (2 or 3 gathered as "re-presentatives" of Jesus, His disciples) is empowered to be the very Body of Christ … to be Christlike.

- *"But just as He who called you is holy, so be holy in all you do …"[153]*

---

149 John 17:17
150 2 Corinthians 13:11
151 John 15:9
152 Matthew 28:20
153 1 Peter 1:15

- *"His divine power has given us everything we need for life and godliness through our knowledge of Him who called us by His own glory and goodness."*[154]

- *"Whoever claims to live in Him must walk as Jesus did."*[155]

The low levels of Christlikeness in and through too much of the church is a blatant demonstration that we have disobeyed Jesus by failing to do what He commanded His disciples to do: make disciples who obey everything He commanded. But the point remains, it is altogether possible for us to be in the tangible presence of Jesus because He is present in and through His Body. He intends to disciple us through His Word-instructed, Spirit-inspired people. We are to embody His will and speak His words to each other, for we are the very Body of Christ.

- *"For where two or three come together in My name, there am I with them."*[156]

- *"Don't you know that you yourselves are God's temple and that God's Spirit dwells in your midst?"*[157]

- *"Remember your leaders who spoke the Word of God to you. Consider the outcome of their way of life and imitate their faith."*[158]

- *"Let the word of Christ dwell in you richly as you teach and admonish one another with all wisdom … And whatever you do, whether in word or deed, do it all in the name of the Lord Jesus, giving thanks to God the Father through Him."*[159]

---

154 2 Peter 1:3
155 1 John 2:6
156 Matthew 18:20
157 1 Corinthians 3:16
158 Hebrews 13:7
159 Colossians 3:16-17

John Wesley, the father of "Methodism," so named for his methodical process for discipling both the lost and the found, wrote, "For, after all our preaching, many of our people are almost as ignorant as if they had never heard the gospel. I speak as plainly as I can, yet I frequently meet with those who have been my hearers many years, who know not whether Christ be God or man. And how few are there that know the nature of repentance, faith, and holiness! Most of them have a sort of confidence that God will save them, while the world has their hearts. *I have found by experience, that one of these learned more from one hour's close discourse, than from ten years' of public preaching.*"[160]

By "close discourse," he meant the meeting of little bands of believers to be questioned and dialogue about our Triune God and all matters pertaining to Him. Under the watchful guidance of a fully devoted and growing follower of Jesus, these meetings enabled sincere followers of Jesus to dialogue (especially to answer questions) about Jesus, His Word, and its application to their behaviors, words, thoughts, attitudes, motives, and values.

How passionately Jesus longs to coach all His followers, by His Spirit through His Word and Body, until they have matured to the point of helping others be similarly coached.[161] To make meaningful progress in this discipling is the prayer of the following chapters.

---

160 Wesley's Works. Jackson, ed. Vol 8, p. 299
161 Ephesians 4:11-16, 2 Timothy 2:2, Matthew 28:20

CHAPTER 5

Do You Want Me to Disciple You? (Part I)

THE BEST COACH

Good coaching is important for those who want to succeed. From grade school through college, I loved football, basketball, baseball, and … well, I ran track. I remember the day that I heard that our new track coach was a "running mate" with an Olympic gold-medal-winning track star. I wanted to be the best I could be, and therefore I wanted the best coach possible, and it sounded like I was getting that in our new coach. I was pumped.

Then I became a coach. When I was called from coaching and teaching to be a pastor, I did not think my dad would be very excited. His only response was this: if you are going to be a pastor, be a good one. That was music to my ears, for that is exactly what I wanted: to be the best I could be. Can you guess what I did? I immediately started a long journey of hunting for the best mentors I could find to coach me in pastoring.

Anyone who really wants to "get ahead," to be truly successful, wants to be coached, and wants the best coach possible. They know they need it. Whether it be swimming, gymnastics, football, weight loss, business leadership, life skills, whatever, people recognize their need for a coach, and they rightly want the very best coach possible.

If coaching is valuable in temporary interests like swimming, drumming, dancing, getting buff, losing weight or job acquisition, does it make sense to secure coaching in that which saves life now and forever? Coaching in knowing and following Jesus? We call it being discipled.

Some need basic life-survival skills. Or relationship skills. Far too many are depressed. Marriages and families are disintegrating like never before. Businesses and government are bankrupting on many fronts. Whole cultures are self-imploding.

"Hey, Coach, can you help me do life well?" "Can you coach me in parenting?" "My finances are a mess. Can you help? In fact, I am a mess. Will you help?"

There is a Coach, a Discipler, who promised to turn ashes into beauty,[162] to make our life abundant,[163] to even make our lives matter. Far more, His coaching leads us to eternal life. Should we consider asking if He would coach us? Or, for some, re-consider Him? Would it be good for Jesus to be our Coach?

Jesus watches our planet. He celebrates much. However, He aches over much more. He knows He can help any and every person, and every situation. He wants to help. He calls to every person on the planet, including you and me: "Come to Me. Learn of Me. Follow Me … I want to save you."[164] He announces, "I love you. I left everything in Heaven to come to you to make relationship with you possible. I would die – and did – to restore our relationship. I came to make you aware of My love. I would love – passionately – to coach, to mentor, to disciple you into life: eternal, abundant, holy, productive life. I have made My Spirit available to you. I have given you My Word. I have given you My Body. In fact, I have given you _everything_ you

162 Isaiah 61:3
163 John 10:10
164 Matthew 11:28-29, 16:24

need for *life* and <u>*godliness*</u> … if only you would be My disciple …
if only you would relate to Me, draw near to Me, if only you would
come to Me – over and over and over, if only you would watch Me
… listen to Me … learn from Me … if only you would follow Me."[165]

Christians don't come to Jesus just one time for eternal "fire insurance."
We enter into a covenant relationship with Jesus as our loving and all-
wise King and Coach. The nature of the covenant is that we come to
Him over and over and over and over to coach and disciple us. To
have the life He promises, we must prepare for and do life under His
gracious guidance and governance, that is, prepare for and do life
under His coaching.

Coming to Jesus over and over, and following Him more and more, is
far more than the <u>*benefits*</u> we acquire through relationship with Jesus.
It is precisely why we were created! We were created for relationship
with Jesus. This is our reason for existence, our "raison d'etre." Doing
life with Jesus as our "life coach" fulfills our purpose – relationship
with Him, including empowering us for partnering with Him and
bearing much fruit, now but especially eternally.[166] From our Creator's
perspective, being discipled by Jesus IS success. Is that your perspective?

Jesus goes on. "The ball is entirely in your court. I want you, I welcome
you, I have made a way, *the* way, for you. The single most important
question for you to answer is this, 'Do you want Me to disciple you?'
That is, do you trust Me enough to let Me be your Coach? I promise
that I can give you every kind of real life: eternal, abundant, holy,
productive life. If you do not let Me disciple you, it is because you
actually trust someone or something other than Me, regardless of what
you say about your 'faith' in Me.' Do you truly trust Me? Seriously? If
so, you will do whatever it takes for Me to disciple you. In short, *do
you want Me to save you*, now and eternally?

---

165 2 Peter 1:3
166 John 15:1-9

"If you do not trust Me to coach you, who do you trust? You do realize that you are being coached by someone, don't you? You are following someone or something. Why do you trust those you are being influenced by (following) more than you trust Me?"

EVERYONE IS BEING COACHED

Like it or not, every person on the planet is being discipled / coached by someone or something. Being discipled is inevitable. The question is not if I am being discipled, but who or what is discipling me. Most waking moments our minds are being influenced ... whether from without or within. Even in solitary confinement, our minds race. Like a river carving out a canyon, what we are thinking digs deep grooves into our soul. These grooves – settled mind sets – shape and profoundly influence how we interpret all that happens to us. Further, these mind sets influence all that we say and do, including our influence on others.

The point: like it or not, aware of it or not, we all are being discipled by someone or something most of the time, even by our own mind sets.

EVERYONE CAN HAVE THE BEST COACH

There is great hope. Jesus, by His Spirit, is profoundly involved as one of the primary and essential discipling influences in every person on the planet.

"But I, when I am lifted up from the earth, will draw all men to Myself."[167]

"When He comes, He will convict the world of guilt in regard to sin and righteousness and judgment ..."[168]

---

167 John 12:32
168 John 16:8

Jesus not only died for everyone; He speaks to everyone. He saves those who respond and trust Him enough to make Him their coach, that is, they become and remain His disciple. When Jesus is received, and is working from within through an open, hungry, obedient follower, that person is empowered for victory[169] and becomes a hope-giver for all who notice. And notice they do.[170]

Can we literally, actually be discipled by Jesus *Himself*? YES! Did His "Come to _Me_ ... learn of _Me_ ... follow _Me_" apply only to persons in the first century A.D.? NO! Is Jesus sufficiently present to disciple us today? YES, overwhelmingly YES!

How? As described in the previous chapters, by the Spirit of Christ, the Word of Christ, and the Body of Christ.

In this chapter, we examine some reasons to be discipled by Jesus, including some of the necessities on our side to be His disciples.

REASON ONE TO BE DISCIPLED AND COACHED BY JESUS

In various ways, Jesus conveys this message: "If you let Me disciple you, I will free you from destroying your own life, and the resulting damage and loss to the lives of all you will influence."

In freeing us from self-destruction, Jesus will simultaneously save us from being destructive to others. "Undiscipled disciples" don't realize how much their unchristlikeness negatively affects others. Unchristlikeness has devastating effects.

"The thief comes only to <u>steal</u> and <u>kill</u> and <u>destroy;</u>"[171]

Those who see themselves as "Christians" yet are failing to be

---

169 1 John 5:4
170 1 Peter 3:15
171 John 10:10

seriously discipled by Jesus will, sooner or later, be destroyed.[172] Simultaneously, to their great demerit, they will negatively influence others with respect to Jesus, whose name these "Christians" are taking in vain.[173]

THE INEVITABILITY OF BEING DISCIPLED

Remember, all of us are being discipled and coached … by someone or something.

Be assured that there exist powerful, destructive forces that will inevitably disciple and form us unless we intentionally say "no" to them by saying yes to Jesus.

> *"For the grace of God that brings salvation has appeared to all men. It teaches us to say "No" to ungodliness and worldly passions, and to live self-controlled, upright and godly lives in this present age …"[174]*

The question is not "Am I being discipled?" The reality is this: every one of us has been, is being, and will continue to be discipled by some combination of persons and circumstances. The issue is "discipled by who or what?" Will we intentionally, proactively, aggressively determine who is going to disciple us, or will we passively allow ourselves to be discipled by those forces we cannot stop from coming our way? Something or someone has and will continue to disciple us! We must make a very conscious, intentional resolve to be led by the leader (Leader) of our choice, or we will inevitably be led by several deceptive, seductive, destructive forces. We live in a rapidly downward flowing river that consists of powerful forces pulling us downward, including: 1) our own flesh, 2) those around us who are not following Jesus, and 3) the seductive, deceiving, tempting influences of evil.

---

172 2 Thessalonians 1:8-9. This strong statement will be discussed in the next chapter
173 The rationale for these hard statements will be provided later in this chapter.
174 Titus 2:11-12

OUR FLESH IS A DEFAULT COACH

Our flesh (mind, emotions, desires, will, body) will powerfully disciple us if we let it. We can't stop our mind (I think), our emotions (I feel), and our desires (I want) from tugging for "their" way. To the degree that the Word and the Spirit have transformed our flesh, this flesh will be "discipled" by Jesus and support us in knowing and following Him, rather than our being flesh-governed. To the degree that Christ is not yet formed in these fleshly components of our heart,[175] they will influence (disciple) us negatively, that is, to be governed by something other than King Jesus. They will pressure us away from Jesus and His will. If what we think, feel, or want is other than what Jesus thinks and wants, and when these thoughts (I think), emotions (I feel), and desires (I want) govern us, then our flesh is functionally reigning as our god. Does our flesh rule? To the degree it rules, it is a deceptive and destructive idol. We are putting our faith in, and giving ourselves to, something or someone other than Jesus. This is idolatry … worshiping an idol that our enemy has counterfeited as "trustworthy" or "good".

THINKING ABOUT OUR THOUGHTS

A special note concerning the assumptions of our minds is in order. We _assume_ that whatever we think is true and right. We don't intentionally believe lies.[176] Why would we allow ourselves to "believe" that which seems to be untrue or wrong? We carry with us many unconscious and untested false assumptions. These assumptions were received and remained because we perceived them to be true. Many of them were and are not true, because the very assumption _excludes_ God's perspective in the assumed idea. An extreme but tragically real example: many young men and women of our culture cohabit, having never known or considered their Creator's intended covenant of marriage. Unknowingly, they assume their views to be accurate, and live (are mind-governed) accordingly.

---

175 Galatians 4:19

176 To be sure, sometimes persons try to believe something they actually believe to be untrue, and sometimes they temporarily succeed. But, in the main, it is true that most of the time most of us think that what we think is true.

The result is that we receive or reject or alter all information that comes to our minds based on what we have already assumed to be true. When an idea from the "outside" enters our mind that is in conflict with what we think, that new idea, to be received, has to "war" with what we already assume. The new idea is accepted, rejected, or altered in great measure by what we already think. Our mind monitors all incoming information, and biases our ability to receive differing perspectives.

I grew up biased badly against Catholics. This bias had absolutely nothing to do with theology or ecclesiology. It had everything to do with football and basketball. The town I grew up in was 90% Catholic (or so I was told). For every public school, there were one or two Catholic schools. The Catholic schools were "our" arch rivals in every sport, which I both observed as a young fan and then participated in as a player.

"My" high school was called Butte Public. Our mascot name was the "Bulldogs." But we were so overshadowed by the Catholic High School that we were not known so much as the Bulldogs; rather we were called "The Purples." What is that about? To be sure, our colors were purple and white, but we were the "Bulldogs." Why did the sports writers call us "the Purples?"

That other school, that despised enemy that too often made us look bad, had no mascot. They were simply "The Maroons." They were the Butte Central Maroons. So because they could not come up with a "real" mascot, we were "lowered" to being called "The Purples."

I loved the color purple. Do you know what color I despised? Yep … maroon. And I had just enough immaturity to identify the Butte Central Maroons, and the color maroon, with Catholic. Thus, though it had no rationality to it all, I superficially distrusted, maybe even was biased against, all Catholics.

One day that all changed. I was eight years old and selling newspapers on the street corner. It was January in Butte, Montana. The temperature on the Metals Bank sign across the street said -10 degrees. To get out of the cold, I went into the Rialto Theater lobby, which was on my corner where I sold my papers. While there, another "paper boy" confronted me. He was seven years older, well over a foot taller, and at least one hundred pounds heavier. He accused me of selling papers in his territory. I retorted that I was only getting warm. He demanded that I give him all my money and my remaining papers to pay him back and to teach me a lesson. I said "No!" He promptly doubled up his fist and smashed me in the nose. It did not take me long to succumb to power. I surrendered the papers and all my money.

Nose bleeding badly, and mixed with all the mess that flows from crying and being very cold, I shuffled out of the theater lobby to the street. I had been beaten, robbed, and was very embarrassed. It made no sense, but I simply crumpled down on the freezing concrete sidewalk up against the side of the building. What a miserable wretch I legitimately appeared to be.

Then out of nowhere, through my tear-blinded eyes, a blurry image appeared. About all I could tell for sure was that she was wearing that hated color. She was wearing a maroon coat, with the big white "M" on the front so there could be no mistaking where she went to high school and where her loyalties lay.

She knelt down on the freezing cement, took out a perfectly clean and folded white handkerchief, and wiped the goo and "maroon" blood from my nose and face. She then asked what had happened. In between sobs, I blurted out enough of the story that she got the general idea. She took my hand, helped me stand, and took me into the doughnut shop. She told me to pick out whatever kind I wanted. Then, she asked for more details on the papers and money. In those days, $.50 was acceptable profit for the day; $1.00 was a great and unusual day. She opened her purse, and took out a $5.00 bill ($50.00 or more today) and put it in my hand. This was unbelievable. I was shocked, stunned, and overwhelmed with gratitude and "love."

Can you guess what my favorite color became? Can you guess how my attitude toward Butte Central, and Catholics in general, changed? Still no theological or ecclesiological rationale. Just a new experience that "changed my mind." I unknowingly repented. I instantly loved maroon, loved Butte Central, and loved Catholics. (Incidentally, enough "maroon" blood was shed on a cross one day that when I saw and even superficially understood, I was dramatically changed forever, quite passionately desiring to live for Him who died for me.[177])

The point I draw from the "maroon" story is this: naïve and erroneous ideas got into my mind, and every new bit of information came through those erroneous assumptions and thus "colored" and biased the new information. It took a major event to "change my mind," resulting in my "hearing" and "viewing" new information through a different mental, "discipling" lens.

Every Christ-follower can testify to having once zealously thought a particular way, and having that way of thinking "judge" or determine his reaction to people or ideas. Then, having been exposed to Jesus' Word, Body, and Spirit, he sees "maroon" in an entirely different light, and responds to "maroon" differently because of his "discipled-by-Jesus" mind.

The ideas we have come to believe are powerful influencers (disciplers) in our life. They not only determine greatly what we feel, desire, and do, but they also distort, or prevent, different ideas that might be truth from being received accurately by our mind. Thus, our mind, which we cannot get away from, is a primary influencer and discipler that

---

177 2 Corinthians 5:15

is always at work in us. We desperately need to examine all that we think in order to test if our thoughts are truly what Jesus thinks.[178]

The greater point: if you listen to many / most Christians, you will hear them saying, "I think … I feel … I want." BUT THIS IS PRECISELY HOW THE WORLD THINKS, AND THUS BEHAVES. As Christ-followers, we died to our old way of living. We have been crucified with Christ. We no longer live.[179] All things have become new.[180] We no longer live "by the flesh."[181] I sincerely mean it when I say, "What I think, or what I feel, or what I want does not matter. I want and am committed to finding out what Jesus thinks and wants." Why? Because my faith is in Jesus! I no longer put my faith in me. I am His disciple. He is my Coach. I am resolved to know and follow Him.

THE WORLD INEVITABLY COACHES OUR FLESH

Our world consists of all the people and cultural forces influencing us that are different from the Word and will of God; that is, those realities that are different from the thoughts, desires, motives, and will of Jesus.

Whatever governs us is our functional "god." When people or other societal pressures influence us in ways contrary to God's, and we allow ourselves to be governed by this influence, we are letting these forces become a functional god, for we bow to them. We would not think of them as "other gods," but by allowing them to "rule" us, we are, in fact, allowing them to be an idol (god). My idols are anything that I allow to rule me other than Jesus. It might be robbing hours from my family in order to be president of the company. The reason I want to be president of the company is to secure things less important to Jesus than my family, for example, applause, prestige, power, or more money than I need. This misuse of time to win others' approval makes "them" an idol (god) in my life.

---

178 1 Thessalonians 5:21-22, 2 Corinthians 10:5, Proverb 3:5-6
179 Romans 6:2-8, Galatians 2:20, 5:24
180 2 Corinthians 5:17
181 Romans 8:1-17, Galatians 5:16-25

The world around us will pressure us to be governed by something we naively deem to be "good" rather than "God's best." If we allow ourselves to respond to this "call of the world," we are in fact being discipled by the world. We are "of the world" in that particular arena. Will we intentionally choose Jesus' higher, narrow way? Or will we "yield" to our perception of the "good," a wider path, motivated by temporal security or significance, that leads to destruction?[182]

> *"May I never boast except in the cross of our Lord Jesus Christ, through which the world has been crucified to me, and I to the world."*[183]

DEMONIC INFLUENCE MALISCIOUSLY SEEKS TO DISCIPLE US

Demonic influence will seek to lead our minds astray from our pure and simple devotion to Jesus,[184] mostly by deceiving or seducing us. We are often deceived or seduced in the areas where we think we are least vulnerable. If or when we are so led, we are functionally "discipled by demons." The primary mission of demonic influence is, by whatever means, to distract us from fixing our eyes on Jesus.[185] The demonic ideal occurs when those being deceived and seduced actually believe they are "walking in light." Think of the Pharisees!

Because of the persistent and powerful influence of the flesh, the world, and the devil, we desperately need Jesus' Word, His Spirit, and His Body to disciple us. "Above all else, guard your heart, for it is the wellspring of life."[186]

Jesus says, "My offer to disciple you will empower you to not be governed by yourself, others, or demonic influence. This results in your being free you from the painful and often devastating fruit of

---

182 Matthew 7:13-14
183 Galatians 6:14
184 2 Corinthians 11:3
185 Romans 1:18-32. 8:1-17, Galatians 5:16-21, Ephesians 4:17-24
186 Proverb 4:23

being discipled by anyone or thing than Me. Some of the fruit of yielding to disciplers other than Me: insignificance, insecurity, pride, arrogance, fear, worry, anxiety, loneliness, isolation, depression, guilt, shame, boredom, addictions, hostility, rejection, malice, hatred, conflict, unforgiveness, division, divorce, suicide, murder and every other kind of destructive evil behavior, along with the complicating, damaging, and multiplying negative consequences."

Our discipler is who or that which we follow. Jesus desires to disciple us by His Spirit, Word, and Body. He seeks to woo and win us, not just once, but over and over and over and over. He seldom overpowers or unilaterally forces His will in our lives. He certainly can, and sometimes does, when it fits His loving, wise, and highest universal purposes. But His forcing His will or controlling us is rare.

To be set free from being a disciple of our own flesh, the world, and demonic influence, we start by intentionally, aggressively determining to be discipled by Jesus. If not, we most likely will suffer the heinous fruit of following the three potential idols of flesh, world, and demonic influence. Though the fruit may not look heinous to begin with, anything that leaves God out leads to eternal death! That is heinous by any definition. Would you be set free from all that will destroy your life? Be discipled by Jesus!

REASON TWO to be intentionally and intensively discipled by Jesus: "If you let Me disciple you, I will lead you to abundant life now."_

> "The thief comes only to steal and kill and destroy; I have come that they may have _life_, and have it to the _full_."[187]

Jesus says to us, "To the degree that you are discipled to walk in the light of My Word, by My Spirit, through the caring and careful coaching of My Body, you will experience the wonderful quality of

---

187 John 10:10

life that I intended in creating you. I came and died, and now live, to restore the 'good' life to you. By good life, I mean the life My Father offers, a holy life of righteousness, peace, joy, meaning, purpose.[188]

"My offer to disciple you into this new, good life will result in the fruit of My Spirit: love, joy, peace, patience, kindness, goodness, faithfulness, gentleness, self-control.[189]

"My offer to disciple you includes inviting you to be My friend and My partner. It includes helping and empowering you to partner in My temporal and eternal works of love. It is so significant that the environment of your family, your church, and your work place will be greatly improved and in some cases transformed by My life through you. Of greater significance is that I can and will empower you to alter the eternal destiny of many lost people, and the quality of life and godliness of your family and church. Your life can and will buzz with passion, purpose and invigorating day-by-day activity as you mature in being discipled by Me. This will take time and work. One day you will see that the time and work were eternally worth it, and be so very glad!"

What we do today, and tomorrow, and the next day will make a great difference on "that" day!

It seems that people would flock to be discipled by Jesus. Is it possible that they don't believe Jesus because they have not seen these promises fulfilled in those who claim Him as Savior but know little or nothing of being discipled by Him?

REASON THREE to be intentionally and intensively by Jesus: "If you let Me disciple you, I will lead you to eternal life."

---

188 Romans 14:17, Ephesians 5:26, John 17:17-19
189 Galatians 5:22-23

"He who believes in the Son has eternal life; but he who does not obey the Son will not see life, but the wrath of God abides on him."[190]

"Do not work for the food which perishes, but for the food which endures to eternal life, which the Son of Man will give to you, for on Him the Father, God, has set His seal."[191]

"Now this is eternal life: that they know You, the only true God, and Jesus Christ, whom You have sent."[192]

"And everyone who has left houses or brothers or sisters or father or mother or children or fields for My sake will receive a hundred times as much and will inherit eternal life."[193]

Jesus will save His followers … forever! How we start the Christ-life is so important that much of this chapter is devoted to a good start. But in any race, the ultimate issue is not how we start, but how we finish.

Jesus calls to all, "Come to Me … let Me coach you … let Me help you get in My purposes and processes with Me … learn of Me … follow Me. I am your Way. I am your Light. I will lead you through darkness into Light, through death into Life Eternal."[194]

Many "Christians" believe in God. But so do the demons![195] The belief in Jesus that leads to eternal life is entirely different than the belief that many who think they are saved possess. Belief that leads to eternal life is in a Person (Jesus). This Jesus is alive, is present and active, is watching and listening and speaking … right now. With absolutely precision, He knows those who actually have faith in Him,

---

190 John 3:36
191 John 6:27
192 John 17:3
193 Matthew 19:29
194 Matthew 11:28-29, 16:24, John 14:6, 8:12
195 James 2:19

as contrasted with those who "take His Name in vain." Those with saving faith are intentionally sensitive and responsive to His Word and voice. They take Him seriously as their God. They take not only His historic death, but His contemporary life, very seriously. Today is the day of salvation.

To be sure, saving faith includes confidence in Jesus as the atoning sacrifice for our sins, but so much more. Jesus knows when the only thing we actually believe about Him is that He sacrificially suffered and died for our sin. He is painfully aware when "believers" are indifferent to the majority of that which He is, says, and does. He knows those who, in their heart of hearts, are unwilling to submit to Him as their living God, including submitting to His authority. To trust Him for forgiving grace, but not for guidance or governance, is to trust in three terrifying hours of Jesus' life, but not to trust in THE living Person named Jesus. Jesus' death for the sin of the world was and is dramatic and glorious beyond imagination. But there is much more to Jesus than the three hours of Good Friday. He was resurrected and lives today! We believe in Him, and we believe Him, which is much more than merely believing for His provision and offer of pardon, as essential as His death for sin is.

> *Jesus' provision of pardon is to establish and develop relationship, not substitute for relationship.*

The faith that saves is _much more_ than simply believing I am prepared for judgment day and eternity because I believe Jesus accomplished pardon on the cross for me. We are saved through faith in a Person named Jesus. He is much more than a doctrine. He did much more than hang on a cross for three horrific hours one Friday. He came, lived, died, was resurrected, and now lives in and has real relationship with His disciples by His Spirit. The reason Jesus "willed" to die included that He knew we had no hope for relationship with God apart from His sacrifice for our sin. However, His death was never intended to be a substitute for relationship, but rather restoration to relationship ... saving, transforming relationship.

Many so called "Christians" simply are not disciples of Jesus. Some of these dare to blatantly oppose the idea that to be saved one must be Jesus' disciple.

To better understand why we need to be discipled by Jesus, we will consider some of the biblical teaching regarding 1) the gospel of the Kingdom 2) repentance 3) the great commission, and 4) obedience. Walk with me through some scriptures that have been ignored or interpreted through a "non-discipleship lens."

THE GOSPEL OF THE KINGDOM OR AN EASIER GOSPEL?

Many well-intended "western culture" preachers of the last century have proclaimed to millions of listeners an easy gospel: "just believe; there is nothing you can do to earn your salvation." There is partial truth in that statement, but it is easily misinterpreted resulting in a conclusion far from the truth.

Jesus and His disciples preached a different gospel, the "full" gospel: the gospel of the kingdom.

> *"Jesus was going throughout all Galilee, teaching in their syna-gogues and proclaiming the gospel of the <u>kingdom</u>, and healing every kind of disease and every kind of sickness among the peo-ple."* <u>Matthew 4:22-24</u>

Consider with me this gospel of the kingdom.

The notable reality in every kingdom is the presence of a King! Citizens of any land understand the requirement to "obey the law of the land," and citizens of every kingdom particularly understand that as kingdom citizens they obey the king.

Jesus is a King, and He has a Kingdom. Everyone is freely invited into Jesus' Kingdom, not based on their own worthiness, but based on the King's desire that all be included[196] and His gracious death that releases all from the consequences of having ignored or rejected this King. Pardon for sin[197] is provided for all; those who actually repent, setting their hearts to know and follow this King, are the beneficiaries of His atoning sacrifice. These are included, celebrated, and welcomed into the Kingdom. In this Kingdom, there is a King, and all who would be in His Kingdom willingly submit to the government of the King.

Much of the contemporary church, along with many of its predecessors, has naively failed to authentically follow King Jesus. Somehow they did not get His message. Because they failed to grasp and practice His message, they invited others into what they themselves knew and practiced. They seldom introduced others to The King and His Kingdom. Thus new recruits were multiplied who did not realize that The King of kings required that in order to be a part of His Kingdom they must change kings.[198]

The authentic Christian community first demonstrates, and then announces, what Jesus and His followers announced: the good news (gospel) about a Kingdom. The King of the Kingdom is named Jesus.

- "Repent, for the _kingdom_ of heaven is at hand!"[199]

- "From that time Jesus began to preach and to say, 'Repent, for the _kingdom_ of heaven is at hand.'"[200]

- "And Jesus went about all Galilee, teaching in their synagogues, preaching the gospel of the _kingdom_, and healing all kinds of sickness and all kinds of disease among the people."[201]

---

196 2 Peter 3:9, John 3:16
197 The core essence of sin is relational: indifference to and ignoring of The King
198 Matthew 7:21-23
199 Matthew 3:2
200 Matthew 4:17
201 Matthew 4:23

- "Blessed are those who are persecuted for righteousness' sake, for theirs is the _kingdom_ of heaven."[202]

- "For I say to you, that unless your righteousness exceeds the righteousness of the scribes and Pharisees, you will by no means enter the _kingdom_ of heaven."[203]

- "But seek first the _kingdom_ of God and His righteousness, and all these things shall be added to you."[204]

- "Not everyone who says to Me, 'Lord, Lord,' shall enter the _kingdom_ of heaven, but he who does the will of My Father in heaven."[205]

- "Then Jesus went about all the cities and villages, teaching in their synagogues, preaching the gospel of the _kingdom_, and healing every sickness and every disease among the people."[206]

- "And as you go, preach, saying, 'The _kingdom_ of heaven is at hand.'"[207]

- "And this gospel of the _kingdom_ will be preached in all the world as a witness to all the nations, and then the end will come."[208]

- "Now after John was put in prison, Jesus came to Galilee, preaching the gospel of the _kingdom_ of God,"[209]

---

202 Matthew 5:10
203 Matthew 5:20
204 Matthew 6:33
205 Matthew 7:21
206 Matthew 9:35
207 Matthew 10:7
208 Matthew 24:14
209 Mark 1:14

- "… but He said to them, 'I must preach the _kingdom_ of God to the other cities also, because for this purpose I have been sent.'"[210]

- "and He sent them out to preach the _kingdom_ of God and to heal the sick."[211]

- "but the crowds learned about it and followed him. He welcomed them and spoke to them about the _kingdom_ of God, and healed those who needed healing."[212]

- "Jesus said to him, 'Let the dead bury their own dead, but you go and proclaim the _kingdom_ of God.'"[213]

- "The Law and the Prophets were proclaimed until John. Since that time, the good news of the _kingdom_ of God is being preached, and everyone is forcing his way into it."[214]

- "… The _kingdom_ of God is within you."[215]

- "After his suffering, he showed himself to these men and gave many convincing proofs that he was alive. He appeared to them over a period of forty days and spoke about the _kingdom_ of God."[216]

- "But when they believed Philip as he preached the good news of the _kingdom_ of God and the name of Jesus Christ, they were baptized, both men and women."[217]

---

210 Luke 4:43
211 Luke 9:2
212 Luke 9:11
213 Luke 9:60
214 Luke 16:16
215 Luke 17:21
216 Acts 1:3
217 Acts 8:12

- "Paul entered the synagogue and spoke boldly there for three months, arguing persuasively about the _kingdom_ of God."[218]

- "Now I know that none of you among whom I have gone about preaching the _kingdom_ will ever see me again."[219]

- "They arranged to meet Paul on a certain day, and came in even larger numbers to the place where he was staying. From morning till evening he explained and declared to them the _kingdom_ of God and tried to convince them about Jesus from the Law of Moses and from the Prophets."[220]

- "(He) has made us to be a _kingdom_ and priests to serve His God and Father—to Him be glory and power for ever and ever! Amen."[221]

Jesus and His disciples preached a gospel: the gospel of the kingdom … the government, the reign, the rule of God. No one is forced into this kingdom, but whosoever would enter must come in on the terms of the King: faith enough in the King to commit to obeying Him and submitting to His government. It goes without saying: to change from one kingdom to another, one must change kings. To enter Jesus' kingdom one must be committed to living a life of submitting to and honoring the new King! The good news of evangelism is about a Kingdom with a good King and a disciplined community. Like children in a family, until individuals mature enough to discipline themselves, they must be lovingly embraced and disciplined by others in the community. Those who enter and honor the King and His community will be saved.

The "bait and switch" gospel of "believe for grace" which then later "insists on" obedience is deceiving and cruel. From the outset,

---

218 Acts 19:8
219 Acts 20:25
220 Acts 28:23
221 Revelation 1:6

Jesus' contemporary disciples must proclaim more than grace for forgiveness. They must proclaim THE King, and His Kingdom, and His invitation to enter His Kingdom by turning from all former kings to submit to the King of kings. This invitation is offered to those who deserve the consequences of indifference to, even rebellion against, the King. But He Himself has vicariously suffered the legal cost of all sin, and welcomes, even commands,[222] "whosoever will" to return to[223] His Kingdom community. If the Kingdom is not preached, it is not the "full" gospel, for it is through the _commitment_ (heart) to grow in submissively obeying King Jesus that we are restored, healed, and ultimately saved.

REPENTANCE: REQUIRED OR OPTIONAL?

The announcement of the Kingdom creates a choice. The choice is to continue to be governed by any or all existing kings, or to commit to the government of a new King. To enter the Kingdom requires changing from every former king, all former kings, to a new King. This is a change of mind. It is repentance. Those who respond to the gospel of the Kingdom by becoming Jesus' disciples must repent, both initially and continuously.

There is a reason that many church attendees fail to live as disciples of Jesus. The reason: failure to hear and/or respond to the requirement of authentic repentance. The King of kings "commands all people everywhere to repent."[224]

To fail to preach repentance is to fail to preach the message of Jesus and His disciples. They proclaimed repentance as a necessary requirement to become Jesus' disciple. Note also the connection of the Kingdom and repentance.

---

222 Acts 17:30
223 "to return to" reflects the author's opinion that children are born safely in the Kingdom. When they are convicted by the Holy Spirit of sin and righteousness, and willfully choose sin instead of righteousness, they rejected the King and thus must return to Him and His rule. John 16:7-11
224 Acts 17:30

- "From that time on Jesus began to preach, "<u>Repent</u>, for the kingdom of heaven is near."[225]

- "Then Jesus began to denounce the cities in which most of His miracles had been performed, because they did not <u>repent</u>."[226]

- "He went into all the country around the Jordan, preaching a baptism of <u>repentance</u> for the forgiveness of sins."[227]

- "But unless you <u>repent</u>, you too will all perish."[228]

- "… <u>Repentance</u> and forgiveness of sins will be preached in His name to all nations, beginning at Jerusalem."[229]

- "Peter replied, "<u>Repent</u> and be baptized, every one of you, in the name of Jesus Christ for the forgiveness of your sins. And you will receive the gift of the Holy Spirit."[230]

- "In the past God overlooked such ignorance, but now He commands all people everywhere to <u>repent</u>."[231]

- "I have declared to both Jews and Greeks that they must turn to God in <u>repentance</u> and have faith in our Lord Jesus."[232]

- "First to those in Damascus, then to those in Jerusalem and in all Judea, and to the Gentiles also, I preached that they should <u>repent</u> and turn to God and prove their <u>repentance</u> by their deeds."[233]

---

225 Matthew 4:17
226 Matthew 11:20
227 Luke 3:3
228 Luke 13:3
229 Luke 24:47
230 Acts 2:38
231 Acts 17:30
232 Acts 20:21
233 Acts 26:20

- "But because of your stubbornness and your _unrepentant_ heart, you are storing up wrath against yourself for the day of God's wrath, when His righteous judgment will be revealed."[234]

- "Godly sorrow brings _repentance_ that leads to salvation and leaves no regret, but worldly sorrow brings death."[235]

- "The Lord is not slow in keeping His promise, as some understand slowness. He is patient with you, not wanting anyone to perish, but everyone to come to _repentance_."[236]

- "Remember the height from which you have fallen! _Repent_ and do the things you did at first. If you do not repent, I will come to you and remove your lampstand from its place."[237]

The word "repent" is a translation of the Greek word "metanoia." "Meta" means "change" (think metamorphosis). "Nous" means mind. Thus, the core meaning of repent is "to change the mind."

Why would anyone want to trust his own goodness, his own wisdom, and his own power to rule his own life when he could change his mind – repent – and trust the goodness, wisdom, and power of Jesus?

Repentance is the most logical of all options when we realize there is a perfect, good, wise, and powerful King who wants to save us. By "save us" I mean far more than "forgive us." I mean deliver us from all that would destroy us (including ourselves) and lead us into all that is truly good, now and eternally.

To repent with regard to Jesus looks like this: once Jesus was not my

---

234 Romans 2:5
235 2 Corinthians 7:10
236 2 Peter 3:9
237 Revelation 2:5

King, my Lord. I was king. But I came to know enough about Him to change my mind (repent) and commit to Him as _my_ King. Whatever Jesus was to me as a pre-disciple, He has now, through the change of mind called repentance, become my God, my King, my Lord, my Master. Through His Kingship He also becomes my Savior, my Deliverer, my Healer, my Provider, my Friend, my Hero, my Passion …and on and on. I grow in knowing and experiencing Jesus in all His ways of "saving" me, but I start by recognizing that He is King, and I am not, and I set my will to follow Him because I have heard enough about Him to put my faith in Him. This is repentance. The early church simplified it all down to one phrase: Jesus is Lord!

The point of this chapter is this: because Jesus is King of His Kingdom, and true repentance is necessary to enter His Kingdom, being coached and discipled by Jesus is more than possible; it is necessary both for eternal and abundant life.

The next chapter considers two more greatly distorted or erroneous perceptions by much of contemporary western Christianity: unnecessary discipleship, which includes unnecessary obedience. Much of the western church assumes that being a disciple of Jesus, including radical obedience to Him, is good, but optional, for Christians, because Christians are saved by grace.[238] Anyone tackling this issue might be considered very naïve, at best. But I invite you to honestly and thoughtfully journey with me as I tackle it in the next chapter.

---

238 Due to this "grace-based, optional obedience" mind set, a "Christian" can survive quite nicely with weekly or casual worship service attendance, and not need to be significantly discipled to be an "authentic Christian."

CHAPTER 6

Do You Want Me To Disciple You? (Part II)

We journey on, thinking about being discipled by Jesus. We wondered to what extent being discipled by Jesus is _possible_ (chapters 1-4). Now we are pondering to what extent being discipled by Jesus is _necessary_. Necessary? Yes, that is the question we are seriously investigating.

The question was considered through the lens of Jesus' Kingdom and repentance in chapter 5. The conversation continues in this chapter as we look at biblical discipleship and biblical obedience.

DID JESUS INTEND TO CREATE "CHRISTIANS" OR "DISCIPLES?"

The core question we now consider is this: "Is being a disciple of Jesus necessary to be a Christian?" Or, can you be a "Christian" if you are not Jesus' disciple?

>   _"Therefore go and _make_ _disciples_ of all nations ..."_[239]

The great commission is about making _disciples_ of Jesus, not just "believers" of a creed, even a creed about Jesus.

There was a time when certain groups of believers built whole denominations around verses like Hebrews 12:14: "without holiness

---

239 Matthew 28:19

no one will see the Lord." Many of those involved lived in constant fear of "coming short" and "losing out" with God. This is the dreaded legalism of "salvation by works." This is not even close to the meaning of the gospel of the Kingdom or being Jesus' disciple.

But now we have drifted to a more dangerous and damaging extreme, sometimes called "cheap grace." Cheap grace substitutes believing an idea or doctrine for becoming an authentic follower and disciple of Jesus. Cheap grace "trusts" any number of ideas or past acts[240] instead of presently trusting Jesus enough to intentionally follow Him.

Grace is costly. It cost Jesus everything to make relationship with us possible. Relationship with Jesus is made actual when we sufficiently believe in Him to respond to His call for relationship.[241] Disciples of Jesus have a very real, life-impacting relationship with Jesus.

Relationships are God's wonderful gift to us for life's highest enjoyment and meaning. They are also work.

Christian discipleship involves a profoundly personal and ongoing relationship with Jesus, precisely because we have come to trust Him. Being Jesus' disciple leads to life's greatest enjoyment and meaning – both temporal and eternal. But there is a cost. The cost of discipleship includes the work of relationship.

THE GREAT COMMISSION

Let us consider the great commission found in Matthew 28:16-20. Question: what did Jesus command His disciples to do? Answer: make disciples! Where does Jesus ever tell His followers to make church goers or church members simply by muttering their agreement to a particular doctrine or creed? Or "hell-escapers" simply by praying

---

240 Baptism, prayer prayed, walk the aisle, sign a card, etc. Faith in these acts, in and of themself, is simply legalism.
241 Matthew 11:28-29

"the sinner's prayer?" Where did Jesus commission His followers to make "Heaven-goers" for having raised a hand or signed a card or gone to an altar? Or to make "professors of faith?" Or to make "doctrine–knowers?" Or to make "Church–goers?" Try this one: "Make Christians?"

Is there any difference between "making Christians" and "making disciples?" Jesus commanded His followers to make disciples. He did _not_ command making Christians, or any of the other above mentioned descriptors. He commanded His disciples to "make disciples." It was disciples who were to be baptized. It still is.

A disciple is one who has been invited into quantity and quality of relationship with a mentor or guru. In this relationship, the disciple gives himself to the discipler to watch, to learn, to be coached and to be mentored. To be sure, the sinner's prayer, a raised hand or signed card, or profession of faith, etc., are NOT in error, so long as these experiences are not substituted for what must truly occur: a repentant heart that turns from trusting all other kings to trusting, thus following, The King ... that is, becoming His disciple.

We are to make disciples of Jesus. By definition, if one is Jesus' disciple, he is being discipled by Jesus.

What did Peter, James, John, and the Jesus' other disciples _hear_ when Jesus told them to "make disciples?" They did not hear "get people to raise their hands" or "pray a prayer." They heard their Discipler say, "Just as I have adopted and worked with and coached you, now you are to work with and coach lost persons until they know enough about Me to make the same kind of commitment to Me that you made when I first invited you to leave your old life to know and follow Me. And that is merely the beginning. You must then disciple them toward maturity just as I did with you." New followers were to be as attached to Jesus as much as Peter was when Jesus called him.[242] This attachment to Jesus is eternity long, and during this life is to aim at the new disciple actually knowing and obeying _everything_ Jesus commanded.[243]

Beethoven was a master musician. If you want help with music, you might see if Beethoven has some openings in his school of discipling. Rembrandt was a master artist. Want help with art? Check out Rembrandt's openings. Jesus was and is the Master in living life as intended. Want life, now and eternally? Become Jesus' disciple!

If we are to be disciples of Jesus, we must do with Jesus what disciples of Beethoven or Rembrandt would have done with them: spend significant time with the Master, the Discipler. We must watch and be taught by Jesus through Jesus' Word, Body, and Spirit. We must be asked to explain what we have learned by someone who is discipling us. We must be watched or give reports to our discipler to assure that we are making progress in believing the words and doing the works of Jesus.[244] This is considerably more than informing new attendees of the church's "systems of belief," and securing an expression of agreement, and calling it good.[245]

Who were the ones Peter and John were to baptize in water? Not hand-raisers or altar goers, but disciples … brand new, infant, baby, immature disciples, to be sure, but knowingly _committed_ to Jesus as their Discipler.

While on a mission trip in Israel, it was my delight to baptize some of our people in the Jordon River. Just up the hill from where the baptisms occurred stood a tower-like facility. After the baptisms, we were told the purpose of this tower. To be baptized in the early church was to violate the dictate of the Roman Emperor. The penalty in this

---

242 That this attachment is to occur, and one way to do it, will follow in this book.
243 Matthew 28:20
244 John 14:12
245 We pastors have usually done the best we can, including membership classes. This book seeks to move us in the direction of progress in being and making disciples of Jesus, knowing by experience the challenges involved.

geographical area was a guillotine-type beheading. This beheading of newly baptized converts occurred in the tower. Those who were baptized knew that they might immediately or as soon as discovered be marched into the tower and lose their temporal life for being baptized into Christ's family. Baptism meant much!

Human babies have the basic genetic code to, when receiving "normal" care, grow into what they are born as – humans. Puppies grow to be dogs, not cats. Failure to carefully communicate what it means to become a disciple of Jesus has doomed many to confusion, disillusion, even destruction.[246] The implications of being a disciple of Jesus must be carefully communicated before new birth, and then built in from new birth on.[247]

Infant disciples must clearly grasp what Jesus has done and will do for them. They must also clearly grasp what it means for them to become a disciple of Jesus, namely, invest much meaningful time with Jesus via His Spirit, Word and Body. Prospective or infant *disciples* must be sufficiently coached in the nature of being Jesus' disciple. They must be taught how it is that He saves them. They must be taught until they can articulate their need for real relationship, both with Jesus and His Body. They must understand the good news of the Gospel to be that Jesus has made possible, at extreme personal cost, a life-saving and transforming relationship with Himself. Jesus loved and loves them with all His heart, mind, soul, and body. He invites them into a reciprocal relationship.[248]

But they must be willing to enter into an eternity long covenant relationship – like marriage. And such a relationship is available

---

246 Destruction: responding to a caricature of the gospel, and being disappointed and disillusioned, throwing out the caricature, having never experienced the real and authentic that saves

247 Matthew 8:18-22, 16:24, Luke 14:25-35. This is explanation must include the nature of grace, authentic faith, heart obedience, and other issues of chapters 3-4

248 To be sure, the reciprocity begins in immaturity. But it is to mature to loving God entirely, including all one's strength. Matthew 22:37-40

and intended! We can talk to Jesus, listen to Him, be comforted by Him, be taught by Him. He is a real Person we will someday meet face to face who has real thoughts, real feelings, real desires and real responses right now. We can truly know Him! New disciples must understand their need to be coached somewhat like Jesus coached His disciples, including knowing and doing all that Jesus had commanded. They need to know the high level of maturity Jesus intends to bring them to, even to the whole measure of the fullness of Christ.[249]

These "baby" disciples must understand that they need committed relationships with Jesus' disciples (two or more gathered in His Name) similar to what Peter, James, and John had been committed to in being with Jesus.[250] They must be discipled – by Jesus' Body – to meet with Jesus and walk by His Spirit. Because they understand and are willing to be discipled by Jesus' Body, they are making provision for Jesus to truly disciple them.

Because many "Christians" around them do not understand their need to be discipled, these who are considering becoming a Christian (disciple of Jesus) must be clearly helped to understand that saving faith includes genuine repentance, heart obedience, and submitting to Jesus as Lord and King of His Kingdom.[251]

The abundant and supernaturally good life that Jesus offers *His disciples* "works," precisely because His disciples are being discipled, coached, and mentored by the Genius who created life and knows how life works. By definition, one is not a disciple of Jesus who is not being discipled by Jesus. One must become and remain Jesus' disciple to experience His promised life.[252]

---

249 Ephesians 4:11-16
250 Mark 3:14
251 In short, I believe the good news of the gospel includes a clear awareness of the issues of chapters 3 and 4 of this writing
252 John 15:1-9

That life is experienced through receiving and responding to Jesus Himself, a Person, dwelling within us. His indwelling presence is not cheaply given; it cost Jesus His life. Nor is it cheaply acquired; it costs us our self-sovereign independence. Nor is it cheaply experienced; it costs us sensitivity, learning to recognize and follow Jesus' voice. But the temporal and eternal benefits infinitely outweigh the costs ... and all alternatives.

To the degree that we draw near to Jesus, He will draw near to us.[253] He who is Life gives Himself to those who truly respond to His invitation to be His disciple. He invites all; some respond. In responding and persevering, they receive far more than temporal abundant life; they receive eternal life, Life Himself.

One way or another, we as Jesus' followers must sufficiently understand that we are responding to Jesus' invitation to eternal covenant relationship. We must make marriage-type vows to submit, trust, and love the King of all kings. But for many, maybe most, there was far too little understanding of, and commitment to, an eternal "marriage covenant" to be started and sustained through "living together." They did not understand that or how the "two were to become One" with Jesus as "Head of the relationship."[254] This must change.

The mandate to make disciples obviously proclaims the love and gracious death of The King for the sins and guilt of His subjects. In so dying, He threw open wide the curtain that had separated indifferent, independent, arrogant, rebellious, sinful humans from a holy God. In dying as the sinless Lamb of God, He made relationship possible that previously was not possible.

What is not being well articulated is that Jesus did not die to give us permission to continue to be very casual in our relationship with

---

253 James 4:8
254 Ephesians 5:31-32, 1:22, 4:15, Colossians 1:18, 2:10

Him. He did not die for us to "believe that He died for our sin" while we continue to walk in the same ways we did before "believing." He died that we might live a _new life_ with Him as our new King and Lord.

> "Go, stand in the temple courts," he said, "and tell the people the full message of this new life."[255]

> "We were therefore buried with Him through baptism into death in order that, just as Christ was raised from the dead through the glory of the Father, we too may live a new life."[256]

> "And He died for all, that those who live should no longer live for themselves but for Him who died for them and was raised again."[257]

> "Therefore, if anyone is in Christ, he is a new creation; the old has gone, the new has come!"[258]

Jesus' disciples earned a nickname!

> "… The disciples were first called Christians in Antioch."[259]

Christian means "little Christ." Considerably after Jesus had ascended, the disciples of Christ picked up a new description, a new name: Christian … little Christs. Why? They resembled their Christ!

Over two hundred times Jesus' followers were called His disciples before this obscure note in Acts 11:26. By then, the church was well established, and those who were a part of the community Jesus started had a name: disciples of Christ. Disciples of Christ was their name;

---

255 Acts 5:20
256 Romans 6:4
257 2 Corinthians 5:15
258 2 Corinthians 5:17
259 Acts 11:26

Christian became their "nickname." They so followed and became like Jesus that they were called "little Christs." But "Christian" was not their primary title or identity; their primary title and identity was "disciple of Jesus."

Back then, I remind us, everyone knew what a disciple was. A disciple was one selected by an expert in a given field (medicine, craftsmanship, theology, etc.). This expert would look for and find the very most qualified persons to mentor and disciple. The expert would invite a prospective disciple to be "with Him,"[260] come to work for him, even move into his home. In that close relationship, the expert could disciple (teach, train, mentor, coach) the disciple until the mentor's level of external expertise and internal values were significantly reproduced in the disciple. These "disciples" would typically be stunned by the rare privilege of being invited into a close, formal, coaching relationship with the expert. They would see it as the highest imaginable privilege to be a "disciple" of the "maestro."

Our "Maestro," Master Jesus, has no pre-requisite capabilities or accomplishments for those He invites. "Come to Me, all ..." He invites anyone, everyone, with no requirement of expertise or potential, but merely enough confidence in the Master to humbly, persistently spend time being discipled. That simply is what true disciples do! The disciple trusts Jesus enough to be with Him, to watch and learn from Him, and to be observed and coached by His Word, Spirit, and Body throughout life.[261] Jesus doesn't call the discipled, but He intends to disciple the called.

Those who had been discipled by The Great Maestro of all maestros were commissioned to do for others what Jesus had done for them.[262] They certainly preached and taught and performed ministries of compassion, but at the core of their responsibilities was Jesus' co-

260 Mark 3:14
261 Matthew 11:28-29
262 Matthew 28:18-20

mission: "do for others what I did for you, and help them to then do the same for others."

So, everyone in the new community was a disciple, including Jesus, the Chief Disciple. No one was ever a better disciple than Jesus, who spent massive time with His Father being discipled by His Father.[263] Further, He did, said and judged nothing apart from securing agreement with His Father.[264] No one has ever been able to claim such a close, discipling relationship as Jesus claimed to have with His Father.

Only two other times in the New Testament are Jesus' followers called Christians:

- Acts 26:28 ... by the pagan King Agrippa, who wonders if Paul is actually trying to persuade him to become one of these "little Christs"

- 1 Peter 4:16 ... by Peter when preparing Christians to be ready for persecution and suffering because of who they are

Well over 200 times, Jesus' followers are called His disciples. Is the point sufficiently obvious? To be a Christian is to be a disciple of Jesus, and to be a disciple of Jesus is to be discipled by Jesus!

The primary name of those who follow Jesus is "Disciple." To call oneself a Christian is to say, "I am a disciple of Jesus, the great Master, and I entrust myself to Him, including all the time He wants with me to teach me, train me, observe me, and coach me for living now and preparing me for eternity." How can anyone claim to be a disciple of Jesus if they are not being discipled by Jesus? That's simply a contradiction. It's not possible! What would we say about a person

---

263 Luke 3:21, 4:42, 5:16, 6:12, 9:18, 11:1, etc.
264 John 5:19, 30, 8:28-29, 12:49-50

who claimed to be a doctor yet had never made the effort to go to medical school?

It is disciples of Jesus, that is, those who have been and are being discipled by Him, who will be saved in this life and for eternal life. To see yourself as Jesus' disciple but not prioritize time for Him to disciple you is a serious denial of what it means to be His disciple. To be with Jesus forever, there must be an authentic attachment, a discipling relationship, with Him now. He calls us to Himself. Discipleship is not optional.

OBEDIENCE: REQUIRED OR OPTIONAL?

The major component of the great commission is *"teaching them to obey everything I have commanded you."* The easy part is the "teaching" component … dispensing of information. The very difficult component is establishing obedience. Disciples are doers of the Word, not just hearers. It is especially difficult when so many Christians have been welcomed into the family of God with an understanding that obedience is optional, because they are saved "by grace alone." Authentic Great Commission evangelism recognizes that everyone who has been baptized must be taught to obey.

This surely means far more than affirming we are saved by grace, so we need not "work." I hear something like this being said altogether too often by both church attendees and church leaders: "We should be grateful for God's gift of grace, but we are not required to obey God. That is legalism. If we are grateful, we will try to be obedient. And God's Word is filled with practical wisdom we would be wise to consider. Of course, many of the commands are far too idealistic for us to seriously embrace, and we certainly must not try in our own strength to obey. That would not be faith, but work. If we are not sufficiently empowered to obey, we trust that God knows what He is doing and celebrate His great grace." In short, our obedience is entirely up to God.

To the contrary:

> "What shall we say, then? Shall we go on sinning so that grace may increase? By no means! We died to sin; how can we live in it any longer?'"[265]

> "For the grace of God has appeared that offers salvation to all people. It teaches us to say 'No' to ungodliness and worldly passions, and to live self-controlled, upright and godly lives in this present age ..."[266]

If we are to "teach them to obey everything" as Jesus commanded, there must exist in the church a climate of grace and truth. This, of course, mirrors Jesus. No one was more full of grace and truth than He.[267]

GRACE AND TRUTH: THE CLIMATE NEEDED TO DISCIPLE OTHERS TO OBEY JESUS

The following story illustrates not only the grace and truth of Jesus, but the necessary grace and truth of disciplers if they are to partner with Jesus in making disciples.[268]

Every Sunday when I was a kid, my parents took me to church. As the years passed, most of those church services disappeared into a crowd of childhood memories, but one Sunday will always stand out.

I was seven years old. That Sunday, when the pastor had been into the message for a while, I fidgeted in boredom and thought about the marbles I'd stashed in my pocket earlier that day. I reached in and pulled out a handful to admire. Realizing my best marbles were still in my pocket, I got greedy and tried to pull out more. Within a

---

265 Romans 6:1-2
266 Titus 2:11-12
267 John 1:14
268 Story taken from author's book, If Jesus Were A Parent

moment, all of the marbles spilled out onto the floor. There was no carpet to muffle their landing.

Bang, bang, bang! Can you hear the marbles hitting the hardwood floor? Can you hear them rolling down to the front of the church and slamming into the altar? Can you see the pastor halting his message to lean over the pulpit and glare his disapproval while the congregation all focused their attention on "the kid?" I slouched in my seat, certain that I was in for the worst whipping any kid ever got for bad behavior in church.

Suddenly, I felt a big hand on my shoulder. In the midst of my fear and embarrassment, my dad had slipped his arm around my shoulders and was patting my arm. I looked up to find him staring straight ahead, his expression declaring,

"This is my son and I love him. Yes, he drops his marbles sometimes and everyone else wonders about him. But I am well pleased with him. I know he was a problem, but he didn't mean to be. I stick by him. I'll speak with him and help him understand. When it's all over, he'll do better than any of you realize. I'll see to it."

I would do almost anything with and for my dad. Even now as I write this memory, tears well up in my eyes. Why? I loved him. I easily submitted to his authority. Why? Like Jesus, he first loved me. He parented me with grace. He was kind, patient, not rude, not easily angered. He forgave me and stood with me. He spent time with me. Like Jesus, he explained things to me gently. He instructed and corrected me kindly. He explained things so they made sense to me. Like Jesus, he gave me specific directions and disciplined me fairly when I failed to obey.

For any of us to make disciples of Jesus, we must be His disciples ... being discipled by Him ... becoming increasingly like Him. Among other things, He is full of grace and truth.

Obedience is first about the heart

"Man looks at the outward appearance, but the Lord looks at the heart."[269]

"You are the ones who justify yourselves in the eyes of men, but God knows your hearts."[270]

Expecting obedience will legitimately be critiqued as legalism unless it is thoroughly understood and regularly communicated that God's understanding of obedience *STARTS* in the heart. We must continually remind ourselves that it is the heart that God observes. A heart *committed* to obeying Jesus is immediately possible by grace. Performing perfectly is, at the very least, an ominous and fearful responsibility. But a Holy God who has graciously provided full atonement for legal imperfection is fully justified and reasonable to expect "aiming for perfection."[271] "Aiming high," knowing how it will delight our Father and with no fear of judgment for aiming and missing, is truly manageable and immediately possible. Rather than condemnation for aiming high and missing, there is heavenly celebration, affirmation, and encouragement to keep on "aiming for perfection." I wonder if our Father, who sees our imperfect performance and heart, yet sees us "aiming for perfection," does not shout a very loud, "*PERFECT*!"

Obedience must be understood relationally. A relational understanding sees obedience as, first, a locked-in attitude of deep resolve toward a Person (Jesus) to do whatever He commands, because He is God, He is trusted, and He is loved. If obedience is merely about performance, and if I am *not* able to obey *all* of Jesus' commands, and if that is a *requirement* for relationship with Him and eternal life, I am hopelessly lost. Obedience as performance is or will become legalism.

269 1 Samuel 16:7
270 Luke 16:15
271 2 Corinthians 13:11

However, my real faith in Jesus, including that I trust what He says, empowers me to commit to and sustain this holy _resolve_ to obey. This is a heart position, and this is what God sees clearly and judges perfectly. It is worth repeating that, though I regularly come short of perfect performance, I can, as Paul admonishes, "aim for perfection …" precisely because I am saved by grace and need not fear losing relationship with Jesus because of coming short of His will. As I "<u>aim</u> for perfection," God is observing and calls it "perfect." He knows my heart, and knows I am "aiming" to obey Him. He knows if my will is set to obey, I will inevitably be making progress. If I am aiming to obey Him, I will secure and receive help, and, over time, I will do better. My intent to obey will turn into successfully performing what Jesus commands. My heart intent to obey has motivated me to secure God's help so I now have the ability to obey. Specific obedience begins when God's will is known to me and, because my will has been set to obey Him, my heart response to recognizing His will is a clear "yes." Particular obedience progresses until the heart intent to obey secures whatever help needed to turn intention into obedient action and character.

To attempt to clarify the distinction between obedience as a heart attitude and obedience as perfect performance, imagine the following dinnertime scenario:

A family is sitting at the table. The father reminds his children that there was a problem the night before when one family member spilled his milk. He tells them to be careful tonight to not spill their milk. Dinner goes smoothly until the doorbell rings. The four-year-old jumps out of his chair. In his excitement, he _unintentionally_ knocks over his glass of milk. It spills across the table and onto the floor. The father helps his son quickly clean up the milk while the mother welcomes their guests into the living room. A few minutes later, while the family visits with their company, the older brother sees an opportunity. He dislikes milk. He knows his parents expect him to drink his milk, but as they visit, off to the kitchen he goes to deposit his milk in the sink. He delights in watching it go down the drain.[272]

Let's analyze this simple scenario. Both boys "spilled" their milk. Were both sons disobedient? The younger brother didn't mean to spill his milk. It was an accident. But by some judging "technically," the four-year-old was guilty of disobedience because he did, in fact, spill the very milk he was told not to spill. And technically, the older brother didn't "spill" his milk. He purposefully poured it in the sink. Did either or both boys disobey their father's direction to not spill the milk? If only one disobeyed, which one was it? For anyone seeing the "heart," the younger boy would be judged innocent and the older as guilty.

> *"But thanks be to God that though you were slaves of sin, you became obedient from the heart to that form of teaching to which you were committed …"* Romans 6:17

IT IS THIS HEART OBEDIENCE TO OUR KING THAT IS REQUIRED IN HIS KINGDOM

Jesus was crucified for claiming to be the Son of God, and for claiming to be a King, in fact, _the_ King. We claim Him as King. Our King. To enter His Kingdom, and come under His loving presence, protection and provision, we recognize, honor, and submit to Him as our King. If we are not _committed_ (*think heart*) to obeying Him, either we do not see Him as King, or we are rebels against the King. In either case, we are not included in His Kingdom. (Remember, when we introduce lost persons to Jesus, they need to know that He is the King above all kings with ALL authority.) Note the clear teaching that follows regarding the necessity of obedience to be a Christian. Please remember: biblically, obedience starts as _resolve_ to obey; this Spirit-guided and Spirit-aided resolve matures into godly action, and ultimately, godly character.

---

272 Another illustration from If Jesus Were A Parent

"Not everyone who says to me, 'Lord, Lord,' will <u>enter</u> the king-dom of heaven, but only he who <u>does</u> the will of my Father who is in heaven."[273]

To enter Jesus' Kingdom, a genuine, holy resolve to obey Jesus must be established. This is repentance. Jesus knows that if the resolve is present, progress in performance will occur. He also knows that the aim, the miss, the painful brokenness of missing, the re-aiming, etc., will all be observed by others and model authenticity.

"He (Jesus) became the source of eternal salvation for those who <u>obey</u> Him."[274]

This could not be more clearly stated. Again, God sees the heart, and knows if the holy resolve is present. The holy resolve is always the first human side of obedience which, over time, becomes tangible and visible.

"We know that we have come to know Him if we <u>obey</u> His commands."[275]

What is the evidence that we know Jesus, whom to know is life eternal?[276] Obedience!

"He will punish those who do not know God and do not <u>obey</u> the gospel of our Lord Jesus Christ. They will be punished with everlasting destruction and shut out from the presence of the Lord and the majesty of His power."[277]

How has this position of Paul, the great apostle of grace, been so heinously confused or ignored?

---

273 Matthew 7:21
274 Hebrews 5:9
275 1 John 2:3-6
276 John 17:3
277 2 Thessalonians 1:8-9

THE COST OF DISCIPLESHIP: REAL RELATIONSHIP BEFITTING THE KING

- *"Enter through the narrow gate. For wide is the gate and broad is the road that leads to destruction, and many enter through it. But small is the gate and narrow the road that leads to life, and only a few find it."*[278]

- *"Many will say to Me on that day, 'Lord, Lord, did we not prophesy in Your name, and in Your name drive out demons and perform many miracles?' Then I will tell them plainly, 'I never knew you. Away from Me, you evildoers!'"*[279]

- *"Come to Me, all you who are weary and burdened, and I will give you rest. Take My yoke upon you and learn from Me, for I am gentle and humble in heart, and you will find rest for your souls."*[280] Note: Jesus's disciples do not come to Him once; they come to Him over and over and over and over.*

- *"Then Jesus said to His disciples, 'If anyone would come after Me, he must deny himself and take up his cross and follow Me. For whoever wants to save his life will lose it, but whoever loses his life for Me will find it. What good will it be for a man if he gains the whole world, yet forfeits his soul? Or what can a man give in exchange for his soul?"*[281]

For me, to deny myself means to say "no" to what I think, and feel, and want in order to say "yes" to Jesus. What does it mean to you?

- *"If anyone comes to Me and does not hate his father and mother, his wife and children, his brothers and sisters—yes,*

---

278 Matthew 7:13-14
279 Matthew 7:22-23
280 Matthew 11:28-29
281 Matthew 16:24-26

even his own life—he cannot be My disciple. And anyone who does not carry his cross and follow Me cannot be My disciple."[282]

- *"I have been crucified with Christ; and it is no longer I who live, but Christ lives in me; and the life which I now live in the flesh I live by faith in the Son of God, who loved me and gave Himself up for me."[283]*

- *"And he died for all, that those who live should <u>no longer</u> live for themselves but <u>for</u> Him who died for them and was raised again."[284]*

REASON FOUR TO BE DISCIPLED BY JESUS:

"If you let Me disciple you, I will help you make progress in becoming <u>like Me</u>, and in the process, you will lay up great treasures in heaven!"

Like Jesus? In what ways? To say we can be like Jesus sounds naively arrogant.

What is written? Can we who are being discipled by Jesus …

- walk as Jesus walked?"[285] We can do one step as Jesus did … then another.

- like Him who called us is holy, be holy in all we do?[286] Could we not have one holy thought, say one holy word, do one holy act! Then two … then four … then eight … and more and more?

---

282 Luke 14:26-27
283 Galatians 2:20
284 2 Corinthians 5:15
285 1 John 2:6
286 1 Peter 1:15

- do what Jesus did, in fact do even greater things?[287] It is through faith. Could we not grow in faith?

- be like our Master?[288] More and more!

- love God the Father with all our heart, soul, mind, and strength, like Jesus does?[289] Yes, starting with willing one thing: knowing Him!

- love our neighbor as we love ourselves?[290] One act at a time.

- make other disciples of Jesus who will be free from the powers of evil, experience abundant life now, receive and retain eternal life, become like Jesus in this life?[291] Follow me as I follow Christ!

- be filled to the fullness of God?[292] By His Spirit, as I yield.

- be perfect as our Father in heaven is perfect?[293] "Really, Jesus?" "Yes, really! I see your heart, and if it is not yet pure, as you behold Me, I will, by My Spirit, make you pure! Is that not perfect?"

For these and other reasons, Jesus stares into our eyes and says to us, "Because I love you, I would do anything – everything – to save you. I invite you to commit to not being discipled by your own thoughts and desires, and by others thoughts and desires. I invite you to intentionally commit to being discipled by Me, far more than ever before. I can save you, but you must grow in being discipled by Me!

---

287 John 14:12
288 Matthew 10:24-25
289 Matthew 22:37-38
290 Matthew 22:39-40
291 Matthew 28:18-20
292 Ephesians 1:22-23, 3:16-19, 4:11-15, 5:18
293 Matthew 5:48

Will you repent of all other governments and fix your eyes on Me as your King? I died for everyone and made salvation available to all, but only those who respond to My invitation to become My disciple will be saved. I beg you, for your sake, other's sake, My sake, come to Me! Learn of Me! Follow Me! I will save you, I promise!

Section B:
Processes Jesus Might Use in Discipling Us Today

CHAPTER 7

Who Do You Say That I Am?

QUESTION 1

One day Jesus and His guys traveled to a different region. They must have scattered and mingled in the shops or other common grounds for a while. When they gathered again, maybe around the evening campfire, Jesus asked them something like this, "So, what is the talk on the street about Me? What do they know about Me? Who do they say that I am?"

Evidently, Jesus had become the buzz of the region. People must have been wondering and discussing who He was. Maybe even arguing a bit?

The sparks flickered upward as someone tossed a twig into the fire. Even the smoke burning their eyes did not deter the disciples from answering. They had plenty to tell. "Some say John the Baptist; others say Elijah; and still others, Jeremiah or one of the prophets."[294]

Then Jesus prepared to ask them another question. Due to the gravity of the question, I imagine a poignant pause. Jesus leaned forward, His eyes darting back and forth from one disciple to another, waiting for their eyes to respond and lock into His gaze.

---

294 Matthew 16:14

"But what about you," He asked. "Who do you say that I am?"

A longer pause. Silence. Big moment. Slight nervous tension.

Then ... "Simon Peter answered, 'You are the Christ, the Son of the living God.'"[295]

If it had been ambiguous to this moment, ambiguity was no longer the case. There it was. Right out in the open. It had to be faced. Peter thought ... and spoke it right out loud: "Jesus, You are the Messiah, the long waited for Deliverer of God's people." Peter actually believed it, and dared to say it out loud: he believed that the Messiah, the nearly mythical dream that so many had nearly given up hope for, was actually sitting right there ... maybe smoke burning His eyes ... with them.

Now the atmosphere was hyper charged. No drifting off to sleep or even day dreaming. All bodies poised, nearly tense due to focused anticipation. All minds simultaneously united in wondering how Peter's proclamation had affected Jesus. Wondering what Jesus was thinking. Wondering if Peter was right. Wondering if Jesus would tell them. Wondering. Waiting.

Finally came Jesus' response. What a stunning response. Something like this: "Peter, do you realize how blessed you are? What you just said did not come from your own observations or imaginations. And you did not get it from any other mere mortal. What you just said were and are the very words of God My Father! He whispered to you, and you heard His whisper clearly enough to do something with it: you spoke what you heard! And I tell you: though you nor others may not see it yet, you are a Rock! And I will empower you, and partner with you, through this magnificently clear revelation you have articulated, to build My eternal family. And nothing, not even the gates of Hades, can stop what we are doing."[296]

---

295 Matthew 16:16
296 Matthew 16:17-18

What a moment. Try to imagine the impact on those listening to Peter as he articulated his answer to Jesus' question ... and then as Jesus responded. I believe Jesus' disciples were all marked like never before and shaped for the future by Peter's answer: "You are the Christ, the Son of the living God."

Some observations:

- Jesus asked His disciples to think about His very essence, His nature, and then to articulate their conclusion about Him, and to Him, in front of each other. When we are gathered, I wonder if Jesus might want to ask us this same question?[297] Would it be helpful for us, His contemporary disciples, to routinely answer this question? How helpful? Why?

- Peter's response had a meaningful impact on Jesus, and certainly had to powerfully impact the other disciples, though no mention is made in Scripture. What would happen if we spent more time together in real dialogue with Jesus, seeking to answer His question biblically, or out of our experience with Him?

- Jesus responded to Peter in front of the others with an unambiguous statement given directly by God's Spirit. If we spoke to Jesus about Jesus might He sometimes respond with a powerful Spirit-given Word from His Father for us?

- The total conversation surely impacted and elevated all the disciples to a much greater clarity, greater faith in, and greater commitment to Jesus and His mission. Could talking _to_ Jesus more _about_ Jesus possibly result in this kind of clarity, faith, and commitment? Is He worth the try?

---

297 Our answer would be praise, and it would come from our relationship with Jesus, not a preacher's message or a writer's song. It would be our very own "song" to Jesus

Jesus surely wants to disciple His contemporary disciples – us – with the same kind of question for the same reasons. He might ask us, "Why do you think I want all of you to answer My question in each other's hearing?"

JESUS' QUESTION ADDRESSES OUR GREATEST NEED!

The more clearly we answer Jesus' question, the greater will be our accuracy in knowing Him. The greater our accuracy in knowing Jesus, the greater will be our faith in Him and our love for Him, thus those He loves. The greater our faith and love, the greater will be our inward and outward Christlikeness, our character and ministry, and our productivity now and for eternity. Knowing Jesus better through accurately answering His question leads to tangible, meaningful, eternal life.[298] "What comes into our minds when we think about God is the most *important thing* about us."[299] In other words, the most important thing about you is your knowledge of God. Jesus said, "Anyone who has seen Me has seen the Father."[300]

Conversely, the more distorted or absent our answer to Jesus' question, the more indifferent to Jesus we will be. Or confused about Him. Even ignorant of Him. The more indifferent to, confused about, or ignorant of Jesus we are, the more we will inevitably default to trusting in someone or something other than Jesus. We will then give ourselves to the someones or something else. This is idolatry and will, sooner or later, destroy our lives. We will later observe this reality identified clearly in Romans 1:18-32.

Our greatest need is to know Jesus as He actually is.

> *"Now this is eternal life: that they may <u>know</u> You, the only true God, and Jesus Christ, whom You have sent."[301]*

---

298 John 17:3
299 This World: Playground or Battleground? by A.W. Tozer, pp. 5-6.
300 John 14:9
301 John 17:3

"What is more, I consider everything a loss compared to the sur-passing greatness of <u>knowing</u> Christ Jesus my Lord, for whose sake I have lost all things."[302]

A denominational discipling director and I were facilitating a meeting to be "discipled by Jesus" in the Midwest of the U.S. It was the first time the "group" met, and it was 6:00am.

Like we start most meetings, we affirmed the actual presence of Jesus. "Lord Jesus, we celebrate Your presence.[303] You are here, and You desire to guide and lead us.[304] We commit to listening for You throughout our time together."

I then asked if anyone would be willing to answer Jesus' question, "Who do you say that I am?" Several were answering meaningfully. The atmosphere was alive with the awareness of Jesus' presence. I asked if any, instead of talking to us about Jesus, would talk directly to Jesus, but only about Jesus, directly answering His question, "Who do you say that I am?"

Some responded. While one person was imagining staring into Jesus' eyes and tearfully answering His question, I involuntarily jumped. I was startled because the table had started to shake. Simultaneously I heard a muffled sob, and then a crescendo of sobbing in volume and intensity. I looked over to see a huge man with bib overalls, head on the table, shaking and sobbing loudly. It was a bit ominous ... eerie. No one tried to pray over the top of the sobs. All became silent except for this giant of a man. Something dramatic was happening because of his awareness of the real presence of Jesus.

He began to blurt out intermittently through the sobs, "Jesus is so

---

302 Philippians 3:8
303 Matthew 18:20
304 John 14-16

ashamed of me." I did not know what to do. So I waited. He repeated his one line statement of what he thought Jesus was thinking about him several times. He went further. "My pastor would be so ashamed of me if he knew."

After a bit, I asked the group (perhaps dangerously), "Does anyone have any idea what Jesus _might_ be thinking about this man?"

Several were quick to respond, and all, one way or another, articulated Jesus' great love and grace for this man, regardless of what he had done. One man across from the table became vehement. His voice rose from normal volume to "preacher shouting" as he tried to "persuade" our sobbing, huge friend. He even stood, leaned over the table, and started pumping his fist in his zeal to make the point.

With almost as much zeal, I interrupted the "preacher," insisting that he stop. When he quieted down, I said, "We all agree with what you are saying, but do you think the way you are saying it is the way Jesus would speak?"

The question obviously jarred him; he instantly changed. Sitting down, he extended his hands palms up, and with tears in his eyes and a gentle voice, he began to explain how deeply and tenderly Jesus valued our brother at the table. The tone and message were almost as if Jesus Himself were speaking the words. The message, and the method, sunk deeply into the heart of our sobbing brother, and healing began.

My point: both the sobbing "giant" and the "preaching" brother were profoundly affected by the conscious awareness of Jesus' presence and who He is. Both had their thoughts, emotions, desires, words, and acts changed because they were aware of Jesus. One was convicted of sin and was outwardly "out of control"; the other, when he stopped to think about "who Jesus is," was changed by the awareness of Jesus' gentleness.

"Come near to God and He will come near to you."[305] God specially makes Himself known as His people are sincerely praising Him.[306] The awareness of Jesus changes us, so very much, in life saving ways. We desperately need to know and answer His question, "Who do you say that I am?"

Paul was the persecutor-turned-missionary through a dramatic encounter with Jesus. Even with this life-reversing exposure, He was not satisfied with His knowing of Jesus. Many years later, after having walked with and suffered for Jesus in extraordinary ways, he could have been satisfied with his abundant knowing of Jesus. But no! While in prison for Christ, having apostolically planted churches and written "mysteries" about Jesus that would later become Scripture, he declares,

"What is more, I consider everything a loss compared to the surpassing greatness of <u>knowing</u> Christ Jesus my Lord, for whose sake I have lost all things. I consider them rubbish, that I may gain Christ ... I want to <u>know</u> Christ ..."[307]

After years of proclaiming the knowledge of Christ, and now while imprisoned for knowing Christ, Paul yearns for more. "I want to know Christ."

Answering Jesus' question compels us to struggle for clarity regarding life's single most important issue. If I, or my family, or my church, can talk articulately about science, or math, or cars, or football, or cooking, or houses, or people, or church issues, but do not know Jesus well enough to articulate even somewhat of who He is, are we naïve and in possible danger of hearing, "I do not know you."?[308] The good news is this: I can stare into Jesus' eyes, and wrestle with Who

---

305 James 4:8
306 Psalm 22:3, KJV
307 Philippians 3:7-8, 10a
308 Matthew 7:21-23

He actually is as revealed through Scripture. The "knowing" gained from this wrestling strengthens my faith in Jesus. It also strengthens our obedience to Jesus, because to know Jesus is to love Him, and if we love Jesus we will grow in obeying Him.[309] This "experiential" knowing of Jesus will save and empower me for life and eternity, regardless of my knowledge of math or science or politics or economics. Consistently wrestling with the question, "Who do you say that I am?" greatly enhances my knowing and responding to Him, whom to know is life eternal.

" Now this is eternal life: that they may know You, the only true God, and Jesus Christ, whom You have sent."[310]

"His divine power has given us everything we need for life and godliness through our <u>knowledge</u> of Him who called us by His own glory and goodness."[311]

"This is what the LORD says: "Let not the wise man boast of his wisdom or the strong man boast of his strength or the rich man boast of his riches, but let him who boasts boast about this: that he <u>understands</u> and <u>knows</u> Me ..."[312]

My wife either figured out on her own or heard a life-changing truth which she tells to church after church. "What we think about Jesus determines what we think He thinks about us. What we think He thinks about us determines what we think about ourselves. What we think about ourselves determines how we feel about ourselves, and how we feel about ourselves determines how we relate to and treat all those around us." How much do we need to take time to think about who Jesus is and what Jesus thinks about us?

---

309 John 14:15
310 John 17:3
311 2 Peter 1:3
312 Jeremiah 9:23-24a

Failure to wrestle with and respond to Jesus' question is the basis for every kind of destruction.

> *"The wrath of God is being revealed from heaven against all the godlessness and wickedness of men who suppress the truth by their wickedness, since <u>what may be known about God</u> is plain to them, because God has made it plain to them."*[313]

Jesus' question created thought and articulation about Him. The church has one essential reason to gather: to help each other know Jesus, with the resulting effect of believing and following Him.

Logically, the conversations in the foyers of the church would be expected to be primarily, if not mostly, about Jesus. But if conversations about Jesus are minimal or non-existent in the homes of church families, the children legitimately perceive Jesus' relative importance to about one or two hours out of every one hundred and sixty eight.

Why are conversations about Jesus so minimal? Is it because we have no place that we practice speaking about Jesus, and to Jesus about Him? That can and must change. "Who do you say that I am?"

JESUS' QUESTION EXPOSES A PAINFUL REALITY

Tragically, too many Christians find it difficult to talk about Jesus. We almost always talk about that which we are knowledgeable of, or that which we care about, or that which we have in common with others. Jesus should fit all three of these categories for the church: we know Him, we care about Him, and we have Him in common. But seldom, in the informal, natural conversation of the church, can one overhear conversation about Jesus. Don't we gather to help each other know Jesus? What is wrong and what can we do?

---

313 Romans 1:18ff. Emphasis added

Jesus is all that the church universally has in common. He is the primary, even single, reason we gather. Why do we not enhance and develop our commonality in Christ by talking together about Him? Who He is? Why do we seldom answer the question He asked His early disciples?

If I asked you to tell me about your mother, you could do it easily and well. You know her. You could and happily would paint pictures of her in my mind by telling me wonderful things about her. And I would honor and trust and care for her more upon having heard you tell about her.

Why don't or can't we paint word pictures of Jesus? Either we do not know Him, or we have so little practice talking about what we know that we are tongue-tied, even among Christians. (Surely we are not embarrassed or ashamed to speak of Him, are we?) Answering His question requires that we wrestle with who He is. Further, we are then better able to articulate well to ourselves and to others who He is. We easily talk with our "natural" brothers and sisters about our mother, whom we know, care about, and have in common. Why not Jesus, whom we know, care about, and have in common?

Seriously. Listen to conversations among Christians. Most of the time, the conversation does not include Jesus. It leaves Him out. That is, it is godless.

> *"Avoid godless chatter, because those who indulge in it will become more and more ungodly."*[314]

Godless chatter, that which omits God from the conversation, leads to more and more ungodliness. Does this explain some of the challenges in our churches and families?

---

314 2 Timothy 2:16

Sometime ago I started inviting church attending men to coffee or lunch with the intention of essentially asking them the question Jesus asked, "Who do you say that I am?" After some small talk, I would say something like, "Tell me something about Jesus … or your relationship with Him, or what Jesus means to you, or who Jesus is to you." Most would stammer, some almost choke, and finally blurt out something about Jesus' love for them, or forgiveness of sins. To minimize being offensive, I would change the conversation because of their obvious discomfort.

Most of these men sincerely believed they were saved, heaven-bound, and serving God as He intends. And they probably were, at least on the first two counts. Yet, to talk about Jesus was like pulling teeth. If we don't know Jesus well enough to talk about Him, it is very difficult to follow Him in our routine of life, or help others know and follow Him. If we don't know Jesus well enough to talk about Him at a quiet coffee shop with our pastor, might we struggle with being too nervous or feeling incapable of talking about Him at home or at work or at school? Is Jesus important enough to be included in our conversations? Why is it so difficult for so many Christians to talk about our King? Our Savior? Our Friend?

> "If anyone is ashamed of Me and My words in this adulterous and sinful generation, the Son of Man will be ashamed of him when He comes in His Father's glory with the holy angels."[315]

The most neglected subject in the Kingdom of God is the King Himself. Instead, we teach, even preach, mostly about topics and doctrines, important to be sure. We teach righteousness and morals, psychological helps, marriage and parenting, money and time, values and vision, ministry strategies, etc. These are all well and good, but they are corollaries to our message, not the core of our message. In our preaching and teaching, we must maximize and stay on message.

---

315 Mark 8:38

Our message is a Person, and this Person named Jesus is our very life.[316]

A seminary professor in a large city told his class that Jesus is seldom the primary topic of a sermon. One of his students did not believe it, so decided to visit 52 different conservative Christian churches for the next year. Upon completion of the year, including Christmas and Easter, the student confessed to the professor that the professor was correct. He had not heard one sermon focused primarily on Jesus: who He is or what He did or is doing. What is wrong? What can we do?

If we experience minimal passion and articulation about Jesus in our pulpits, it is not surprising that in the foyers of the church, in the "natural" and "normal" conversations of the church, seldom is He mentioned who is the very reason for our gathering.

In the few minutes per week that the church gathers to help each other know and follow Jesus, is there anything more important to talk about than Jesus? Why do we include and honor and glorify Jesus so little in our conversations? What is wrong and what can we do?

> "For I resolved to know nothing while I was with you except Jesus Christ and Him crucified."[317]

Paul was fixated on Jesus. What do you think about that? Can you imagine anything more important we could talk about than our answer to Jesus' question: Who do you say that I am? We talk about weather, sports, people, problems, politics, and where does it get us? If we talk even somewhat accurately about Jesus, He is glorified, honored, valued, trusted, and loved. We grow in faith, in love, in wisdom, and are transformed. Who is Jesus to us? We must answer,

---

316 Colossians 3:4, Acts 8:12, 18:5, 28:31, 2 Corinthians 4:5, Ephesians 3:8, Philippians 1:18
317 1 Corinthians 2:2

and answer well. And in answering to each other, we will be far better equipped to articulate our answer to our family and friends, to say nothing of our praise to Jesus as we dialogue with Him, our Resident King, throughout each day.

> *"But in your hearts set apart Christ as Lord. Always be prepared to give an answer to everyone who asks you to give the reason for the hope that you have. But do this with gentleness and respect ..."*[318]

If Jesus is set apart as Lord in our hearts, He would logically be set apart as Lord in our conversations. Why is it so hard for us to talk about Jesus?

HOW CAN WE BEST MAKE PROGRESS?

For all the above reasons and more, we must strategically determine ways to improve in answering this question Jesus asks His disciples. How shall we do it? Of course, it will be helpful to have strong preaching and teaching on "who Jesus is." Even when it was more in vogue for pastors and teachers to talk about the plethora of Jesus' activities and the mysteries of His nature (not primarily His grace), the public proclamation did not have sufficient effect to create conversation about Jesus in the foyer and families of the church. Jesus' current disciples need to be able to answer His question for themselves, not just hear the answer from another source.

The simplest solution seems to be to *prioritize* meetings where the first priority of the meeting is for the facilitator to ask "Who do you say that Jesus is?" and for the group members to grow in knowing and articulating their answers. Thus, it is my practice in meetings to be discipled by Jesus to start by imagining Jesus asking us the question, "Who do you say that I am," and learning to answer in each other's presence.

---

318 1 Peter 3:15

It is not enough to merely proclaim one of Jesus' names or attributes we have heard or memorized, though that is a good beginning point. We must learn to articulate an expansion of the reality and the ramifications of Jesus' personality. The ramifications might include how His nature and personality (who He is) determines what He does, and how what Jesus does affects us, and our response to who He is and what He does.

Can you imagine the hour-long discussion and praise that resulted when a group member proclaimed, "Jesus is our High Priest"? If all we did in a meeting was to dialogue with Jesus about who He is, would that be a good meeting of His disciples?

Our speaking about Jesus and to Him _about Him_ is praise. Our verbal and behavioral responses to who He is are called "worship," and are to be practiced all week long, not just while the musicians are singing. The result: others see our good works and give praise to our Father in Heaven.[319]

As we meet together, we intentionally work at being aware of being in Jesus' presence. We seek to stare into His eyes and answer His question, "Who do you say that I am?" Our answers are often rough and ugly, but we are on our way. By simply taking time to sit together, contemplating the real presence of Jesus, and talking to Jesus about Jesus, very good things happen.

A group of 30 men from a fairly large church were "practicing His presence" by "talking to Jesus about Jesus." They were wrestling to answer Jesus' question, "Who do you say that I am?" It was a meaningful meeting.

Then, just when things were going well, a younger man in the congregation changed the topic. With each word carefully measured,

---

319 Matthew 5:16

he asked permission to raise an issue. Permission was granted. He proceeded to affirm all the men present for what they were saying and doing, but then he confronted the whole group. "For several years, there has been an unwillingness to support our pastor. We can make all the commitments and plans we want to lead our families and our church in the things we are learning, but until we – the men of our church – change our attitude and determine to loyally submit to our pastor, nothing of significance will occur. As long as we are unwilling to submit to God's leader, He will not honor or help our well-intentioned efforts." Ouch!

The perceived "warmth" of the meeting suddenly turned frosty. An older, very influential member of the church began to speak, in what seemed to be a "condescending" spirit toward the younger man, or at least what he had said.

The facilitator of the meeting held up his hand: "Please wait! I ask that before any of us respond to what has been said, that every one of us imagine ourselves staring into Jesus' eyes. Tell Him what you are thinking or what you want to say. Ask Him if it is what He is thinking. Ask Him if He wants you to say what you are thinking."

The silence was deafening ... and long. After several minutes, another longtime leader in the church spoke up, identifying how wrong and how prideful he had been in his critical spirit. Then another. And another. By consciously focusing on the presence of Jesus, and talking directly to Him "as if" He is a real Person (and of course He is), and "as if" He is listening (which He is), and "as if" His opinion matters, (which, of course, it does), and "as if" He might speak (which He promises to do by His Spirit), the whole meeting changed. Instead of defensiveness, or argument, or resentment, the conversation was full of introspection, honesty, humility, and "gentleness of Spirit." Soon tears of repentance and words of reconciliation flowed freely. Why? Blend together the awareness of

Jesus' presence, add good men choosing to be responsive to Jesus, and season with the power of Jesus' Holy Spirit. It is a recipe for transformation in marriages, families, and churches ... and then communities and cultures.

If we would formally practice Jesus' presence far more, starting by talking to Him about Him, we would experience far more stories like the above.

Another good thing happens in these meetings. Remember the idea of telling me about your mother. When you do, I hold her in high or higher esteem. I "see" her more clearly. When you tell me about Jesus, I will know, trust, and love Him more. Peter and John got to watch Jesus; I am able to "watch Him" through your stories and dialogue with Him.

By gathering week after week, and starting our meetings wrestling to articulate some new or growing aspect of who Jesus is, we grow in the knowledge of Jesus.

> "But grow in the grace and knowledge of our Lord and Savior Jesus Christ. To him be glory both now and forever! Amen."[320]

Growing in the knowledge of Jesus will certainly be an eternity-long process.

> "My purpose is that they may be encouraged in heart and united in love, so that they may have the full riches of complete understanding, in order that they may know the mystery of God, namely, Christ, in whom are hidden all the treasures of wisdom and knowledge."[321]

---

320 2 Peter 3:18
321 Colossians 2:2-3

In her holy resolve to grow in the knowledge of Jesus, my wife Debbi determined to look for, record and memorize the names, attributes, and activities of Jesus. As her list lengthened, she determined to organize the list alphabetically. This gave her a memory tool by which she could recall and rehearse to Jesus, alone or with others, the answer to His question, "Who do you say that I am?"

For example, under A she has listed Advocate, Almighty, Almighty God, Alpha, available, Anointed One, Author and Completer of Faith, Author of Eternal Salvation, etc. She reads these in contexts, gets a mental picture of the meaning and implications of the name, and then "stares into Jesus' eyes," telling Him who He is.[322]

Debbi teaches this in all the churches we work with. In one of our 6:00 am meetings to be "Discipled by Jesus," she shared the idea. That night at the evening meeting, a 10 year old who had been at the 6:00 am meeting came up to Debbi. The 10 year old had used every spare moment all day to make her list of Jesus' names for every letter of the alphabet. She asked, "What do you have for Q?'" Debbi replied, "Quick to listen." She smiled and said, "I found quintessential."

A woman heard the same idea in March of 2011. On a return visit to her church in June of 2012, she came to me with a big smile, and handed me several pages of paper with over 400 names of Jesus she had discovered that year in her times with Jesus. She was aglow with the glory of Him on Whom she was focused.

Are you persuaded of the value of Jesus' current disciples answering Jesus' question, "Who do you say that I am?"? Chapter 8 models how Jesus can disciple His followers today around the same question He used long ago.

---

322 31 names of Jesus, one for each day of the month, is listed at the end of the appendix section

Who Do You Say That I Am? (Part II)

QUESTION 1 (CONTINUED)

We have talked about Jesus' question, "Who do you say that I am?" in the last chapter. Now you are invited to enter in to an early morning gathering of ten of Jesus' disciples. Jesus is here to disciple us.[323] I, Hal, am facilitating the meeting.

Hal: "Good morning, everyone. You came ... again. Way to go! And good morning to You, Lord Jesus. Thank You for letting us join You. Oh, that we could adequately honor You this morning. Thank You for being here with us. I am always in awe when I think that You, the Creator and Superintendent of the universe, are here with us ... listening, willing and wanting to speak when we will listen. So ... we do honor Your being with us.

"Let's start by again answering the question that Jesus asked His disciples, 'Who do you say that I am?'"

TIME OUT

We start immediately by talking about Jesus. By asking this question at the very beginning, we do our very best to get and keep the meeting laser-like focused on Jesus. This helps us think about Him. It helps us

---

323 Matthew 18:20

to better articulate who He is. It helps us better know Him, thus better trust Him and better love Him. In short, we start the meeting in praise and worship.

TIME IN
Alivia: "I have been thinking about how Jesus has provided for me. It is overwhelming to me that He speaks to just the right people to help me."

Hal: "What does that tell us about Jesus? What does that reveal about His personality?"

David: "He is caring. He is our Provider."

Maddie: "He knows what we need."

The group chimes in with various ramifications of Jesus' activity and personality.

Hal: "Thank you. Can someone think of a time in the Bible that we have record of Jesus providing? If not, can anyone look up a time?"

TIME OUT
When the group is talking about Jesus, it is usually better to thoughtfully investigate and meditate on one particular name[324] in scriptural contexts than to quickly throw out several names. We need to experience far more depth regarding who Jesus is than a mere _recitation_ of several of His names or attributes.

TIME IN
Justus: "He fed thousands with just a few fish and loaves."

Murray: He provided wine from water when the wine ran out at a marriage celebration.

---

324 In this case Provider

Hal: "This is great. As great as it is for us to talk about Jesus, why don't we talk to Him. 'Jesus, we do remind ourselves that You are sitting here, and we do not mean to leave You out. We want to speak directly to You in answer to Your question.' Let's all picture Jesus – however you like to see Him. I often imagine being with Him like Nicodemus was. Imagine looking into His eyes and telling Him about being your Provider."

TIME OUT
A most important shift needs to occur. It is a "critical shift."

The facilitator needs to lead the dialogue from horizontal discussion *about* Jesus to vertical discussion *to* and *with* Jesus.

This shift often results in those present realizing that they are being encountered by Jesus. The facilitator normally, even repeatedly, needs to remind the group that Jesus truly is present. As good as it is to talk about Jesus, it is better to talk directly to Him.

Made in God's image, we have imagination, that is, the ability to "see" in our minds what we cannot see in the natural. We can thus imagine "seeing" Jesus. Imagination is a precious gift to be used carefully and thoughtfully.

The facilitator can encourage all present to imagine *STARING* into Jesus' eyes and answering the same question He asked His first disciples. "We are going to talk to a real Person, Who is delightedly listening, thinking, feeling, and wanting to talk with us." By imagining staring into Jesus' eyes, plus speaking to Him *only about Him*, an environment is often created where His Holy Spirit powerfully works to enable life-transforming encounters with Jesus.

TIME IN
Hal: "Just like Nicodemus or the woman at the well, imagine that you are sitting with Jesus, and staring into His eyes. Then He asks you,

'Who do _YOU_ say that I am?' Be sure to talk mostly about Him, not yourself, unless it is a statement of worshipful response to who He is.

Eden: "Jesus, I think You are so special to take care of that problem at the wedding ... when they ran out of wine. It makes me think that maybe You might care enough to provide some things for me that I don't have to have, but they sure would be nice."

TIME OUT
The Holy Spirit can reveal who Jesus is and all that Jesus said.[325] He can also speak to us about what Jesus is thinking or even wants to say.[326] One of the things Jesus' Church must mature in is learning to listen for and recognize what He is saying to us by His Holy Spirit. This discipling meeting is a time to be encountered by the living God and to practice listening for and to Him. The primary way we recognize Him is in a _GOOD THOUGHT_. It might be Him. As we intentionally "practice His presence" by examining our thoughts in discipling meetings, we are being equipped to better know and follow His voice in the majority of our hours which cannot be spent sitting at His feet.

So, in order 1) to experience His presence by hearing His voice,[327] and 2) to practice and get better at hearing His voice, and 3) to practice identifying with Him and by imagining what He is thinking ("crawling inside His skin"), I sometimes dare to say: "Let's put ourselves in Jesus' place. Are any thoughts coming to mind that might be what Jesus is thinking?"

When we care about others, we spend time thinking about how what we say and do affects them, and how they might respond. Is Jesus worth imagining how we are affecting Him, especially since He dwells in us to help us know what He is thinking and wanting? The

325 John 14:26
326 John 16:14
327 John 10:27

reason there is so little fruit of His Spirit in many churches and many Christian families is that we have not been discipled to meaningfully meditate on what Jesus is thinking and feeling and wanting.

TIME IN

Hal: Let's slow down and test our minds for some good thoughts about what Jesus might be thinking. Maybe the Holy Spirit is actually revealing Jesus' thoughts or words to us ..."[328]

Dawson: "I think Jesus wants to tell us that He really likes us trying to think about Him and what He is thinking."

Hal: "Does anyone else think that what Dawson just said is actually what Jesus wants to say to us? Is anyone concerned that this is not what Jesus is thinking or wanting to say?"

TIME OUT

When someone "dares" to respond, and someone usually does, I always try to use it as an opportunity to train us all to "test the Spirit."[329]

I certainly want to get the Holy Spirit's immediate guidance right. Of greater importance, I am using this process to disciple Jesus' followers not only to relate to Him, but in how to relate to Him so they can be discipled by Him in private, and increasingly throughout the day.

This meeting with Jesus to be discipled by Him is a powerful _equipping_ meeting.[330] By answering Jesus' question, "Who do you say that I am?" we (Jesus' disciples) are developing a new language skill. The new skill: the ability to articulate truth about Jesus to ourselves and to others. I repeat: far too many sincere Christians do not experience a climate where Jesus' nature and attributes are the topic of the

---

328 John 14-16
329 Romans 12:2, 1 John 4:1
330 Ephesians 4:11-16

conversation, including too many Bible studies! We may care deeply about Jesus, but if we do not experience relationships where Jesus is naturally the topic of conversation, it is very difficult to develop the mental process needed for internal dialogue with Him. Nor do we develop the verbal skills to talk about Him with our families, our church, or anywhere else. That is one key reason that this "equipping and discipling" meeting to answer Jesus' question is so important.

We will dig more truth out of scripture later, but by starting with this question, we start with the very best of the best, that is, our biblical knowledge of Jesus.

Let's listen in on another meeting.

TIME IN

Hal: "Who do you say that Jesus is?"

Elle: "The Good Shepherd."

Debbi: "The One who is near."

Emma: "Our sovereign King."

Hal: "This is great. Thank you. Let's slow down and look at one of these a bit more in depth. How about everyone telling us something about Jesus as the 'Good Shepherd.'"

Justus: "He is good means I have no wants with Him as my Shepherd. He actually takes care of me."

Avila: "He makes me lay down in green pastures. I am able to rest in a good place, not rest in a hard place or be restless in a good place."

Hal: "That is special. Let's talk a bit more about that. Anyone?"

Silence.

David: "It hit me that maybe He gives me the miracle of rest, not only in green pastures, but in a hard, arid place."

Hal: "How does that work?"

Addie: "I'm not, sure, but that kind of rest takes work to experience in the hard desert place."

Justus: "My Good Shepherd reminds me to think about Him in the desert and that helps me rest."

Hal: "It is so good to talk about Jesus. We could spend the whole meeting doing this and it would be a great meeting. Let me remind us again that we also want to talk to Jesus. Let's take a few more minutes and imagine ourselves sitting somewhere at our Good Shepherd's feet. Maybe we are at a campfire, or your living room. Imagine staring deeply into the eyes of Jesus, and tell Him 'who He is' to you as your 'Good Shepherd.'"

Debbi: "Oh, Jesus. You really are my Good Shepherd. You have watched over me in very dark and painful places, even through the valley of the shadow of death, protecting me from more than I could bear. You even provided for me in the very presence of my enemies. How grateful I am to You."

Phoebe: "Jesus, You are my Good Shepherd, for You speak to me and I hear Your voice. You said that your sheep hear Your voice, and I know it is true. You pulled me away from worse than a bear and a lion. You called me loudly enough to get me out of the wrong relationship. It seemed worse than miry clay. Morning by morning I hear You speak to me, and I am eternally blessed and grateful."

David: "Lord Jesus, as my Good Shepherd, You lead me so wonderfully. You do go ahead of me, and call me to follow. You make it possible for me to walk away from all I have lived in and lived for to follow You into a very new, very exciting, and sometimes very scary place."

Hal: "How do you think this affects Jesus? Is anyone sensing what Jesus is thinking, or feeling, or even wanting to say to David?"

TIME OUT

The purpose of asking this question is to help us put ourselves in Jesus' place and imagine what is literally going on in Him right now. We have the Holy Spirit to actually help us do this. We want and need to "know Him" as a real Person. To be His disciples, we need to know Him. As long as no one gets arrogant, either about knowing for sure how Jesus is being affected, or, in being "arrogantly critical" of anyone daring to think out loud about what Jesus might be thinking or feeling, the practice is constructive in knowing the real Jesus. We have the Scripture, the Holy Spirit, and each other to balance or question anything that seems unbalanced or questionable. We are actually able to know what Jesus thinks and feels and wants by the presence of the Holy Spirit. Jesus said the Holy Spirit would take what is of Jesus and make it known to us.[331] Which is more dangerous, to idly chatter about football, or to help each other imagine what Jesus might be thinking?

It is important to practice examining our thoughts, to discern if the Holy Spirit might be revealing Jesus' thoughts about what we have just said to Him.[332] Asking the above question is one of the ways we practice *bringing every thought captive into obedience to Christ*.[333]

---

331 John 16:14
332 John 16:13-15
333 2 Corinthians 10:5

TIME IN

Eden: "I can't imagine Jesus being anything but delighted with David's words to Jesus … to say nothing of his leaving everything to follow Jesus. In fact, I can't begin to imagine how very delighted and thrilled Jesus is with David."

Hal: "Isn't it great to try to think about what Jesus thinks and feels? Does anyone agree with what Eden said about Jesus?"

Debbi: "Of course that is what Jesus is thinking. How could He not be?"

Hal: "Would anyone dare to try to say to David what you think Jesus might want to say to him, 'if He were here?' which, of course, He is by His Spirit, and in and through His Body. Maybe someone even had a thought come to mind that actually _was_ the Holy Spirit revealing what Jesus is thinking or wants to say. It's OK to say what you think Jesus might say … we are here to "practice His presence." We are here to help in case someone seems to be a bit off."

Eden: "David, I think Jesus does want to speak to you. I think He wants to say something like this, 'David, I gave you a great mind, and you could be so proud and independent of Me, but instead you have humbled yourself by seeking to find and follow My way. You are delighting Me in your pursuit of My highest. I have blessed you to make you a blessing, and you have responded humbly. I will make you a blessing.'"

Maddie: "Eden, that's amazing the way you remembered scripture. Thank you. I think it is exactly what Jesus wants to say to David. Thank you so much."

David, with tears: "I did not realize what it would be like to imagine what Jesus might be saying to me. Thank you."

Hal: "Does anyone think we are being coached and discipled by Jesus? Would He want to say encouraging words like that to us?"

Group unanimously agrees.

Hal: "I think it would be good for us to celebrate both the presence of Jesus by His Spirit, and the sensitivity of the group to listen to Him and speak what we think to be His word."

Group: joyful applause!

WHAT HAPPENS AS DISCIPLES GROW IN ANSWERING JESUS' QUESTION WELL?

A most helpful statement came to my attention a few years ago: if you desire to change the culture, you must change the conversation. Why? Conversations are words that penetrate the mind, and as a man thinks, so is he.[334] Or as a family or group or church thinks, so it is.

Our thoughts and words are powerful. They are a power for good or evil. They are so important that Jesus says we will give an account for every thoughtless, idle word.

> "But I tell you that men will have to give account on the day of judgment for every careless word they have spoken. For by your words you will be acquitted, and by your words you will be condemned."[335]

Godless words are powerful missiles that, slowly or quickly, destroy cultures. Conversely, godly words, especially words that reveal Jesus, are powerful truths that set hearers free from destructive lies. Godly words create faith and love. Those who speak truth about Jesus in ways that are received change cultures for the better.

---

334 Proverb 23:7, James 1:26, NKJV
335 Matthew 12:36-37

NEW SELF-TALK

As we mature in articulating "who Jesus is" in a group, we get better at telling ourselves the truth. We are more aware of Jesus, and experience less "I think" and more "Jesus, what do You think?" And we are better at knowing what Jesus thinks, because we know Him better.

The "culture" of most minds needs great change. To change the culture of our own minds (ways of thinking, mental positions, attitudes, motives), we must change the conversations in our minds.

> "... Do not be conformed to this world, but be transformed by the renewing of your mind ..."[336]

> "Finally, brothers and sisters, whatever is true, whatever is noble, whatever is right, whatever is pure, whatever is lovely, whatever is admirable—if anything is excellent or praiseworthy—think about such things."[337]

> "Sanctify them by the truth; Your word is truth."[338]

Self-talk greatly makes and breaks each of us. As Christians we are no longer alone in our minds. We have invited Jesus into our "heart." As we think in our hearts, so are we. By the presence of the Holy Spirit, we have the provision to actually know the mind of Christ.[339] But He seldom speaks so loudly that we cannot help but hear. It is usually through our intentionally seeking to think "with Him" that we are reminded of who He is, or of scripture, or realize what is true and right, and thus come to know and agree with Jesus' thoughts.

We can aggressively, proactively destroy the lies that destroy us by

336 Romans 12:2
337 Philippians 4:8
338 John 17:17
339 1 Corinthians 2:16

proclaiming to Jesus who He is. What we practice and learn in our group time, or in our own time with Jesus, we can better proclaim at other times.

One of the best little habits of my life happens in my early morning shower. In the mornings, I am normally groggy, often feel weary, occasionally a bit "down" with the challenges I face. I stick my face directly into the flow of water, and imagine looking into Jesus' eyes. I answer His question, "Who do you say that I am?" I proclaim to Him what I have come to know about Him, and soon my mind is renewed as I tell Him the important truths about Him – He is gracious, powerful, faithful, my King, my Light, my reason to live. This is "hallowing His name," for He and the Father are One. These few minutes of proclaiming who He is usually, in fact almost always, transforms my emotions and desires through the renewing of my mind, and this results in instant faith, serious passion, and holy purposes. To change your life, change your interior "soul" culture. To change the culture of your soul, change your conversation from self-talk to talk with and about Jesus.

NEW FAMILY TALK

To change the culture of our families, we will need to change the conversations. Much of my book, *If Jesus Were A Parent*, is a testimony to the power of talking naturally and routinely about Jesus, "as if" He were alive, present, important, listening, and desiring to participate in the conversation ... which of course He was and is. To "talk naturally" about and to Jesus normally requires regular meetings with your family, something like the meeting being described in this book. In these meetings, talking about and talking to Jesus is practiced routinely and intentionally.

At the young age of three, our son Dan asked Debbi, "Mommy, is Jesus' last name Perkins?" Jesus was so included in our conversations and our decisions that Dan assumed Jesus to be an important family member, which of course He was and is.

Including Jesus in the conversations at home must convey an accurate picture (tone, expression, language) of Him.[340] Our conversations can convey Jesus as graciously caring for our best, knowing what is best, and gently desiring to help us know and do what is best for everyone. If our family members hear us (both in formal meetings and the rest of the time) talking about our Jesus, who is present, caring, gentle, and humbly truthful, then the probabilities of authentic faith being formed in them are highly maximized. This authentic faith will then result in ease of dialogue about Jesus, commitment to knowing and following Him, including genuine desire to do His will. To change the culture of your family, change the conversations.

NEW CHURCH TALK

What is true of the family is true of the church. To change the culture of the church, change the conversations. When our conversations include and honor Jesus, growth in knowing Him, believing Him, and loving Him occurs. He inhabits the praise of His people. Relationships are influenced by His love, grace, and wisdom flowing in and through the Body. Governing decisions are the fruit of agreement with Him. Ministries are empowered by Him. When the conversations of the church are about any and every thing other than Jesus, inevitably the "godless" flesh of the church dominates: cars, gardening, football, last year's picnic, new health food phenomenon, etc.

"Avoid godless chatter, because those who indulge in it will become more and more ungodly."[341]

Godless chatter – leaving God out – leads to increasing levels of ungodliness: selfishness, pride, fear, envy, conflict, division, manipulation, domination … and on and on. Intentionally talking about Jesus by the church's groups (praise), and to Jesus about the church (intercession), brings transformation.

340 Remember how the lay "preacher" misrepresented Jesus to the "giant" of a man until the lay preacher thought about how Jesus would speak to the man
341 2 Timothy 2:16

I am thinking of one of my dear friends, a church leader with many people under his supervision. In his time alone with the Lord, he started staring into Jesus' eyes while answering the question, "Who do you say that I am?" In so doing, he was regularly encountered by the Holy Spirit in such power that his relationship with Jesus was greatly enhanced. His sensitivity to Jesus and others increased. He changed the way he prayed in public. Most of his prayer became simply "talking to Jesus about Jesus." This was often followed by the heart-felt worship of Jesus that comes from "seeing" Him: "how I honor You; how I long to please You; oh, how I love You (often in tears). His preaching style changed, as he gave much message time talking to Jesus about Jesus or to Jesus about the Word from Jesus. Relationship with Jesus was modeled for the congregation, and soon experienced by the congregation. Soon reports started coming of the people being changed through watching and listening to their renewed spiritual player/coach. All because he voraciously practiced answering Jesus' question, "Who do you say that I am?"

When we have learned to tell Jesus who He is in private or in a group, we have developed greater language skills and ease of communication to talk to others informally about this Jesus. As we do, we are ministering to them in powerful ways, for the knowledge of Jesus is the single most important knowledge available for life (eternal and temporal) and for godliness.[342] It is ministry of the highest order. "Sir, we would see Jesus."[343] To change the culture of your church, change the conversations.

NEW EVANGELISM TALK

As we grow in our ability to articulate to Jesus who He is, and the many-faceted implications of what we are learning, we are preparing to minister to our lost friends. How? As they see our good work[344] and

---

342 2 Peter 1:3
343 John 12:21
344 Matthew 5:16

the hope that is ours, they will ask us for the reason for our hope.[345] We will be equipped to tell them, for the gospel is about a Person, a King, and we are growing rapidly in knowing and following Him. We are developing skills, not only in talking to Him, but about Him. And the more we talk to and about Him, the more we trust and love Him. Imagine introducing your lost friends to your best Friend, a Person, as contrasted with (and I am being careful here) introducing them to a series of principles or abstract truths. I have found that even strangers enjoy dialogue about Jesus. Talking about Jesus and Who He is almost inevitably leads to...

1) discussion about relationship with Him, and that leads to ...

2) identifying the relational issues of ignoring God, and living a God-ignoring life, which leads to ...

3) the pain to God and cost to make reconciliation possible, and ...

4) the possibility for a real, tangible life-altering relationship with Jesus the Christ and King, and the Kingdom lifestyle to which authentic repentance and saving faith lead.

Everyone wins, including our Triune God, when we are able to naturally yet sensitively think and speak much of Jesus. Without a place and time to practice this "talk," we typically do not engage others in conversation about Jesus, or even think that often about Him ourselves. We must be discipled to think and speak more of Jesus, and a very good way to do that is to routinely stare into His eyes and answer His question, "Who do you say that I am?"

---

345 1 Peter 3:15

CHAPTER 9

Do You Understand What I Have Done? (Part I)

SECOND QUESTION

Jesus loved His disciples.[346] He was profoundly aware of His imminent death and departure, and the painful impact of both on His guys. In order to make outward the depth of His inward care and concern, He did the unthinkable. The Master served the servants.

The household servant must have been absent who normally would assist guests in that time and culture with the needed foot washing. None of Jesus' disciples thought of the unthinkable ... doing the servant's job. Or if they did, they did not act on the idea. It seems that someone would have recognized that at least their King, their Messiah, needed His feet washed. If anyone did, timidity, or something else, overruled the idea.

But Someone was present and thought of the unthinkable, and acted on it.

Dinner was about to start, and there they were, not talking about the "elephant in the room" – each other's obviously dirty feet. They actually started eating ... in close proximity to those feet. Finally, right in the middle of dinner, Jesus stood up and proceeded to take off His outer garments. Can you imagine what Jesus' disciples were thinking?

---

346 This event is recorded in John 13:1ff

Some of them undoubtedly were wondering what Jesus was thinking. But none of them had thought about stooping to wash each other's feet.

Their Master, their King and Messiah, was essentially different. He loved all. He was not class conscious. All were under His power, but because He was and is essentially love, He used His power – not to dominate or intimidate or in any other way unilaterally control – but to lower Himself under those He had power over.[347] The Messiah King proceeded to wash the feet of His subjects.

His subjects had to be shocked. This is absurd. The Master is serving His servants! What is up with that? At least Peter had the presence of mind to try to resist his Messiah-King bowing before him to wash his feet. Jesus quickly won that debate.

It got very quiet. All the clatter of mindless dinner-time chatter, dishes scraping the table, and lip-smacking, open-mouthed chewing dissipated. Silence emerged and reigned, except for the soft sloshing of a towel being dipped into a basin of water, and being rubbed against dirty feet. The disciples are, yet again, stunned by Jesus, surely wondering, "Why is *He* doing this? What is He thinking?"

Yet again, Jesus strategically plants into their wondering minds a question that begs for an answer.

"Do you understand what I have done for you?"[348]

Now the silence was complete. Deafening. Long. No one, not even Peter, dared to gamble a guess. They legitimately did not know how to answer what Jesus asked.

---

347 John 13:3
348 John 13:12

With no response forthcoming, Jesus proceeded to answer His own question.

> *"You call Me 'Teacher' and 'Lord,' and rightly so, for that is what I am. Now that I, your Lord and Teacher, have washed your feet, you also should wash one another's feet. I have set an example that you should do as I have done for you."*[349]

Jesus not only washed His disciples' feet; He washed their minds. The ideas He put into their minds were upside down, counter-intuitive, unworldly perspectives.

- "In My Kingdom, the greatest are to be the servants."

- "My disciples follow My example, for they are to be like Me. You are to be My servants by washing the feet and minds of those I love."[350]

- "What I do for you, you are to do for others … wash both feet and minds!"

> *In Jesus' Kingdom, the language of the lofty is "How may I help?" The posture of the powerful is bowing.*

Jesus' Kingdom subjects bow before Him and then obediently bow down to serve those made in His image as He directs.

Jesus has good reason to ask His present-day disciples the same question:

> *"Do you understand what I have done for you?"*

---

349 John 13:13-15, cf. Matthew 20:20-28, Mark 10:35-45, Philippians 2:4-9, 1 Peter 5:1-3
350 For example: Matthew 10:7-8, 19-20, 27, 32, 42

I believe this question which Jesus asked *desperately needs to be* regularly asked of Jesus' contemporary disciples. More importantly, I believe it needs to be answered by today's disciples of Jesus! How often? Weekly. Daily!

The failure to be asked and to sensitively respond to the essence of this question normally results in a cancerous-like disaster in Jesus' church – His Bride, His Body. This failure leads to …

- unintentionally drifting into a "lukewarm" relationship with Jesus, at best

- greatly squandering many of life's most important opportunities for Him

- floundering naively in fruitless "service" for Him, much of which He has not even asked us to do

Conversely, by consistently answering Jesus' question, we are able to …

- see the manifest activity, presence, and glory of Jesus in our present situations

- experience life-giving faith in and passionate love for Jesus

- recognize the very Spirit of Jesus speaking into our minds

- celebrate how much Jesus accomplishes through His Body

- recognize if or when our tangible relationship with Jesus has drifted, and our words and behaviors are increasingly of the flesh and not of the Spirit

You might say "Wow! That question must be much more important than it seems."

Obviously, I would agree with you. If the above benefits of answering Jesus' question are even remotely accurate, how much would it be worth to you to take the time to learn how to answer Jesus' question, and then to persistently answer it?

So, when we gather to be "Discipled by Jesus," we are going to look back to see …

- how Jesus has washed our feet (the good He has done for us)

- how He has washed our minds with His truth (the good He has said to or done in us)

- how we are following His example to do for others what He has done for us by "washing their feet" (serving others in love) and "washing their minds" with Kingdom truth (speaking the truth in love)

We have completed a very meaningful beginning in our time of being discipled by Jesus. We have responded to His question, "Who do you say that I am." But there is much more. We must be led to the next focus of the meeting. Our meeting must move from dialogue with Jesus about who Jesus is to dialogue about what Jesus has done … not only 2000 years ago, but last week, or yesterday. We move from who Jesus is to what Jesus has done by answering another of Jesus' questions,

"Do you understand what I have done for you?"

Pull up a chair and join a group of Jesus' disciples as we are being discipled by Him. Watch and listen as we work through this second question Jesus asks. I will again facilitate the meeting, and some of my special friends will be joining me. My best friend, and my constant encourager and helper, Debbi, is sitting in her normal position, right beside me.

Hal: "Well, thanks to each of you who helped to answer Jesus' first question. Lord Jesus, we could spend our whole meeting doing nothing but responding to Your question, "Who do you say that I am?" It would be a wonderful meeting. Thank You, Holy Spirit, for bringing such clarity to these who spoke, and to those who helped us sense Jesus' responses to our responses.

"Now, we need to move on to another question You asked Your disciples, and want to ask us. Here it is: 'Do you understand what I have done for you?'

Jesus said, *"My Father is always at His work to this very day, and I, too, am working."*[351]

Let's look back on our last week to observe what Jesus did. Holy Spirit, we welcome You to show us some things Jesus did in this last week. Remember, silence in our meeting creates space for the Holy Spirit. Does anyone see anything Jesus did for you, or in you, or through you?"

Silence.

Phoebe: "I am getting no thoughts revealing anything that Jesus did. What does that mean?"

Hal: "I'm not sure. Let me ask: are you aware of how to see what Jesus did in your life?"

---

351 John 5:17

Phoebe: "No. I never heard anyone say or imply that there is a way to see what Jesus is doing."

Hal: "I understand. Let me ask all of you. Are there good gifts, and if so, where does every good, even perfect, gift come from?"

Almost everyone started to answer that question. So I pointed to Hudson.

Hudson: "Well, Jesus said that even human fathers give good gifts to their children, and so how much more will our Father in heaven give good gifts to those who ask Him."[352]

Murray: "Where does it say that every good gift comes down from the Father?"

Hal: "Anyone know?"

David: "I've got it. James 1."

Hal: "Thanks, David. Please read it."

David: "Don't be deceived, my dear brothers. Every good and perfect gift is from above, coming down from the Father of the heavenly lights, who does not change like shifting shadows."[353]

Hal: "So, Maddie, you are being very quiet tonight. May I ask you a question?"

Maddie: "If you promise it's not too hard."

Hal: "I promise. How can we recognize what the Father and the Son are doing?"

---

352 Matthew 7:11
353 James 1:16-17

Maddie: "That's not too hard. If there is something good in our life, it is from the Father."

Hal: "What do all of you think about that? Can we be certain of that? And how do we know what "good" is?"

David: "If someone was given $1,000,000, would that be good?"

Alivia: "I'd call it a good thing. And take it."

Hudson: "Not necessarily. It depends upon if the $1,000,000 has a good effect on you."

Hal: "What do you mean?"

Hudson: "Well, if the $1,000,000 has the effect of causing you to not rely on the Lord, and you buy a bunch of "toys" that destroys good priorities, that wouldn't be good."

Hal: "So … someone help us. Let's try to think with Jesus to sense what He thinks is good."

David: "I think good has mostly to do with right relationships, with truth, with morality and righteousness."

Phoebe: "And with everything that enhances eternity, I mean, with people getting to heaven and laying up treasures on the way. Maybe the best way to know is by simply thinking about what Jesus would call good."

Hal: "Awww. That's great. But to be practical, let's list some specific things we think Jesus would say are truly good gifts from His and our Father."

Matt: "Sunshine!"

Dan: "Food."

Phoebe: "Eternal life."

David: "God's only begotten Son."

Renata: "Our own sons … and daughters."

Deborah: "The Holy Spirit."

Debbi: "The fruit of the Spirit."

Justus: "Memory."

Dawson: "The ability to think."

Hal: "Are thoughts good or bad?"

David: "It all depends on if they are from God or not."

TIME OUT

We went on and on. Over time we concluded three categories of gifts we wanted to watch for:

1. Good gifts Jesus does for us

    a. eternal (typically ways the Body of Christ helps us better know and follow Jesus)

    b. temporal (sunshine, ability to see, food, etc.)

2. Good gifts (usually thoughts) that Jesus does in us

   a. all the things He teaches us from His Word

   b. all the times He helps us remember His Word

   c. all the times His Spirit convicts, guides, corrects, encourages, enlightens, teaches, inspires, etc.

3. Good gifts Jesus gives through us:

   a. Praying for others

   b. Demonstrating Jesus' character and personality: love, forgiveness, grace, mercy joy, peace, patience, kindness, goodness, gentleness, faithfulness, self-control … especially in our relationships

   c. Washing feet: helping, serving, giving, blessing,

   d. Washing minds: encouraging, affirming, listening, seeking to understand, asking questions to better understand, asking permission to share perspective, speaking the truth in love, etc.

   e. Helping others wash feet and minds

Having settled these concepts, it became easier for the group to "see" and talk about what Jesus had done in the last week, or even in the last 24 hours. Let's visit a later meeting of the group.

TIME IN

Hal: Let's move on now to the question Jesus asked His disciples after He washed their feet: "Do you understand what I have done?" How has Jesus washed your feet since we last met? Or … what did Jesus do for you, or in you, or through you this past week?"

IN YOU

Renata: "He taught me about being His inheritance in Ephesians."

Hal: "He spoke into your mind by His Word and Spirit?"

Renata: "Yes. It is so meaningful to me that Jesus' inheritance – what He lived and died to inherit – includes me. The great Creator and King of the universe died to have me with Him."

Hal: "Group, do you think this is good, from the Lord?"

Dawson: "How could it not be? It is straight from scripture."

Hal: "Can we celebrate with Renata the goodness of the Holy Spirit for speaking to her in such a meaningful way? Would someone give thanks to Jesus for speaking so meaningfully to Renata?"

Deborah gives great and joyous thanks to Jesus for speaking so clearly to Renata. Many "amens" from group members. Good meeting happening!

TIME OUT

When we answer the question, "What has Jesus done _in_ us" like Renata just did, we are reflecting on and reporting the most critical component of our existence: "our heart."

The condition of our heart determines our eternal destiny. God is not willing that any should perish, but people are perishing.[354] Jesus died for everyone, but many do not believe.[355] The Holy Spirit is convicting everyone of sin,

---

354 2 Peter 3:9
355 John 3:16

righteousness, and judgment, but many are not repenting.[356] Why? The condition of their heart. The condition of our heart determines whether we respond to all that God does to save us or not.

We are exhorted, above all else, to guard our hearts.[357] Our relationship with God occurs primarily in our heart – the extent to which we receive and respond to His revelation to us. It is the heart that God observes and judges.[358] The condition of our heart is also the primary determiner in how we receive and respond to all that happens to us.

So, in responding to the question, "What has Jesus done *in* us?" we are taking time to reflect and report on "the state of our heart" ...

- progress in awareness of Jesus[359]

- progress in dialogue with Jesus[360]

- progress in joy, prayer, and thankfulness[361]

- progress in faith[362]

- progress in bringing every thought captive into obedience to Christ[363]

- progress in selfless, Christlike motives and attitudes[364]

- progress in godly desires[365]

---

356 John 16:7-11
357 Proverb 4:23
358 1 Samuel 16:7
359 Philippians 3:8-10
360 John 15:1-9, 2 Corinthians 13:14
361 1 Thessalonians 5:16-17
362 Hebrews 11:6
363 2 Corinthians 10:5
364 1 Chronicles 28:9, Philippians 2:5-9
365 Romans 8:5, 2 Peter 1:4

At all costs, we must know and talk about our heart condition. Answering, "What has Jesus done in us" empowers us to get the help we all need to examine and know the condition of our thoughts, our attitudes, our desires, our motives, that is, our hearts. In being discipled by Jesus together, His question, "Do you understand what I have done for you?" must be applied to what He has been allowed to do in our hearts! In our "Discipled by Jesus" meetings, we are being equipped to think about and evaluate our thoughts by accounting for our thoughts.

We are learning to think and talk about what we are thinking.

This is CRITICALLY IMPORTANT in being transformed.

"Do not conform any longer to the pattern of this world, but be transformed by the renewing of your mind. Then you will be able to test and approve what God's will is —his good, pleasing and perfect will."[366]

TIME IN
Hal: "What else happened that was good this week?"

David: "We sold our house!" (Bursts of applause.)

Hal: "Wow! How many were praying?" (Most of group lifts hands.) "Can we assume this is good and a gift from Jesus, and if so, why?"

David: "Anyone who knows how much we needed to sell it would think that it is good."

Matt: "Jesus said that if we would seek first His Kingdom and righteousness, that He would take care of the other stuff. I don't know how anyone could more carefully be seeking first Jesus' Kingdom than David is. This has to be a blessing from God." (More applause.)

---

366 Romans 12:2

Hal: "How great to be seeing the ways Jesus is 'washing our feet.' What is your response when you realize Jesus has done something good for you?"

Matt: "For selling David's house? Thank You, Lord. THANK You. Thank YOU! THANK YOU, LORD!!!!!

TIME OUT

Genuine gratefulness that leads to sincere thanksgiving is paramount in our relationship with Jesus. He is the Author of everything truly good in our lives. That which is truly good is that which is the BEST for us in the light of our circumstance and the circumstances of all around us. When Jesus does something good (for us, in us, or through us), it is His present-tense expression of His love for us. When I recognize His good gift, and trace the gift back to Him as the Giver, I become aware of His tangible, present-tense love for me, and my heart is touched. I feel His love, and that ignites love in me for Him.

Was your family like mine on Christmas day? Weeks of thought, gift purchasing and preparation went into getting ready for a couple hours together opening gifts around the Christmas tree. A thoughtful gift would be unwrapped. The recipient would look at the gift and squeal with delight. Immediately, the gift-recipient would run to the gift-giver, feeling the love that motivated the gift-giver to give such a good gift. Feeling love from the gift-giver, the gift-recipient's heart would be profoundly warmed with love for the gift-giver.

So with Jesus. When we recognize His good gifts, and then recognize the good gifts are the expression of His love for us, our hearts are profoundly touched. Gratefulness normally wells up into passionate love for the Giver of the good gifts. A significant part of the reason we are commanded to give thanks in and for everything[367] is to help us to slow down, look at the perpetual good gifts of Jesus, see His gifts as expressions of His

---

367 1 Thessalonians 5:18, Ephesians 5:20

love, and truly thank Him. Result: we feel His love, experience love for Him in return, and are bonded to Him in the bonds of love. His good gifts, recognized and appreciated, empower our hearts with reciprocal passion for Him. We love Him because He first loved us.[368]

The converse is equally – but destructively – true. When my wife Debbi blesses me with something good, and I take the gift for granted or do not even notice it, I am ignoring the demonstration and evidence of her love for me. Her love exists in her heart; it is very real. For her love to become tangible, to get it out into the open, she has to say or do something good for me to experience her love. When I fail to notice the gift, or meditate on the love that motivated the gift, I fail to experience her love. When I do not experience her love, reciprocal love is absent. My heart is untouched. That is a dangerous place in a husband-wife relationship.

How much more dangerous it is when Jesus, motivated by love, does good things for us, and we fail to notice the good gift, and thus we sever from our heart the love of the Lover who gave the gift. In so doing, we shut down our experience of His love. When we fail to recognize His love, we fail to experience it, and when we fail to experience His love, our hearts grow distant. Then we inevitably chase after other lovers. Idolatry has occurred.

The human heart _will_ seek to be loved. If we do not experience Jesus' love, we will chase around looking in all the wrong places. Paul uncovers this very truth in Romans 1. When anyone fails to recognize the truth of what can be known about God, and thus fail to give Him thanks, it leads to disaster.

> "For even though they knew God, they did not honor Him as God or give thanks, but they became futile in their speculations, and their foolish heart was darkened."[369]

---

368 1 John 4:19
369 Romans 1:21

Failure to see what God has done and be thankful is tragically, often eternally, detrimental to our relationship with Him. Jesus is perpetually "washing our feet and minds," doing good for, in, and through us. If we recognize it and are thankful, we experience His love. If we fail to recognize it, we quench His love. Either way, there are serious and eternal consequences. Most of us need great help to develop this habit: "in everything, give thanks."[370]

As we grow in following Jesus, it is of paramount importance that we learn to thank God for hard circumstances and difficult people. When circumstances are easy, we can coast which easily entices us to drift toward lukewarmness. But when circumstances are hard, we are tempted to complain, criticize and even doubt God. It is a test. We either pass or fail. By daring to believe that our Lord is good, and is at work in all things to bring good for those who love Him,[371] we can choose to thank Him for this trial, for at the very least, it is strengthening our faith, which is far more precious than gold.[372] Just like Jesus looked straight into the eyes of Pilate, so we honestly face our problem, and choosing to thank God that He is for us and at work in and through this problem. It is like doing "faith pushups." We don't usually get strong in faith in the soft, easy, so called "good" times. We dare not waste our opportunities to grow spiritual "faith muscles."

Similarly, we want to learn to truly be thankful for difficult people. Jesus clarified that anyone can love those who are good to us. If we are to grow in likeness to Him who clearly loved and loves His enemies, we must learn to love those who behave like enemies.[373] We cannot grow in this level of love until we have real enemies to love. When people act like enemies, we dare not waste the opportunity to grow in love. We can very sincerely give thanks to our King for them, for they

---

370 1 Thessalonians 5:18
371 Romans 8:28
372 1 Peter 1:7
373 Matthew 5:43-48

are our "training ground" in love. In being genuinely thankful, we are empowered to grow in love.

The next chapter allows us to continue to look in on and listen to Jesus, a group facilitator, and a group of His disciples as they meet around His question, "Do you understand what I have done for you?"

CHAPTER 10

Do You Understand What I Have Done? (Part II)

QUESTION 2 (CONTINUED)

Today, this very day, Jesus is proactively "washing the feet" of His friends and His foes. He asks those who are paying attention, "Do you understand what I have done for you?" It is of utmost importance that we, Jesus' contemporary disciples, recognize what He has done since we last met. He has been at work for us, and in us, and through us. He wants us to be aware of what He has done and to realize why. We not only look "up" to answer who Jesus is, we look "back" to answer what He has done. We typically look back 2000 years, but must determinedly look for the many things He does for us each day. Join us again for this meeting of Jesus with some of His contemporary disciples, already in progress.

CONTINUATION OF MEETING: WHAT HAS JESUS DONE THROUGH YOU

Hal: "I'm wondering if Jesus was able to do anything good _through_ any of us this week. Doing good is exactly what He went around doing in His first body.[374] I am sure He spoke to all of us to serve or encourage or bless people we were with this week. Anyone getting help in remembering something good Jesus did through you?"

Long silence.

---

374 Acts 10:38

Hudson: "I don't really feel good about talking about the good things I did last week, even though I know Jesus made it possible. It sounds like I am bragging."

TIME OUT

It is challenging for most of us as followers of Jesus to tell about good things Jesus accomplishes through us. We feel like we are bragging or glorifying ourselves. It seems to be pride. And it can be.

But to not tell what God has accomplished through us can be motivated by not wanting others to think we are bragging, which is also self-centered, thus pride. Motive is everything, and if the speaker's motive is truly to recognize what Jesus has done, and to honor Him and thank Him, the right message will come through.

In fact, the Apostle Paul, who said, "Follow my example as I follow the example of Christ"[375] set a clear example for us in reporting the good things that Jesus has accomplished through him.

"Paul greeted them and reported in detail what God had done among the Gentiles through his ministry."[376]

"I will not venture to speak of anything except what Christ has accomplished through me in leading the Gentiles to obey God by what I have said and done—"[377]

Without pride, or fear of being judged as having pride, Paul would tell what Jesus accomplished through him. In fact, he preferred to stay silent unless he was telling what Jesus got done through Him.

---

375 1 Corinthians 11:1
376 Acts 21:19
377 Romans 15:18

The early church regularly gave and received reports of what God had done through each other.

> *"On arriving there, they gathered the church together and <u>reported</u> all that God had done through them and how He had opened the door of faith to the Gentiles."[378]*

> *"When they came to Jerusalem, they were welcomed by the church and the apostles and elders, to whom they <u>reported</u> everything God had done through them."[379]*

Jesus reported what He had done to His Father.[380] Jesus' disciples – in each other's hearing – gave reports to Jesus of all they had done.[381] On <u>that</u> day, we will all give a report for our acts and words.

> *"But I tell you that men will have to <u>give account</u> on the day of judgment for every careless word they have spoken. For by your words you will be acquitted, and by your words you will be condemned."[382]*

> *"For we must all appear before the judgment seat of Christ, so that each one may be recompensed for his deeds in the body, according to what he has done, whether good or bad."[383]*

John Wesley admonished his followers to keep "short accounts." This routine "accountability" helps prevent us from drifting from our "sincere and pure devotion to Christ." [384] I cannot overstate the importance of supportive reporting!

---

378 Acts 14:27
379 Acts 15:4
380 John 17:4
381 Luke 9:10
382 Matthew 12:36-37
383 2 Corinthians 5:10
384 2 Corinthians 11:3

TIME IN

Hudson: "OK. I appreciate that all of you promised to pray that my 20 year old son would go out to dinner with me and that I would be able to listen without correcting or confronting him. Well … it happened. We went out on Friday night. It was a very good time. He even talked about some of the mess he is in. The Lord reminded me not to lecture him again, but to keep seeking to simply know and understand him. We both enjoyed the night, and your prayer that our relationship would improve was answered. I believe we will be able to grow in relationship and he will feel that I truly care and want to help him, not manage him."

Hal: "So, the Holy Spirit spoke to you right during dinner, you recognized His voice, and responded by not lecturing but listening. Sounds like Jesus threw the ball to you, you caught and ran with it, and our team moved forward. What do you think, team?"

Great applause, for both Jesus and Hudson: Jesus, for working in Hudson by guiding him, and Hudson, who sensitively listened and obeyed.

Hal: "Jesus, did You get anything else done through us this week? We need You to help us see it."

Debbi: "You remember that I thought the Holy Spirit was guiding me to spend very specific time in prayer for my grandchildren. I want to thank you all for praying. I asked the Lord to help me get up 15 minutes earlier each morning to increase my time with Him so I could have more time to pray for each one. He helped me, and it was wonderful to invest that time in praying for each grandchild much more consistently."

Celebrative applause! The whole "team" (army) makes progress when one does well. We were thanking both Jesus and Debbi for the

Kingdom good that was done through her Spirit-guided prayers last week.

Hal: "We have heard that Jesus was at work in selling a house, revealing that we are His inheritance, and helping us pray and make progress in our family relationships. Did He help anyone make progress in relationship with any lost persons?"

Silence.

David: "I remembered to pray for my friend who is lost, but I did not get around to sending him the e-mail I told you last week I thought the Lord wanted me to send."

Addie: "Hey, we celebrate that you prayed. And thank you for honestly reporting that you forgot to send the e-mail to your friend. It helps me to hear that kind of honesty."

Hal: "Does anyone have any thoughts come to mind, maybe from the Holy Spirit, about what Jesus might be thinking, or even wanting to say, to David?"

Silence.

Debbi: "I am not sure what the Lord is thinking, but I know I am so grateful that David is seeking to connect with a lost friend, and praying for him. I think the Lord is highly pleased that David cares for his lost friends and is committed to getting better at connecting with them."

Hal: "Thank you. I remind us that we are practicing thinking from Jesus' point of view. We are practicing His presence, attempting to grow in knowing Him and sensing what His Spirit is saying to us. As we "practice" here, we are being equipped to think and behave as the Body of Christ out there. We need practice to be led by His Spirit in all we say and do. So, thank you, Debbi, for wrestling with your answer. What do the rest of you think about what Debbi said?"

Renata: "I think she has said pretty close to what Jesus wants to say to David. Maybe Jesus would ask David if he is willing to commit again to e-mail his friend this week."

David: "For sure. I hate it that I let a whole week go by and did not do the one simple thing I thought the Lord asked me to do."

Justus: "Join the club. I promised you I would pray for you last week, and I forgot. I am so sorry. I promise the Lord and you to pray for you this week. In fact, if you want, I will e-mail my prayer for you to you, and the Lord could use that to help you remember to e-mail your lost friend."

David: "You are amazing. Thank you. But I hate for you to feel like you …"

Justus: "Quit it. It's no big deal. Besides, the Lord told me to e-mail you to help you remember."

Hal: "Wow! Justus thinks Jesus spoke to him. What do all of you think? Would his e-mailing David probably be good? If so, it well could be the Lord. Do you think it was the Lord who gave him the thought to e-mail David?"

Eden: "I think it was the Lord."

Hal: "Let's vote. All who think it was the Lord applaud Him for speaking to Justus."

Applause.

Hal: "And all who are glad that Justus is on our team … in our army … as one who sees and catches the pass Jesus throws to him, and then runs with it, please celebrate his partnership in our Jesus-called mission."

More applause. It is good to be discipled by Jesus' Spirit through His Word and Body.

TIME OUT

It is my task as the facilitator of the meeting to NOT be the teacher. "Teaching" is good if the "facilitator" has given others a chance to speak, and when that which is being said needs some clarification, or when no one responds to the facilitator's question. In a group setting, we "teacher-types" must remember (or learn) that the goal of teaching is not to tell. The facilitator's task is to listen in order to find out if the learners can articulate the Truth well enough to do what has been taught. So, the good facilitator (whose life, responses, and questions are profoundly discipling those present) learns, with much practice, to listen by asking better and better questions.

To facilitate those present in being discipled by Jesus, facilitators need to regularly ask questions that remind the group that Jesus is present and might be speaking by His Spirit. To test for the Holy Spirit, we learn to observe our minds for _good_ thoughts and to dialogue with Him. For example:

- "Are you willing to tell Jesus what you just told us?"

- "Has anyone had a good thought that might be given by Jesus' Spirit?"

- "What are you thinking? Do you think that thought was from the Holy Spirit?"

- "What do you think Jesus is thinking?"

- "Does anyone think that what Hudson said was given him by the Spirit?" How can we test it?

Further, it is paramount that Jesus' contemporary disciples be in a supportive and accountable environment like Jesus provided His original twelve.

"When the apostles returned, they gave an account to Him of all that they had done."[385]

Jesus was full of grace and truth. Surrounded by His grace, Jesus' contemporary disciples must be asked for the truth about their communication with Jesus since the last meeting. "Do you understand what I have done _IN_ you?" The answer reveals the degree of awareness and dialogue with Jesus. Our thoughts are either with Jesus or without Him. Our goal is to persistently increase our awareness and dialogue with Jesus, so that His truth in us and life through us increase as our independent-of Him ideas, words, and acts decrease.[386] We must learn to examine and talk about our thoughts, for it is in the thought life that we experience relationship with Jesus, or fail to experience relationship. Jesus speaks to us through many avenues, especially the Bible and other Christians, but we receive and relate to Him in our minds. Each thought is either a thought we have received from Him, or not. If it is not from Him, it is independent of Him and we do not want it to govern us. The table of our heart pictures this. (Chapters 1-2)

THROUGH YOU

In the context of great grace, we must also be asked the question, "Do you understand what I have done _through_ you?" Jesus' contemporary disciples desperately need to experience profound, persistent,

---

385 Luke 9:10
386 John 3:30

long term "parental" love that _listens_ as the disciple answers Jesus' question, "Do you know and understand what I have done through you this past week?"

If we have a hard time remembering any good things that Jesus accomplished through us, we must be helped to be far more intentional in following Jesus in our families, our church family, our work places, our schools, and our communities.

> *"Anyone, then, who knows the good he ought to do and doesn't do it, sins."*[387]

Jesus in us – His Holy Spirit – will be guiding us to go "around doing good,"[388] to intentionally pray, listen, affirm what is good, rejoice with those who rejoice, weep with those who weep, encourage, serve, etc. Jesus was intentional and proactive, doing nothing apart from His Father.[389] We need much help in becoming like Him in everything we do.[390]

TIME IN

Hal: "Is there anything else about last week before we move to listening to Jesus speak to us through His Word?"

Justus: "I've been wondering if I should say anything. I think the Lord wants me to, because I need help. I am so embarrassed … thought I would quit doing this. I blew up at my son again this week. I hate it. It's ruining our relationship. I wish you would all pray for me."

Hal: "Thank you. Bless you. We will pray, won't we?"

Group: Nods and affirmations of support.

---

387 James 4:17
388 Acts 10:38
389 John 5:19
390 1 Peter 1:15, Colossians 3:23

Hal: "Justus, can I ask a couple questions that you don't need to answer if you don't want to?"

Justus: "Of course."

Hal: "Thank you for that response. I was almost certain that is what you would say. What happened after you blew up?"

Justus "Well, his eyes were glued to the floor. I'm sure he wanted to walk away or holler back at me."

Hal: "What happened next?"

Justus: "I realized what I had done and told him I was very sorry, and hoped he would forgive me. I was surprised that he just shrugged his shoulders and said, 'No big deal.'"

Hal: "Did you talk with Jesus about it?"

Justus: "Oh, yes. I felt so badly, and told Him I was so sorry and I would do my best to quit blowing up but that I desperately needed His help."

Hal: "Well, everyone. What did Justus do right?"

Renata: "He confessed the unchristlikeness ... didn't just admit. He agrees with Jesus that Jesus loves him but hates the behavior, and he intends to turn away from what is not Christlike."

Hal: "You are such an encourager, Renata. Thank you. Is there anything else Justus needs to do?"

Debbi: "Justus, are you able to celebrate what happened?"

Justice: "Celebrate?"

Debbi: "Yes. After we confess our sin by turning from it, we need to celebrate that Jesus is the One who showed us our sin, and is still with us. We need to celebrate that we hurt so badly which shows how sensitive we are to Jesus. If it does not hurt when we fail Him, we are moving toward luke-warmness in our relationship with Him. And we need to celebrate that we are saved – in spite of our weaknesses – because of Jesus' loving sacrifice for us. We can sincerely aim for perfection,[391] because we are not saved by our ability to perform perfectly, but by Jesus' grace.

Hal: "Sounds like a sermon to me."

Debbi: "I've heard it lots of times."

Hal: "Hmmm, I wonder where ... Anyhow, Justus, what are you thinking?"

Justus: "I'm thankful for all of you and for your help as I am growing up."

David: "Let me read this. *'Brothers and sisters, if someone is caught in a sin, you who live by the Spirit should restore that person gently. But watch yourselves, or you also may be tempted.'*" [392]

Well, enough of that meeting.

One final note regarding accountability and reporting to Jesus and His disciples: We are prone to focus on and produce results in those areas for which we are held accountable. There has been considerable accountability in the typical church in two areas:

---

391 2 Corinthians 13:11
392 Galatians 6:1

1. Attendance (especially numerical church growth or decline)

2. Finance (including ability to build buildings, provide quality events, hire staff, etc.)

If the church is large numerically, both leadership and attendees and outsiders are prone to think of the church as successful. If the church is growing numerically, regardless of size or Christ-focus, almost everyone applauds. If the church is declining numerically, many assume that something is very wrong, and sometimes they are right. But not always.

Reports of numerical progress – be the progress "good" or "bad" – are kept and given by most churches to leadership bodies. Because largeness and numerical increase of the church are generally perceived to be the sure evidence of God's blessing, and people's applause, largeness and numerical increase is that to which most church leaders give themselves. At almost any cost. Every Sunday, some trained and dutifully loyal parishioners can be observed carefully counting every possible person on the premises, and then recording the numbers to be reported to the appropriate authorities. And most will hear the report and feel its impact … for better or for worse.

Financial strength and progress is perceived in almost the same light as numerical strength and progress. Plans are carefully made and communicated to maximize necessary income to support perceived needs and important ministries. Offerings are received and special campaigns engaged. Proceeds are carefully counted, evaluated, dispensed – sometimes through very time consuming, even agonizing and painful processes, and ultimately a report, an accounting, is given.

Massive amounts of time and relational energy are invested by the best of the best church leaders and ministers simply in planning and accounting for improved results in attendance and finances.

Far more than the accounting for numbers and finances is the desperate need for careful planning, training, and accounting for results in personal, relational ministry. This includes being discipled by Jesus: listening and responding to Him, growing in knowing, believing, obeying and loving Him. It also includes making disciples of Jesus: listening and responding to our family, our church family, and our lost neighbors until all are consistently being influenced to take yet another step toward Jesus.

It is much easier to keep track of worship attendance and offerings than relational transactions between Jesus and His disciples, and between His disciples and others. We are prone to focus on that for which we must give a report. Therefore, we must create environments, methods, and strategies to give reports concerning those issues for which we will give an ultimate account. This must be done, regardless of the cost. We will ultimately account for …

- our relationship with Jesus, or lack thereof, including our acts and words, and our thoughts, attitudes and motives. These are reflected in all our relationships, identified below.

- our relationships with and ministry to our family

- our relationships with and ministry to our church family

- our relationships with and ministry to our lost neighbors.

Current disciples must do better at the great need for accountability in these areas that matter most. I am not arguing against accountability regarding attendance and finance, but for far greater relational ministry-planning and ministry-accounting for relational transactions between Jesus and His contemporary disciples, and those disciples and their families, their church family, and lost sheep.

One major purpose of group gatherings to intentionally be discipled by Jesus is to be equipped for the work of the ministry. I conclude this chapter on reporting what the Lord has done in and through us with an illustration of a man who learned how to facilitate answering Jesus' question, "Do you understand what I have done?"

A pastor's son got in a little hassle at school. When being pushed, he retaliated by hitting the boy who pushed him. He got reported, had to meet with the principal, and his behavior was reported to his father, a well-known pastor in town. The pastor was a former Marine, and then became a bar tender. After a difficult illness, he repented and returned to God, becoming a devoted follower of Jesus. Then he was called to become a pastor, which he did. However, he carried some of his "marineness" into his new life with Jesus, including how he disciplined his son.

Upon hearing of his son's behavior from the principal, the pastor went home. In typical marine-like fashion, he ordered his son to go to the son's room until Dad got there to administrate justice. His son knew what was coming: a whipping with a belt.

On his way to the room, the pastor started to pull off his belt. He then remembered that though Jesus is ready to discipline as appropriate, [393] Jesus was first full of grace and truth. So the pastor determined to have a "meeting with Jesus" before punishing his son for the son's behavior.

When the pastor entered his son's bedroom, his little buddy was quivering in fear. He was fully aware and painfully anticipating the punishment that was about to occur. But the pastor had been thinking much about how Jesus would discipline (and thus disciple) his son. He got down on one knee, and very gently asked a wonderful question, "Can you tell me what happened at school?" (Though asking for an

---

393 Hebrews 12:5-7

accounting, he obviously did not ask the question, "Do you know or understand what Jesus has done for you?" This was not the time for that question. But he did ask for a report.)

The son, a bit surprised by his dad's humbly kneeling down and the gentle tone of his question [394] might have been slightly relieved by at least the postponement of "the belt." He explained to his dad how the other boy had started the altercation, but yes, he had retaliated and hit the other boy.

The Dad asked his son another question. "So ... how did you feel when you hit the other boy?"

The son must have temporarily forgotten that he was on trial and probably facing "sure and just" judgment and consequences. His countenance lightened, and a smile of glee emerged as he responded, "It felt really good, Dad."

Dad, skipping some other questions he might have asked, instantly dropped down to the bottom line. "How do you think it made Jesus feel when you hit the other boy?"

Just as quickly as it had appeared, the gleeful smile was gone. The son looked deeply into his Dad's eyes, then down to the floor. Tears started to trickle down his cheeks. "It made Jesus sad."

Dad asked another good question. "What do you think about making Jesus sad by what you did?"

The son, with authentic repentance that flows from remorse, quickly articulated, "I don't ever want to make Jesus sad. I am so sorry."

The story is far from completed, but the point is clear: good things

---

394 Matthew 11:28-29

happen when we give an account to a grace-giving and truth-seeking coach. Good things happen when we get and give help in being discipled by Jesus' Word, Spirit, and Body.

We have spoken of and illustrated two questions Jesus asked His disciples back then and still may want to ask us today. By answering them, we see Jesus' nature ("Who do you say that I am?") and we see His activity ("Do you understand what I have done for you?"). Just as His first disciples saw His activity and came to know His nature, and thus were discipled, we are making progress in knowing and being discipled by Jesus.

Now we move to knowing Jesus in greater depth. We have watched Jesus; now we listen to Him. He wants to explicitly tell us about Himself, His Father, us, our relationship with Him and each other, our purpose, our destiny, our character and activity, and on and on. We have the privilege of sitting at Jesus' feet, listening to Him talk to us through His very Words that have been recorded for us. Let's get to it …

CHAPTER 11

Do You Listen to Me? (Part I)

THIRD QUESTION

"Peter, James, John … I need to talk with you for a second. See that high mountain? I'm going up there to pray.[395] I'd like you to go along with Me."

So up the mountain they climbed with Jesus leading and His inner circle following. Upon arriving, Jesus began to pray. As He was praying, His face was, how would you say it, well … transfigured … literally. His face shone like the sun.[396] His clothes were also transfigured, becoming dazzling white, like a flash of lightning.[397]

But the drama had only just begun. Moses and Elijah somehow appeared … in stunning glory. They spoke with Jesus about His upcoming Jerusalem experience, including His departure.[398]

The disciples had been half asleep, but who could sleep through the dazzling light, or Moses and Elijah conversing with Jesus? Peter probably was not yet fully awake. He did not realize what he was saying, but spoke anyhow.[399] "I'll build a shelter for each of you."

---

395 Luke 9:28
396 Matthew 17:2
397 Matthew 17:2, Luke 9:29
398 Luke 9:30-31
399 Mark 9:6, Luke 9:33

I wonder how often I just blurt things out … anything. Oh, there are lots of "explanations" … I was not "fully awake," not really thinking, or being fearful, or wanted to impress those present. Foolish and godless chatter are particularly identified as serious errors to be avoided.[400]

Before Peter got more words out of his mouth, a cloud enveloped them, and from the cloud came a voice … The Voice. "This is My Son, whom I love; with Him I am well pleased. _LISTEN TO HIM_."[401]

Have you ever been confronted in public, and gravely embarrassed? I can't imagine what Peter must have felt.

But that is not the point. The point is this: In one of the very few times we have record of the audible voice of God the Father, He commands that we LISTEN to His Son whom He loves and with whom He is well pleased.

Or maybe Peter's embarrassment and pain is actually part of the point, a component of the bigger picture. Why do we not recognize our Shepherd's voice? Probably too much noise going on … too many words. Out of our mouths. From others' mouths and into our ears. Inside our minds. Too much noise. "This is My Son. Listen to HIM!"

For many years while getting ready for the day I listened to the Bible on an old cassette player. I kept the volume fairly low to not wake other family members. But keeping the volume low created a problem. When I turned on my electric razor, the Bible tape was drowned out; I could not hear it at all with the noise of the razor. When I turned on the water, the same reality occurred – I could not hear the Bible tape. Brush teeth? Too loud to hear my Bible.

We have a very hard time listening to Jesus because of all the noises –

---

400 Ephesians 5:4, 1 Timothy 6:20, 2 Timothy 2:16, 23, Titus 3:9
401 Matthew 17:5, emphasis added

distractions of every kind. The noise is not just in our ears from outside sources. In fact, it is mostly internal noise that hinders our listening to Jesus. The thoughts and emotions and desires in our souls relentlessly rumble, louder than a razor, drowning out our ability to listen to Jesus.

When does Jesus talk? Where do we listen to Him? How can we listen?

For starters, let's state the obvious.

When I am talking, it is very difficult for me to listen to Jesus. Even when I am talking while praying, when I am intentionally communicating with God, I don't hear Him because it is me who is talking. Peter was talking when Jesus' Father said, "This is My Son. Listen to Him!" The typical conception of prayer is that we do all the talking and God does all the listening. Because this is almost entirely the normal practice of prayer, when we think of prayer, we almost always think of talking to God, not listening to Him.

> *"The trouble with nearly everybody who prays is that he says 'Amen' and runs away before God has a chance to reply. Listening to God is far more important than giving Him our ideas." Frank Laubach*

> *"The Desert Fathers did not think of solitude as being alone, but as being alone with God. They did not think of silence as not speaking, but as listening to God. Solitude and silence are the context within which prayer is practiced." Henri J.M. Nouwen*

> *"The more we receive in silent prayer, the more we can give in our active life. Silence gives us a new outlook on everything. We need silence in order to touch souls. The essential thing is not what we say, but what God says to us and through us. Jesus is always waiting for us in silence." Mother Teresa*

When I am in God's presence (and I always am) and talking like Peter was, it is hard for me to listen to Jesus.

It is very hard to listen to Jesus when others are talking, even Christians. When I attend church gatherings, I try to listen for Jesus speaking through His Body. It is still a stretch for me. So much noise and distraction. I need much greater discipline to remember that God's Son dwells in His church by His Spirit, and then to carefully remember to listen for Jesus through His people. "This is My Son. Listen to Him!"

When televisions and iPods and other noise generating devices are pouring into my ears, it is very difficult to listen to Jesus, though He surely can and does speak through all sorts of noise.

Even when I am alone, and thinking, I am listening to someone. Who? What? My mind races. I am listening to myself. Noise. My emotions respond to my mind with peace or pain, compassion or anger, joy or fear. Loud noise. My desires want this and that. Noisy and powerful distractions.

In the midst of all the noise, from without and within, Jesus is waiting to speak, or even speaking, but the "water" or the "razor" drowns out the sound of His voice in my soul. The genuinely awe-inspiring provision of Christian experience is that listening to Jesus speak by His Holy Spirit is intended to be normal. Jesus' disciples listen to and follow His voice.[402]

> "But when He, the Spirit of truth, comes, He will _guide_ you into all truth. He will not speak on His own; He will _speak_ only what He hears, and He will _tell_ you what is yet to come. He will bring glory to Me by taking from what is Mine and _making it known_ to you."[403]

---

402 John 10:3, 4,16, 27
403 John 16:13-14

> *"My sheep LISTEN to My voice; I know them, and they follow Me."*[404]

The provision for Jesus' contemporary disciples to listen to Him through His indwelling Holy Spirit has not been sufficiently honored. I am pained and concerned because much of Christ's Body is unintentionally but detrimentally disconnected from our Head.

> *"He has lost connection with the Head, from whom the whole body, supported and held together by its ligaments and sinews, grows as God causes it to grow."*[405]

We fail to honor the Holy Spirit greatly. The promises and provisions of listening to Jesus via His Spirit are a treasure worth pursuing far more than our hurried Christian culture experiences.[406]

However, there is a certain legitimacy to this marginal pursuit of listening to Jesus speak to us via His Spirit. In spite of all who say, "God told me," I know of hardly anyone who experienced what Peter did on the Mount. Peter clearly heard the voice of God without trying to listen. We diligently listen, hoping to hear, and the harder we try, the less it seems we hear. So, we quit seeking to "listen" to the Holy Spirit. It is easy to give up on fishing if it seems that catching fish will never happen.

However, there is a way to multiply the probabilities that I can listen to Jesus. In fact, there is a way we can – with clear certainty – listen to Jesus. How? We can listen to Him through His Word, the Bible.

When I am reading the Bible, I can be certain that I am listening to

---

404 John 10:27, emphasis added
405 Colossians 2:19
406 See Chapter 1-3 for the greater discussion of being led and discipled by the Holy Spirit

Jesus.[407] There is significant and sufficient reason to believe that the Bible, properly interpreted, is the foundational way the Father intends for us to LISTEN to His Son.

To be sure, we must give due diligence, no, extreme diligence, to not add to, detract from nor misinterpret the Scripture. But ultimately, in all our diligence to properly interpret, we must be careful to remember that we are listening to a Person speaking to us through His agape letter.

The passion of this chapter is to influence all of us, especially those of us who doggedly claim the Bible to be the inspired Word of God, to give extreme effort to LISTENING to JESUS speak to us through His Word.[408] Even when we take time for Bible study, it is easy for us not to be aware of listening to Jesus. It is easy to drift into dutifully doing what Christians are supposed to do ("devotions," "quiet time," "Bible study"). It is altogether too easy to drift into listening, not to Jesus, but for our ideas or desires to be supported by the Bible, that is, getting God on our side.

This leads to a most challenging passage of scripture from John 5. But before investigating, I must share three core realities from my story.

1. My sister gave me a Phillips New Testament when I was a high school freshman. I started reading the written Word of God (Matthew) and was transported from relating to laws to becoming a follower of my new Hero, a real Person named Jesus. My life and eternity were forever changed, from dark to light, from drab to color, from death to life by listening to Jesus through His Word.

---

407 2 Timothy 3:16. This is not the place to seek to establish the rationale for the inspiration of Scripture. Many resources are available. Consider Josh McDowell, Evidence That Demands A Verdict

408 Too many "battle for the Bible" but do not seriously LISTEN to Jesus, including His clear words about battling

2. It was through studying the written account of Jesus in the garden[409] as a college senior that I came to love Jesus with all my heart, mind, soul, and strength. Responding in love to Jesus with all my heart has thoroughly transformed every part of my life, including hundreds of thousands of "small" Kingdom choices that "saved" me, plus purpose and blessings both now and eternally. I am unspeakably grateful.

3. It has been through devotionally "eating" the written Word of God as spiritual food before eating physical food most mornings for the last 42 years that my life has been over-proportionally blessed for time and eternity.

The point: I love, love, love the written Word of God. As I hold my tattered Bible that is literally falling apart, I have to be careful not to "worship" it. When it was stolen for a few days, I grieved the loss like losing a dear loved one.

All of the above statements about loving the written Word of God were said in order to address the "challenging" passage from God's Word in John 5.

Jesus healed a crippled man on the Sabbath. Healing a cripple is good, but not on the Sabbath, or so thought the Pharisees. Then Jesus claimed that God does that sort of thing ... right there in the Pharisees' hearing. Not smart by conventional wisdom. Then Jesus made the worst claim imaginable: He claimed to be the very Son of God. Those moral policemen of the day judged Jesus guilty of crimes deserving death, and were trying to execute that judgment, that is, get Jesus killed.

Love for these enemies reigned in Jesus' heart. He wanted His

---

409 Luke 22:39-46

persecutors to be saved.[410] It was nothing less than this great love for them that spilled out as He warned them of the desperate plight of their relationship with God. They assumed they were the "righteous ones." But Jesus looked below their study of the Scripture, their scrupulous external law-keeping, and their presumed righteousness before God.

"You have never heard His voice nor seen His form ..."[411]

This might seem to be acceptable, after all, how many have "heard His voice" like Peter did on prayer mountain, or seen the very form of God?

"nor does His word dwell in you ..."[412]

But what about this? The religious leaders may not have heard God's voice, or seen His form, but surely God's Word dwelled in them. They studied the Scriptures continuously, even professionally. Jesus even says it below. These professional, best-of-the-best religious leaders ...

"diligently study the scriptures ..."[413]

But, oh, oh! Look at their motive, and at what they had come to believe about the scriptures:

"... because you think that by them you possess eternal life."[414]

These were highly sincere, intelligent, diligent, and morally disciplined leaders. Unknowingly, they believed a lie. The lie was a very subtle twist from the truth, but a spiritually fatal twist, unless they listened

---

410 John 5:34
411 John 5:37
412 John 5:38
413 John 5:39
414 John 5:39

to Jesus and repented. They had unwittingly come to believe that to know and master the scriptures determined their eternal destiny. Thus zeal to know the scripture dominated their lives. They studied, knew, and relied on the words about God, but did not know God. They were relating to ideas and behaviors, not to God! *Really?* Actually, that makes them a lot like a lot of us. Do you know any Christians who mostly relate to and interact with biblical ideas and ethics, but not so much to a Person named Jesus?

Jesus confronted this very issue. Their faith was in the scripture, not in Him whom the Father had sent.[415] The scriptures are God's Word, intended to reveal a Person. It is this Person that scripture reveals has been sent from God and is to be known, trusted, and followed.

> *"These are the Scriptures that testify about Me, [40] yet you refuse to come to Me to have life."*[416]

The inspired Scriptures, a priceless and honored gift, are the very best means we have to objectively know God. It is these very Scriptures that have been given in order to make God known. But for these religious leaders, the means had come to take the place of the Omega – the End. Faith had drifted from the God of the Scriptures to the scriptures of God. Result: the preoccupation with Scripture pushed the God of the Scripture into the background. So subtle, but so devastating. They trusted in their knowledge of the Bible, not their knowing of the God of the Bible. They had come to rely on their knowledge, their "doctrines and theology," not their communion and union with God. Even though they knew the Scriptures, Jesus lamented that God's Word did not dwell in them.[417]

Is it possible for us to know the Scripture and yet God's Word not dwell in us? Surely not! Jesus says, "Yes, it is possible." Terrible, but possible.

---

415 John 5:38-39
416 John 5:39-40
417 John 5:38

Diligently studying the Bible is a very good thing. But Bible study is a means, not the end.

We study the Bible in order to listen to a Person.

We study the Bible in order to listen to a Person. His name is Jesus. This chapter is given to motivate everyone possible to carefully, diligently study the Bible, but as a means to the end of knowing The Person whom to know is eternal life.

We all know people who don't care enough about knowing God to diligently study His Word. But we also probably know some people who care enough to "diligently study the Scriptures," but knowing and even mastering the Bible is their unrecognized objective. Bible study has become, for them, an end rather than the means to the end. They might even be just like those religious leaders Jesus was addressing in this regard: their faith has been placed in their knowledge and theological understanding, instead of in a Person. Their faith is in their faith. They are not listening for a Person speaking through the Scriptures to them. They are seeking to know, and understand, master and live by, even teach, the Scripture. When they "talk about God," they don't really talk about God. They talk primarily, if not entirely, about the "things" of God … doctrines and theology, morality, church growth, even making disciples. Their conversation does not include a Person named Jesus. It seems if they were in close, confiding, caring, working relationship with Jesus, their conversation would include Him. They persistently stop one step short – just like the Jewish leaders – of letting their scriptural knowledge lead them to Jesus. In all their study and analysis and teaching, they stop short of the God-given intent of the Scripture, to know Him whom to know is life eternal.[418]

"The Bible is not an end in itself, but a means to bring men to an intimate and satisfying knowledge of God, that they may enter

---

418 John 17:3, 1 John 5:13

into Him, that they may delight in His Presence, may taste and know the inner sweetness of the very God Himself in the core and center of their hearts." A.W. Tozer

The intent of this entire chapter is simply this: we desperately need to intentionally and persistently listen to Jesus.[419] The most foundational, primary way to do this is to carefully study the Scripture, but with the conscious awareness that we are listening to the Living Christ speaking to us through correctly understood Scripture. We study the scripture diligently as the necessary pre-requisite to do what Jesus' Father commanded Peter: "listen to My Son." We dare not stop one step short in merely "studying diligently." We must study because the Father commanded us clearly, "This is My Son, LISTEN to Him."

The next chapter will model some helpful ways to listen to Jesus, and respond. It will identify some challenges and possible solutions in being discipled by Jesus, both in groups and privately.

---

419 Matthew 17:5

CHAPTER 12

Do You Listen to Me? (Part II)

THIRD QUESTION (CONT.)

What does it look like when a group is listening to Jesus speak through His Word? Let's join a group just starting to study through Philippians. We are about to move to the third question Jesus might ask us, "Do you listen to Me through My Word?"

Hal: "As we study through Philippians, we will examine each word to make sure we are carefully listening for what Jesus wants to say to us through His Word.[420] So, the first word here is 'Paul.' Will someone in the group tell us briefly about Paul, or anything you think the Lord wants us to hear about Paul."

Group: Two or three people made some comments about Paul.

Hal: "Thank you. Let's go ahead. How about Timothy. Who is he? What do we need to know about him?"

Group: Again, several made brief comments identifying various things about Timothy. Then, an abrupt comment was made by the pastor of the church, who was sitting immediately to my right. His name is Randy.

---

420 This is the "Analyze" process described below

Randy: "You skipped a word."

Hal: "Uhhh … oh, sorry. Paul _AND_ …" (I did not think Randy was trying to be "cute" or funny or point out an error on my part. I turned to look at him, truly wondering what he was going to say.) "Do we need to define 'and?' Or is the Lord saying something to you through the word 'and?'"

Randy did not answer. He could not. He was staring down at the table, obviously choking back tears. We all waited. He finally spoke.

Randy: "I was just doing what you said, thinking about each word. As I thought about '_and_' I very clearly heard Jesus speaks to me." Again, he looked down … tears now streaming down his cheeks. He finally was able to talk.

Jesus said, 'You don't have an "_and_" in your life.' Another long pause. Jesus showed me that if I were writing this letter, I could not say, 'Randy and _____.' I don't have a Timothy.'"

Several of us were in tears as we watched and listened to the account of Jesus, by His Spirit and His Word, discipling one of His special guys. The sweet silence of Spirit-encounter continued. After a while, I spoke, hoping that I did not rush the process.

Hal: "Has Jesus said anything else?"

Randy: "Oh, yes. My 'Timothy' is to be Kenneth." Kenneth is Randy's 8 year old son. Now most of us were in tears. There was no need to ask if the group thought that Randy had accurately heard the voice of God. It was obvious that all present perceived that we were observing a holy encounter, almost as if Moses and Elijah had just shown up. It will take years, in fact eternity, to reveal the significance of Randy's sitting at Jesus' feet that morning, listening to Him speak through

Scripture to a father about his son.

Since then Randy and Kenneth sit together at Jesus' feet most mornings. Dad asks his son the kinds of questions (and better) that were being asked during those meetings to be discipled by Jesus. Together they listen for Jesus' Word and Spirit, even through each other. Together they respond, make commitments, pray, and go into their days separately, but together in Jesus. The "Kenneth stories" that have occurred in the past year beg to be told. Hopefully they will be. Kenneth meets with Jesus on his own when his dad cannot be with him. Kenneth sacrifices temporal pleasures for eternal values, a discipline difficult for anyone, to say nothing of a boy his age. He receives correction and coaching in following Jesus. Other parents want Kenneth to come to their home to have Kenneth's influence in their family. He leads others in meeting with Jesus, and encourages adults that they too can do what he has learned to do.

Of course, not every meeting has that kind of instant life-changing drama. But many do.

In facilitating a meeting where we seek to listen to Jesus through His Word (a primary way of being discipled by Jesus), it is my practice to work straight through a book of the Bible. I have led groups through almost every New Testament book, including Revelation, and many Old Testament books.

There are three very important reasons for this practice:

1. To be best discipled by Jesus, His followers need to be helped to study the Bible carefully in order to accurately listen to God's Son. They typically cannot or will not do this on their own. They need someone to do this primary spiritual discipline with them.[421] Since listening directly to Jesus is

---
421 Mark 3:14

critical to being _His_ disciple, then being discipled to listen directly to Jesus through His Word is essential to making disciples of Jesus.

2. Jesus' contemporary disciples need to be trained and coached to be discipled by Jesus in private, not just in group meetings. When two or more gather to study the scripture in order to listen to Jesus (#1 above), attendees are being _trained_ and _equipped_ to effectively meet and listen to Jesus on their own, independently of the group, throughout the week.[422] They are being discipled to be Jesus' disciples.

3. Jesus' disciples who have been trained (#1 above) to listen to Jesus on their own (#2 above) are now much more able to help and facilitate family members or others in listening to Jesus through His Word. The way that Disciple A has learned to be discipled by Jesus can be passed on to Disciple B (#1 above), who then is able, after meeting with Jesus on his own (# 2 above), to help Disciple C be discipled by Jesus. This begins a multiplication of disciples becoming disciplemakers.

Let's visit another meeting.

Hal: "I love these times of 'sitting at Jesus' feet.' Thanks to each of you for relating and responding so meaningfully to Him. I think this would be a good time for us to move on to another question Jesus wants to ask us, 'Are you listening to Me through My Word?' Let's open our

---

422 Side note: I am amused and irritated that we hand new converts a Bible and say, "You need to read this every day," but when a Sunday School class or small group is encouraged to study through a book of the Bible, a group of 20 long-time church members will lobby for a contemporary or popular book, saying that "the Bible is too hard to understand." What are we thinking? We need to "equip the saints" to listen to Jesus speak to all of us through His Word. This training is intended to happen through this small group meeting of Jesus' disciples.

Bibles to Hebrews 5. We worked with verse 6 last week. Did anyone work through the rest of this chapter this week?"

Alivia: "Yes, and I am sure looking forward to hearing what everyone is sensing the Lord is saying to us through it."

Hal: "Great. Justus, will you very slowly and thoughtfully read verses 7-10? You are reading the message Jesus wants us to hear from Him tonight."

Justus reads.

Hal: "Thank you. Let's take it one word or phrase at a time, to make sure we are not missing anything. 'During the days of Jesus' life on earth ...'

Do we understand the meaning of each of these words or are there any questions?"

Emma: "Just that I am always in awe that the uncreated God, who created everything and had absolute ease and comfort, would truly empty Himself as Jesus did, and come to live as a poor servant, knowing He would be crucified. I guess I am thinking about Philippians 2."

Hal: "Is anyone hearing Jesus saying anything through what Emma is saying?"

Silence.

TIME OUT

I desperately desire that we – Jesus' disciples – slow down and practice bringing at least a few of our thoughts captive into obedience to Him, "as if" He were present, important, and might have something to say.[423] We need to learn this habit, and by practicing together we can coach each other in accuracy. Further, we are creating relationships around the activity of "including Jesus." The biblical name for this is fellowship. If we experience a football game together, we can later talk about the game; if we experience Jesus together, we can later talk about Jesus together.

TIME IN

Hal: "Does anyone want to say anything to Jesus about what Emma said about Him?"

Debbi: "Oh, Jesus. I lift my voice in honor of You ... our great King who created all things and owns all things and yet suffered all things because of Your great love. You are so worthy of all praise and honor and love."

TIME OUT

As facilitator, my task is to guide and monitor group members in listening and responding to Jesus. I am seeking to sensitively turn talk about Jesus or ideas or theology into conversation with Jesus. "Is anyone willing to talk to Jesus about this idea?" "Does anyone think you have heard Jesus speak in this discussion?" "Are you willing to respond to Jesus based on what you think He said to you?"

Note that I simply asked if anyone had thoughts or questions about the first phrase in Hebrews 5:7. Emma did, and it turned into a meaningful interchange between the entire group and Jesus.

TIME IN

Hal: "Are we ready to go on in verse 7? It says that Jesus 'offered up prayers and petitions with loud cries and tears to the One who could save Him from death, and He was heard because of His reverent submission.' Look at each word. Keep observing your thoughts for the

---

423 2 Corinthians 10:5

possibility that the Holy Spirit might be speaking to you through these words and ideas. Any questions or comments?"

David: "What is the difference between 'prayers' and 'petitions?'"

Hal: "Good questions. Anyone know?"

TIME OUT

Even though the facilitator may have the answer to a question, he/she is generally wise to not give an answer to the group, except as a last resort when it is apparent that no one else is able to answer correctly. When the facilitator is the "teacher" who answers all the questions, it teaches the group to be dependent on the facilitator. It teaches the group that they cannot lead because they do not have all the answers.

But more importantly, when the facilitator answers the questions, it robs every group member of the opportunity to examine their own understanding, and to grow in articulating their thoughts about Jesus and all matters pertaining to Jesus.

When group members are encouraged to speak about Jesus and to Jesus in front of the group, that very process of thinking and articulating is a training process, not to just talk about Jesus with others, but to be able to change "self-talk" that leaves Jesus out to "internal, heart-talk with Jesus."

We desperately need to learn to include Jesus in internal conversations. For example, instead of the mind simply wandering aimlessly or selfishly or fearfully, those who learn to include Jesus in conversations in a group are better equipped to include Jesus in their self-talk. "Jesus, I catch myself thinking, '_____.' What do You think? What do You want?" To change a culture (of a heart, or a family, or a church), change the conversation.

ANALYZE

To listen to Jesus, we must do careful and honest Bible study, which I have titled, "Analyze." It is the necessary start, for if we do not understand the words and concepts, we cannot receive God's message accurately. We simply want the plain meaning of the passage, not more or less or other than what is written. We dare not be satisfied, however, with ONLY "figuring out" the meaning. We must be certain to move to listening to the Author of the Word speaking through the Word, and then respond to the Author. If not, we make the error of the religious leaders of John 5 described in the previous chapter.

To listen to Jesus speak to us through Scripture, it is paramount that we know the plain meanings of words and ideas. As a group we *analyze* each word, and each idea, looking up unknown words or concepts in a Bible or regular dictionary.[424] We carefully distinguish between the plain meanings of the text and comments which are being added to the Scripture. These additions might be of the Holy Spirit, but must be identified as such and evaluated appropriately. If questions or disagreements arise about the meanings of the text, the facilitator generally should ask for a postponement of that particular issue until outside study or consultation with a leader can occur.

CATEGORIZE

To help in practically applying the message of Jesus to our lives, it is useful for the facilitator to have the following questions – categories – ready to ask:

Does anyone see a …

- Truth to believe, especially about God (T)

---

424 It was the carefully analyzing of EVERY word that enabled Randy to think about "and," consequently hearing the Holy Spirit that he, Randy, had no "and" in his life he was discipling.

- Promise to claim (Po)

- Command to obey (C)

- Example to follow (Ex)

- Error to avoid (Er)

- Warning to heed (W)

- Condition to meet (Cn)

- Prayer to pray (Pr)

- Fact with no obvious significance (F)

Every group member can be provided this simple list.

TIME IN (LATER IN STUDY OF HEBREWS 5:7-10)

Hal: "We have fairly thoroughly analyzed the words and ideas of verse 7. Are there other questions? Are we ready to start applying this verse?

Group nods that they are ready

Hal: "Does anyone see an example in this passage?"

Eden: "For sure. Jesus submitted to His Father reverently. For Him that meant being willing to go to the cross. I am to follow His example of denying myself and taking up my cross."

Hal: "How do any of you take up your cross?"

Emma: "Every time I do what Jesus wants that is different than what I want."

Avila: "Like being quiet when I want to tell certain people how irritating they are."

Dan: "I think for me to follow Jesus' example means I am to at least be willing to go more regularly to "my garden of Gethsemane" and ask Jesus about what He wants me to do."

Hal: "Does anyone think Dan is hearing Jesus' Spirit in what he is thinking?"

TIME OUT

The group facilitator wants to persistently keep drawing the group to the awareness that Jesus, by His Spirit, is present and might be speaking. If it is my thought, it is actually not that important. But if I truly believe the thought to be from the Holy Spirit, I have an authoritative word from God to believe and act on.

Further, the facilitator must help speaker and listeners to evaluate if what is being said is "fleshly" or actually from Jesus. One of the primary purposes of the group is to intentionally sit at Jesus' feet, seeking to learn to recognize His voice in their minds or through others' words.

TIME IN

Justus: "Well, it certainly would be hard to argue that Jesus doesn't want Dan to spend more time with Him in 'his garden.'"

Hal: "Does Dan's thought seem to be a good thought? Good things come from the Lord. Does anyone see any reason to question if this is the Lord speaking to Dan? (Silence.) Dare we conclude that Dan has heard from the Lord?"

Group nods consent.

Hal: "Dan, let's assume it is the Lord. Are you willing to speak back to Him in response to what He said to you?" (Note: facilitator keeps seeking to keep the group awareness of Jesus' presence and dialogue with Him. When the group is aware of Jesus being present, and that He may be speaking, it not only heightens the meaning of each statement, it influences the group toward many positive postures: sensitivity, carefulness, alertness, guarding words and thoughts, authenticity, humility, honesty, truthfulness, etc.)

Dan: "Lord Jesus, I think You did make me aware that my primary step in following You is to regularly go to 'my garden.' So I will."

Silence.

Hal: "Dan, should or could you be a bit more specific about where your garden is and/or when you will go to it?"

Dan: "I was thinking about that, and I don't know. I have made a lot of promises and did not keep them and want to be very careful."

Hal: "That's so good. Would you at least be willing to commit to talking to the Lord about when and where this week, and see if He guides you?"

Dan: "Sure."

Hal: "Anyone sensing anything the Holy Spirit may want you to ask Dan before we move on? Nothing?

TIME OUT
Let's leave the meeting to discuss the next component of our Bible study.

PERSONALIZE

We dare not finish "Bible study" until we have intentionally made it possible for Jesus to speak directly to us through His Word. This component protects us from "mere" Bible study that stops short of relationship. It literally escorts us into the awareness of Jesus and His speaking to us. This is of utmost importance. I call it PERSONALYZING the study of scripture.

Personalizing Scripture seeks to intentionally avoid the problem for which Jesus confronted the religious leaders: studying the scriptures but not knowing Him.[425] Personalizing simply means placing the words and ideas that have been carefully studied into the mouth of Jesus and having Him *personally* speak His words to the group or individuals in the group. For example, instead of "He was heard because of His reverent submission,"[426] personalizing sounds like this: "Hal, My Father heard Me because of My reverent submission to Him." Personalizing must never change the plain meaning of Scripture. It simply puts the plain meaning into Jesus' mouth and pictures Jesus saying to me what He inspired Paul to write to one of the churches, or what any writer of Scripture wrote to the recipients. "Personalizing" simply makes the Scripture personal (from one Person to another) without changing the meaning of Scripture.

BEYOND THE SCRIPTURE

The Holy Spirit certainly could provide greater and/or more specific messages or applications, and it be very much from Jesus. The danger is in the one who "heard" Jesus speak by the Spirit dogmatically, even arrogantly, affirming that the "application" is from Jesus. Instead, Jesus' current disciples must be trained to humbly recognize and confess that their "message" _might_ be from Jesus. This is another reason it is good for us to do this "Bible study" together.

---

425 John 5:39-40
426 Hebrews 5:7

TIME IN

Hal: "Dan, I don't need to keep you on the 'hot seat,' but I was wondering if it would be helpful for you to personalize what you said, as if Jesus Himself were speaking directly to you? Just think of Jesus looking at you, speaking your name, and saying exactly what you said about His example to you."

Dan: "Well, I know we have done this before, but I am always a little nervous to actually have Jesus say something to me."

Hal: "Thank you so very much for being honest. We really understand. It still makes me nervous at times. But, if we are not changing the plain meaning of Scripture, and since Scripture is the very message God wants us to know, it helps me to think of Jesus saying His Word directly to me. Would anyone else be willing to personalize Jesus' possible words to Dan from what Dan said about Jesus' example?"

Dan: "Oh, I can do it, and I will, since all of you are here to help me if I don't do it very well. 'Dan, this is Jesus. When you were looking for an example in Hebrews 5, and you recognized the example I set by submitting to My Father in the garden, and you had the thought of following My example by at least going into your garden more often to find out My will, it was very good thought, and I agree. I do call you to follow My example and go into your garden more often."

Hudson: "Wow, Jesus. How Dan just said Your words to him was so good. I heard You talking directly to me through what Dan thinks You said to him. Thank You!"

TIME OUT

Often as Jesus' disciples, like Dan, verbalize Jesus' clear Word or applied/practical Word from Himself to the disciple, the disciple does not get as far as Dan did. Why? The Holy Spirit convicts and convinces them that the Living Jesus truly is speaking to them, and they are overwhelmed with His Presence and message. Time after time we have observed contemporary disciples of Jesus break down in tears when they actually recognized that His Holy Spirit through His Word had actually spoken to them. This "hearing of our Shepherd's voice" is supposed to be normal for "Spirit-filled, Bible believing" Christ followers.

Is this dangerous? Could this lead to error or extreme? Of course. However, this disciple is sitting in the presence of a maturing facilitator-discipler, and also a sincere and growing group of disciples. Those surrounding the "Dans" are there to help protect each other from error, and are being constantly made aware of the presence of the Living God. Having led thousands of these meetings, no one has suggested to me any concern about "personalizing Scripture." But we all know of the "God told me" abuses.

Which is more dangerous, Dan attending this "Discipled by Jesus" meeting, or sitting at home watching TV that totally washes his brain with godlessness?

Or is it more dangerous than sitting in a more typical "Bible study" that usually ends up with those present coming to all kinds of conclusions every bit as much as Dan did, and more? Those conclusions are also about God, theology, values, and other important life issues, and assumed to be true. However, those conclusions are usually arrived at with less caution than is being given in what I am suggesting. Several factors greatly help in protecting participants from distorting Jesus' Word through the Scriptures: 1) the humility and sensitivity that comes from a profound awareness of being in Jesus' presence 2) the profound honoring of Scripture that dares not add to or detract from it 3) the caring supervision of each Spirit-filled Christ-follower present. Back to the John 5 issue, is the point of Bible study merely to secure more knowledge or to actually hear from God?[427]

427 Chapter 10

To what degree dare we honor and trust the Holy Spirit of Truth to guide us? Teach us? Remind us? Convict us? Was it really better for Jesus' disciples that Jesus go away because He would then send the Holy Spirit to be in us? I long to so honor and fellowship with the Holy Spirit that I am aware of Jesus, and making progress in knowing what Jesus is thinking, wanting, doing, and saying to me. I believe that while I am carefully studying Scripture in the conscious awareness of the Holy Spirit, and the literal presence of Jesus' authentic disciples, His Body, I have my best opportunity to obey My Father's directive about His Son: "Listen to Him!"

TIME IN

Dan: "Jesus, as I sit here in Your presence thinking about You in the garden, I am overwhelmed with Your response to Your Father, and Your many, many hours alone with Him. I don't need to wait further. I am pretty sure You want me to re-commit to getting up each week day morning at 5:30 so I can have one hour alone with You before I take off for work. I am going to assume that You gave me a sense that that would be best. Thank You. I believe it was You, and that really helps me to commit with great seriousness."

Hal: "Whoa! What an assumption. And what a commitment. Thanks, Dan. Group, do any of you have any concerns? Do you think Dan is biting off too much?

Phoebe: "Dan, the worst thing I can see is if you try to get up and find it too hard and give up, and then feel like a phony or failure. I will pray that you will do this and that it will be meaningful for you. Will you promise to keep talking to us about how you are doing and what you are thinking?"

Dan: "Yes, and with gratefulness to have all of you."

TIME OUT

Behind every course of action there is a cause. Identify the cause, and you identify your "discipler" in that situation. In our meeting, Dan was being discipled, by someone or something. Was he discipled by Jesus? Did he hear his Shepherd's voice? Did the Word of Christ dwell in him to change his thinking and behavior? If Jesus spoke to him (cause), and he obeyed (actions), then it was Jesus who discipled him.

Someone is discipling you non-stop. For each of your actions, there is a cause. The cause is your discipler. How much is Jesus discipling you?

In our meeting to be discipled by Jesus, we have looked at His nature, and His activity, and listened to His Word. Next, we look forward to discerning His will for us as His disciples.

CHAPTER **13**

Do You Truly Love Me? (Part I)

FOURTH QUESTION

The discussion was difficult to have in the presence of the other disciples, so after breakfast, Jesus may have invited Peter to go for a walk. Or maybe Jesus and Peter had a very intensive "heart-to-heart" conversation in front of the other disciples. We don't know for sure.

Neither do we know if or how much Jesus and Peter had talked since the resurrection. We don't know if they had already talked about the resurrection, or the crucifixion, or Peter's denials of Jesus. We don't know if they had talked about Peter's claims that even if everyone else left Jesus, he would not. In fact, Peter claimed, he would go to prison for Jesus, even die for Him.

Did Jesus enter into a little small talk before confronting these big issues? You'd think He would, but we have no record of it.

What we do know is this: Jesus asked Peter a very searching, heart-opening question. "Simon, son of John, do you truly love Me more than these?"[428]

Peter might have heard Jesus asking, "Do you love Me more than these

---

428 John 21:15

friends?" Or, "Do you love me more than these fish?" The fish might have represented Peter's occupation, or maybe just his recreation.

Or Peter might have heard a more pressing question: "Would you ever tell Me again that you are ready to go to prison for Me or even lay down your life for Me?[429] That you actually have agape for Me like I have for you?"

Jesus knew the answer to the question because Jesus knew Peter. The real issue was this, "Did Peter know Peter?" Was Peter persuaded that he loved Jesus, or did Peter so loathe his past failures that he wondered about his future?

Hundreds of times, maybe more, Peter had shuttered with the terrifying memory of those cursing, and cursed, denials, "I am not one of His disciples!"[430] His mind would go elsewhere, but most things he saw, or heard, or dreamed about, brought back that horrendous night of betrayal and consequent pain. He hated what he did; loathed himself for doing it. Now Jesus has to stick it right in his face, or maybe so Peter felt.

"Yes, Lord," he said, "You know that I deeply honor and like You."[431] Peter was not ready to again promise the kind of love – agape – that would vow to lay down his life, the vow he so miserably failed to keep before the denial. He could only say that Jesus was a dear friend.

In all his recent pain, confusion, and drama, including the drama of resurrection, it would not be a stretch to assume that Peter had forgotten Jesus' words to him. "You are Peter, and on this rock I will build My church."[432] Or worse, maybe he had not forgotten, but assumed that he had forever blown his assumed "worthiness" which

---

429 John 13:37
430 John 18:15-27
431 John 21:15 … phileo
432 Matthew 16:18

led Jesus to make the pronouncement. But Jesus had not forgotten nor changed His mind.

"Feed My lambs."[433]

Two more dramatic times Jesus asks if Peter loves Him. Notice that Jesus did not require mature love to feed His lambs or care for His sheep. He commissioned Peter based on Peter's confession of "brotherly love:" "I sure like being with You, Lord, and doing things with You." Peter was not asked to have the love identified as agape –"I will go to prison or die for You, Jesus, regardless of what is in it for me." Nor was Peter required to go to Bible College or seminary to care for and feed Jesus' sheep. Having been with Jesus and wanting to continue to be with Jesus was sufficient to be commissioned.[434]

Fast forward over 2000 years.

Most of us, like Peter, have made strong proclamations and promises to Jesus. "You are my Lord and Savior! I will trust You." "You are my Shepherd! I will follow You." "You died for me; I will live for You. In fact, I will lay down my life for You! I'll even go to prison for You or die for You."

Jesus hears our confession of love, delights in our response to Him, and calls us into eternity-changing partnership with Him.[435]

Most of us, like Peter, have denied our grandiose profession, if not with our mouths, at least by our lives. Peter very publicly denied our Lord. Our denials are normally not so public. But they are every bit as obvious to our Lord who sees the heart. Like Peter, we weep with the recognition of our denials. Like Peter, we wonder if we are so

---

433 John 21:15
434 Acts 4:13
435 Matthew 11:28-29, 16:24, 28:20, John 14:12, 20:21, 1 Corinthians 12:27, Ephesians 2:10, 4:11-16, etc.

unworthy that we might have lost Jesus' invitation for us to partner with Him in His eternal Kingdom enterprise.

Then Jesus invites us into a heart-to-heart conversation, graciously probing the most important issue of our soul. He asks us that same question He asked Peter. "Do you love Me?[436] Truly? More than these? Are you still willing to lay down your life for Me?"

Not realizing that He sees the scream in our heart to say, "Yes!" we assume that His love is more like ours. So we sheepishly answer, "Jesus, I messed up so badly. I promised You once that I so loved You that I would lay down my life for You. I'm embarrassed to even bring it up. How about if I confess that I love You[437] as a very dear friend?"

It is almost as if Jesus did not even notice our failures and does not take note of our stumbling attempts to be humble. "Feed My sheep." "Care for My lambs." It is as if He says to us, "I knew how weak you were when you thought you were strong, and I know how strong I can empower you to be now that you perceive some of your weakness. You take care of My lambs.[438] I will work in and through you to build My church."[439]

"Do you love Me?" We, Jesus' contemporary disciples, also need to give Jesus an honest answer to this question which He asks of all His disciples. We must be every bit as honest as Peter was. And we must answer the question quite regularly.

CHILDISH LOVE

We could answer, "Lord Jesus, You know that I love You," and mean it most sincerely. But many would unknowingly mean the innocent but untested, immature love of a child. A little five year old boy sincerely

---

436 agape
437 phileo
438 Matthew 28:18-20
439 Matthew 16:18

loves his daddy, for his daddy is good to him. In fact, the little boy obeys his daddy, doing whatever his daddy tells him he must do, partly because of the consequences of not obeying, but partly because he actually does want to please his daddy. In short, his motives are multiple and mixed.

But most of the boy's day is spent playing ball, riding his bike, watching videos, and generally "goofing off." The little guy is oblivious to what his daddy is doing, and what his daddy is pressured by, or working on, or dreaming about. The little guy is not yet "about his father's business." He is oblivious to his daddy's work, and the reasons his daddy works. And that is normal. He *should* be oblivious to all his daddy is carrying. He is a five year old and five year olds do not carry their daddy's concerns on their shoulders or passions in their hearts.

Does the little boy love his daddy with all his heart? Probably not. Given his level of maturity, does he love to his legitimate capacity to love? Probably.

DIVIDED, TRANSITIONING LOVE

Jesus asks, *"Do you truly love Me more than these?"*

The newborn, immature Christian is not asked nor expected to be mature, including caring for and feeding Jesus' sheep. However, an inevitable process is at work in every one "born from above." The Holy Spirit indwells these "newborns."

> *"God has poured out His love into our hearts by the Holy Spirit, whom He has given us."*[440]

The Holy Spirit is LOVE. Selfless love. He dwells in the immature newborn. He calls to selfless caring, draws and woos, and unless

---

440 Romans 5:5

quenched and grieved, influences the immature Christ-follower toward mature, dying-to-self love for Jesus and His purposes.

Further, the Holy Spirit reveals the Person of Jesus relentlessly to all believers, including these immature ones.[441] It is through realizing who Jesus is – more and more – that Jesus' goodness and greatness captures our hearts, purifying us from lesser and secondary loves.

It is reasonable that immature Christians would mature into fully devoted followers of Jesus, loving Him with ALL our heart, soul, mind, and strength. But it is not normal, nor is it without a transition … a sometimes very painful transition … from predominant love of self to pure love for Jesus.

The Holy Spirit intends to navigate newly-born, immature Christians from self-preoccupation to fully loving Jesus … full maturity.[442] The navigating is normally lengthy and often tricky.

For example, millions take communion each Sunday, many with tears. At the very least they genuinely believe Jesus' death has saved them from eternal condemnation and provided for them a place in Heaven. They are at the very least truly appreciative to Jesus for what He did for them. Do they love Jesus? At the very least, no one would want to call them "enemies of the cross of Christ." But Jesus, through Paul, says that those whose mind is on earthly things are, in fact, enemies of the cross of Christ.

> *"For, as I have often told you before and now say again even with tears, many live as enemies of the cross of Christ. Their destiny is destruction, their god is their stomach, and their glory is in their shame. Their mind is on earthly things."*[443]

---

441 John 14-16
442 Ephesians 1:23, 3:19, 4:13, 5:18
443 Philippians 3:18-19

If your mind is on earthly things are you literally an enemy of the cross of Christ? *Only on earthly things? Mostly on earthly things? Normally on earthly things?* We obviously must deal with many earthly things. However, if we actually love Jesus "more than these," we grow in seeking first His Kingdom and righteousness, and in the sensitivity that inquires of Jesus regarding His way of caring for our earthly needs.

> *"But seek first His Kingdom and His righteousness, and all these things will be given to you as well."*[444]

> *"And whatever you do, whether in word or deed, do it all in the name of the Lord Jesus, giving thanks to God the Father through Him."*[445]

> *"Whatever you do, work at it with all your heart, as working for the Lord, not for men…"*[446]

Jesus (through Paul) further says that those who give themselves to securing the quantity or quality of food they desire are enemies of His cross.

> *"For, as I have often told you before and now say again even with tears, many live as enemies of the cross of Christ. Their destiny is destruction, <u>their god is their stomach</u>…"*[447]

Seriously? Enemies of His cross? How many who partake of communion each Sunday forget about Jesus all week, precisely because all week long their minds are on earthly things, with what they will eat often at the top of the list, including thinking about what they will eat during the communion service? Are they enemies of the cross of Christ or lovers of Jesus?

---

444 Matthew 6:33
445 Colossians 3:17
446 Colossians 3:23
447 Philippians 3:18-19

Again Jesus asks, *"Do you truly love Me?"* Paul identifies some who are truly lovers, but not of God.

> *"But mark this: There will be terrible times in the last days. People will be <u>lovers of themselves,</u> <u>lovers of money,</u> boastful, proud, abusive, disobedient to their parents, ungrateful, unholy, <u>without love,</u> unforgiving, slanderous, without self-control, brutal, <u>not lovers of the good,</u> treacherous, rash, conceited, <u>lovers of pleasure</u> rather than <u>lovers of God</u>— having a form of godliness but denying its power. Have nothing to do with them."*[448]

These folks were lovers of themselves, lovers of money, and lovers of pleasure. They even had a form of godliness. They were probably church attendees who were respected in the community. Maybe even big givers? But they gave themselves to that which many, many contemporary "believers" give themselves. They love themselves. They love money. They love pleasure. But not God. How would they stare back at Jesus and answer His question, *"Do you truly love Me more than these?"*

The answer to Jesus' question is tricky. *"Do you truly love Me more than these?"* Does our love for Jesus make Him and what He wants more important to us than anything else?

As we grow in knowing Jesus, we grow in knowing ourselves. The Holy Spirit graciously helps us to see how badly our heart is divided. We see that our glib claim of loving Jesus with all our heart was naively inaccurate. We see that what we do, what we say, what we think, and what we want is typically more about us than Jesus. Perhaps we see that we love Jesus, not primarily because of Who He is, but primarily for what He does for us, which is still more about self-love than laying down our life for Him. We see that it is for ourselves that we became His disciples. We want to be saved from wrath, for

---

448 2 Timothy 3:1-5

ourselves. We want to inherit eternal life, for ourselves. We want to experience abundant life now, for ourselves.

The Holy Spirit graciously increases our awareness of the multiple "loves" of our very divided heart. We become acutely and painfully aware of the selfishness of our motives. Some things we do for and because of Jesus; much of what we do is for ourselves. Our acts and words are mostly for ourselves. We see time as "our" time and money as "our" money. We realize that we value money, things and positions more than we value Jesus and what He values. Jesus' question to Peter, "Do you _truly_ love Me more than these?"[449] relentlessly, tenaciously haunts and exposes our badly divided hearts. We come to recognize how much we live for ourselves, including the securities and pleasures of this life. We start to realize how much our self-centeredness is overruling living for Jesus moment-by-moment. His compassionate zeal to "seek and save what was lost"[450] and discipling them until they are obeying everything He commanded[451] has little space in our heart, to say nothing of our calendar.

But the story has not ended. As already noted, the Holy Spirit helps us see Jesus. Seeing Jesus draws our heart toward Him. As we grow in knowing Jesus, we become increasingly aware of Who Jesus is, what He did and what He is doing, and why. His humility and gentleness grow on us. His nobility and stunning righteousness captivate us. We come to realize His eyes are on the entire world, not just us. Or on the other extreme, maybe we come to realize that we are not just lost in the crowd of the billions He died for, but that He actually is sensitive to and cherishes us very personally.

Then, the realization begins to grow in us that there is much He has determined NOT to do without us. That is, He has determined that much of what He will do for others He does primarily through His

449 John 21:15, emphasis added
450 Luke 19:10
451 Matthew 28:20

Body … us … His Bride … His disciples. We come to realize that we have extreme worth and significance to Him and His mission. We are cherished, wanted, even needed and invited by the King of all kings.

Now these three realities are in play: 1) the revelation of the glory and goodness of Jesus, 2) Jesus' invitation to eternally significant partnership, and 3) the awareness of multiple loves in our own heart. The Holy Spirit's uses these three realities (and others) to help us to entirely and radically offer everything we have and are as a living sacrifice to Jesus.

> *"Therefore, I urge you, brothers, in view of God's mercy, to offer your bodies as living sacrifices, holy and pleasing to God—this is your spiritual act of worship."*[452]

Why would anyone ever "offer their bodies as living sacrifices?"

> *"And He died for all, that those who live should no longer live for themselves but for Him who died for them and was raised again."*[453]

> *"We love because He first loved us."*[454]

The Holy Spirit has graciously been at work to purify our hearts, and to keep us pure. But as is normally the case, He does not force or coerce, manipulate or dominate. He reveals, exposes, invites, draws. We respond by offering, and He in response purifies and empowers.[455]

MATURE LOVE

When in fact the great commandment to *truly* love God with all our heart, soul, mind, and strength moves from being a theoretical

452 Romans 12:1
453 2 Corinthians 5:15
454 1 John 4:19
455 Acts 1:8, 15:9

concept to a profound heart reality, we love to sit at Jesus' feet to be with Him, and to find His desires for us. To be sure, there are many immature Christians with divided hearts who are disinclined to proactively seek, and to find, and to follow Jesus' highest for each day. But just as surely, there are many, many who truly so love Jesus – with all their hearts – that they devotedly seek Jesus to find and follow His high calling for the details of their days. They have reached an intended level of maturity.[456] The normal evidence that we love Jesus is that they obediently care for and feed His sheep. "Do you _truly_ love Me? Take care of _My_ sheep."[457] "Do you love Me? Feed _My_ sheep."[458]

Mature love for Jesus normally takes time. Jesus did not ask Peter this question at their first conversation by the fishing boats.

Even Peter's level of love for Jesus led to Jesus giving him responsibility for the caring and feeding of His lambs. How much more will Jesus commission those with mature love? Jesus wants His lambs being coached by those who truly love Him. Truly loving Him, not necessarily theological astuteness nor moral maturity, is what Jesus wants in those He calls to care for His sheep. Theological astuteness and moral maturity are nice, but not necessary, to adopt and nurture some of Jesus' sheep, be they lost, brand new to the fold, or simply without a "spiritual coach." Which of us as parents were astute in parenting concepts or even mature in parenting performance when we began the parenting process? But because we truly loved our children, astuteness and maturity were sought and strengthened.

Mature love for Jesus does not mean that we are perfect in performance. It does mean that we recognize and openly repent of imperfect performance. It does mean that we are intentionally making progress in performance. These are good "spiritual food" for lambs to absorb into their spiritual systems.

---

456 Matthew 22:34-40
457 John 21:16
458 John 21:17

An equally sure evidence that we *truly* love Jesus is that we are devotedly finding and obeying His commands:

- *"If you love Me, you will obey what I command."*[459]

- *"Whoever has My commands and obeys them, he is the one who loves Me. He who loves Me will be loved by My Father, and I too will love Him and show Myself to him."*[460]

- *"If anyone loves Me, he will obey My teaching. My Father will love him, and We will come to him and make Our home with him."*[461]

- *"He who does not love Me will not obey My teaching. These words you hear are not My own; they belong to the Father who sent Me."*[462]

- *"If you obey my commands, you will remain in my love, just as I have obeyed my Father's commands and remain in his love."*[463]

- *"You are My friends, if you do what I command."*[464]

The distinction between heart obedience and ability to perform must always be remembered.[465]

There are many reasons to obey Jesus. In this discussion of transitioning from childishness to full maturity, it is beneficial to understand three particular motivations to obey Him.

---

459 John 14:15
460 John 14:21
461 John 14:23
462 John 15:24
463 John 15:10
464 John 15:14
465 See Chapter 5

1. _Fear of disobeying the King_: All true Christ-followers are at the least resolved to obey Jesus because we fear being a rebel against The King. We are not afraid of Him, but we are afraid to rebel against Him. We recognize that He is King and God, and that rebels will not be allowed entrance into His Kingdom. _Our motive: we risk eternal judgment if we are unwilling to obey The King._

2. _Personal benefits_: Christ-followers are resolved to obey Jesus, not only because He is in authority as King, but also because we trust Him as a good and wise King. We believe Jesus wants and knows what is best for us. Therefore, whatever He commands is for our ultimate best. _Our motive: we benefit temporally and eternally when we obey Jesus._

3. _Jesus' benefits_: Christ-followers are resolved to obey Jesus, to be sure because we fear being a rebel against the King, and certainly because we know that what the King commands is best for us. But we are resolved to obey Jesus at the highest level when we actually love our King with all our heart. We love Him because we know Him – at least we know enough about Him. Everything we know is good. We know enough about Who He is, what He has done, is doing, and will do to love Him. We know enough about why He does what He does, and does not do what He does not do, that we respect, honor and adore Him. We know enough about His love and wisdom and justice to be captured by Him. _Our motive: Jesus benefits when we obey Him._

It is instructive to observe that the angels have not been redeemed or saved from the heinousness of their sin as we have been. Yet, the mere observation of this God-Man Christ Jesus draws them to unceasing praise and adoration. The level of our passion for Jesus reveals the level of our knowing Him. To love Him more, spend more time "staring" at Him.

"Turn your eyes upon Jesus. Look full in His wonderful face and the things of earth will grow strangely dim in the light of His glory and grace."[466]

By regularly answering Jesus' questions in the previous three chapters, the Holy Spirit makes possible establishing and sustaining whole hearted love for Jesus.

- "Who do you say that I am?" invites us to stare at and articulate who Jesus is. Knowing and remembering Jesus' goodness, grace, genius and glory can stun and renew our hearts in love for Him day by day.

- "Do you understand what I have done for you?" helps us to tangibly see how Jesus demonstrates His love for us, not only 2000 years ago, but in the last days and hours. He washes our feet, and then our minds, and we are re-captured with His glory.

- "Do you listen to Me?" takes us ever deeper into knowing Jesus, His nature, His purposes and processes, including His desire and delight to include us as partners in His eternal enterprise.

PURE MATURING LOVE

Pure, maturing loves says, "Jesus, I love You, to be sure because You first loved me. But I won't just say I love You; I will *intentionally* live for You, entirely, regardless of the pleasure or pain that comes to me. I am entirely Yours. I know that if I lose sight of You, my love for You could drift toward lukewarmness. I will fight to focus my attention on

---

466 Turn your eyes upon Jesus, or "The Heavenly Vision" was written by Helen Howarth Lemmel, 20th century

You, to keep my first love white-hot. I will sit at Your feet to know You, to be with You, and to find and follow Your highest for each moment of the life that You gave to me that I have now given back – entirely – to You.

One last word about transitioning from immaturity to maturity. Every season of our walk with Jesus is to be about growing in deeper awarenesses and levels of love: Jesus' love for us, our love for Jesus, and our love for others.

One effect of loving Jesus is this: we aggressively enter into conversation with Him, not about what we want, but about what He wants. "What do You want to do in me? Through me? How can I obey You this day? How can I care for and feed Your sheep this hour? Which ones? When? Where? How?"

Suppose my wife, Debbi, and I were together and neither of us were required by other commitments to do something. I would think it careless, even offensive, to not ask her what she would like us to do. To simply do what I wanted, and expect her to go along without engaging her in the conversation to come into shared agreement as to what would be best would be a violation of love for her.

Logically, we would all engage Jesus, our Lord and King, the One we love with all our hearts much more than we would ask even our spouse. Surely we will delight in sitting at His feet, finding out what He wants to do with and through us this week, this day, this hour, this word, this thought. Having invited Him into our "heart" to be Lord of our lives, surely we would never tolerate independently and unilaterally doing what we want, making Him follow us around as if He had no preference, or worse, as if He were not even present.

Jesus' question, "Do you truly love Me?" has been answered emphatically by a young African pastor in Zimbabwe. This written prayer was found among his notes, papers and books after he was martyred.

> "I'm a part of the fellowship of the unashamed. The die has been cast. I have stepped over the line. The decision has been made. I'm a disciple of His and I won't look back, let up, slow down, back away, or be still.

> "My past is redeemed. My present makes sense. My future is secure. I'm done and finished with low living, sight walking, small planning, smooth knees, colorless dreams, tamed visions, mundane talking, cheap living, and dwarfed goals.

> "I no longer need preeminence, prosperity, position, promotions, plaudits, or popularity. I don't have to be right, or first, or tops, or recognized, or praised, or rewarded. I live by faith, lean on His presence, walk by patience, lift by prayer, and labor by Holy Spirit power.

> "My face is set. My gait is fast. My goal is heaven. My road may be narrow, my way rough, my companions few, but my guide is reliable and my mission is clear.

> "I will not be bought, compromised, detoured, lured away, turned back, deluded or delayed.

> "I will not flinch in the face of sacrifice or hesitate in the presence of the adversary. I will not negotiate at the table of the enemy, ponder at the pool of popularity, or meander in the maze of mediocrity.

> "I won't give up, shut up, or let up until I have stayed up, stored up, prayed up, paid up, and preached up for the cause of Christ.

"I am a disciple of Jesus. I must give until I drop, preach until all know, and work until He comes. And when He does come for His own, He'll have no problems recognizing me. My colors will be clear!" (Source: The Voice of the Martyrs)

This prayer of our martyred brother from Zimbabwe brought me to tears. It also led to my "blurting out" the following prayer in print. You are welcome to read what actually happened in response to Jesus speaking to me by His Spirit through an African brother.

"Oh, Jesus, my living, loving Lord. Your mercy and grace overwhelm me. I, who have been given so much of Bibles and church and holy comrades, to say nothing of food and shelter and jobs and cars and air-conditioning, should be so much more like You by now.[467] I know that You know to what extent I actually love You, and I know that You actually love me, regardless of the extent to which I have responded to Your love. Does it help that I *think* that I *want* every moment of my life to be for You and for YOUR benefit? By now, I should have so grown up into You that I never leave You out of my deciding processes,[468] nor say words without knowing they are Your words,[469] or take action without consulting You first.[470] I should never make You follow me as I walk by my flesh instead of deferring to and following Your Spirit.[471] Do I *really* love You? You know I want to, I mean, I intend to, that is … "

"Hal, this is Jesus. It is good to answer My question, but don't fixate on it. Fix your eyes on Me.[472] Glance at your heart when I ask you, but then gaze persistently into My heart for you and others.[473] It was watching and listening to Me that captured your heart initially, and it

---

467 1 Peter 1:15, Matthew 10:24-25
468 John 5:30
469 John 7:16-18, 12:49-50
470 John 5:19
471 Romans 8:5,13-14, Galatians 5:16-25
472 Hebrews 12:2
473 John 13:1

is by keeping your eyes fixed on Me that your heart will be strengthen and matured in love."

"Thank You, again, Lord. I fully agree, and will seek to obey. I will try again to answer Your question, 'Do you truly love Me?' Because I do love You, I renew my resolve – my holy resolve – to increase in being aware of Your presence, to be discipled by You, to listen to You before I decide or speak or act. I renew my resolve to trust in You with all my heart, not leaning on my own understanding, but in all my ways entering into agreement with You, knowing You will direct my paths.[474] I do not understand why I am so slow to mature, but I am unspeakably grateful that You do understand. I offer my body to be Your body, as a fully-alive sacrifice ... dead to myself, but alive to You.[475] I offer, again, everything I know of to You for Your purposes, not passively assuming You will overpower me, but actively taking responsibility to bring every thought captive to You, to listen and to follow You in everything.

"I will seek to steward the life You gave to me that I have given back to You by the priorities I believe You have taught me:

- Time with You for You to disciple me by Your Word, Spirit, and Body

- Time with my family, to disciple them by loving, listening, and leading them toward and to You ... over and over and over

- Time with my church family, to disciple them by loving, listening, and leading them to You over and over and over

- Time with a focused few lost friends and neighbors to disciple them by loving, listening ... and in the right ways and time ... leading them to You and into Your family"

---

474 Proverb 3:5-6
475 Romans 6:11, 12:1-2

The next chapter focuses on how to respond to Jesus' commission for those who love Him. "Care for My sheep. Feed My Lambs." It demonstrates a way that Jesus helps His contemporary disciples live out love for Him through the above listed priorities.

CHAPTER 14

Do You Truly Love Me? (Part II)

FOURTH QUESTION (CONT.) – DISCIPLED BY JESUS TOGETHER

Please join us again in another meeting to be "Discipled by Jesus," in progress.

Hal: "This has been a very meaningful time of listening to Jesus speak to us through Ephesians 4:1-3.

"Now, we need to intentionally let Jesus talk to us about His preferred future.[476] Let's respond to Jesus' next question, 'Do you *truly* love Me?' If so, we need to work through how to obey Him by feeding and caring for His sheep. Do you think Jesus wants to ask us if we truly love Him?"

Dawson: "Of course. It is so easy to be pulled away to giving ourselves to something else."

Hal: "Anyone want to stare into Jesus' eyes and answer His question?"

Eden: "Jesus, You keep showing me how You actually denied Yourself … moment by moment … to know and follow Your Father. You are … well, awesome. I do love You and do want to get better at feeding Your sheep."

---

476 John 16:13

Hudson: "Lord Jesus, I forget about You so much. I am so sick of it. It is hard to believe that You keep loving me in spite of how I fail You. But I do love You. I do intend to be sensitive to You this week."

David: "Can I ask a question?"

Hal: "Of course. We love questions."

David: "Well, it feels to me that Jesus' question sort of puts me in a corner. If I cannot say, 'I love Him,' that is not good. But if I do say I love Him, then He tells me to work with His sheep. And I don't feel like I am ready to work with anyone else yet. What am I to do with all that?"

Hal: "Thank you. Great observations. Great honesty. I think Jesus is thrilled with your questions. Does anyone want to ask David a question to help him work through this? Or does anyone think the Lord might be giving you something for David to consider?"

Addie: "Dave, what are you thinking or feeling when you wonder if you truly love Jesus?"

David: "Well, I'm not sure. I think I love Jesus … but I'm not sure I'm ready to say I'd go to prison with Him, or die for Him, like Peter did. For sure I don't want to make big promises and then blow it."

TIME OUT
This conversation might go on and on. The big point is this: David, with the help of the Holy Spirit and the group, has entered into one of the greatest conversations imaginable, and it can happen every week and more. Some people trace their entire spiritual life to one or two meaningful conversations about Jesus, or eternity, or morality. They remember well those very "uncommon" conversations … around a campfire or on a painful walk. But they are not supposed

to be uncommon. They are intended to be normal in the Christian community.

TIME IN

Hal: "Let's think about feeding Jesus' sheep. As you think forward to this coming week, what do you sense Jesus might want to do with you and/or through you?"

Justus: "I know He wants me to get back to my early morning times alone with Him. I hate that I commit to being with Him, do it for a few weeks, and then somehow drift away."

Hal: "Thank you. That was quick and to the point. Do you have a time in mind that will work best for you?"

Justus: "I think 5:30 AM."

Alivia: "Some people will think that is too early, but I know you and the Lord can do that."

Hal: "Do you have a place in mind?"

Justus: "Yes, my kitchen table."

Hal: "This is great, Justus. Are you willing in front of all of us to talk to the Lord about what you believe He wants to do with you?"

Justus: "Sure. 'Lord Jesus, I so want and need to be consistent in being with You. I want to be discipled by You far more than I have been. I again commit to getting up and getting ready so I can meet with You at 5:30 AM Monday through Friday. I so need You to help me. I ask, and believing this to be Your will, am confident that we will together do this. Thank You.'"

Hal: "Thank you, Justus. Friends, how many of you would be willing to commit to praying for Justus this week for him to be faithful to this commitment?"

Several raise hands.

Hudson: "Justus, I know how hard this is. Would you like to call me each morning at 5:29? I am always up. If you don't call, I will connect later to see what happened."

Justus: "That's a good idea. Yes, I will."

Dan: "Hey, Huds, can I call you at 5:28 each morning? I need that kind of support."

Hudson: "Sure. We will have 30 seconds."

Hal: "This is great. Justus, Huds, and Dan ... would you tell us all next week how all this is going?"

Agreement occurs, helping all to report their time to be discipled by Jesus, and even their commitments to each other.

TIME OUT

Note that if just one person in the group makes a commitment for the following week, that specific commitment in front of the whole group will be used by the Holy Spirit to speak to everyone. Time seldom allows for all to share what the Lord is calling them to, or to secure clarification of why, what, when, where, how, etc., or to secure prayer and accountability. But just one person being led through that process will be used by the Holy Spirit to help others in the group strengthen or establish their own commitments regarding being alone with Jesus to be discipled by Him throughout the week. This is equally true as one member of the group works through ministering to family members, and church family, and lost persons. The Holy Spirit will be talking to all about their ministry at home, in the church, and the world as one shares in any of those ministry areas.

TIME IN

Hal: "Again, thank you Justus for so quickly identifying Jesus' call for you to come to Him in specific ways. Let's take time to think and talk about what Jesus wants to do through us in our families. Anyone?"

Long silence.

Dawson: "I haven't been taking my boys out. When school started, we lost our evening times together because of activities and did not replace them. I think the Lord is guiding me to get back into the practice of having alone time with each one each week."

Hal: "Thank you. That is exciting. Huge! Do you have an idea of when you will try to get with each one?"

Dawson: "I think Tuesday night after homework would be good for Jacob and Wednesday night after youth group would be good for Jonathan."

Hal: "Great. Do you think they will want to do it, or will it be a battle?"

Dawson: "No, they like it and it will work if I don't drop the ball."

Hal: "What will you do with them?"

Dawson: "Well, I'll try to ask good questions – I am supposed to say that, right? – to catch up on what they are going through and how they are responding. Hopefully, we can do some of the things together that we do in this meeting."

David: "And you had to say that, too. Seriously, I think we are all getting the idea that we can make disciples of our kids the way we are being discipled in these meetings."

Hal: "May your tribes increase. And I am serious about that. In fact, it is my prayer. Thanks, Dawson. Let me ask two more questions: Group, would all of you pray for Dawson, and all our fathers here to intentionally and effectively disciple their children this week?"

Group: "Yes."

Hal: "Second question ... Dawson, will you tell us next week how it went this week? This is such a big deal, and we really want you to succeed."

Dawson: "Of course. I was already planning on it. I knew you would ask."

TIME OUT

Ephesians 4:11-16 clearly affirms that those given oversight in the church are to "equip the saints for the work of the ministry." The ministry of the church is far, far more than programmatic. It must intentionally create ways for Christ-followers to relate to Jesus together, including what Jesus is specifically calling each to do as His Body. By creating space in group time for Jesus to direct His disciples into ministry (somewhat like He did in Luke 9), and by clarifying through dialogue what the ministry is to be, the Word, Spirit, and Body work together to send Jesus' current disciples into their world to "feed and care for" His sheep.[477]

The effect of this discipling and equipping is stunning. Jesus' contemporary disciples are to help each other mature all the way to "the whole measure of the fullness of Christ."[478] Every disciple is to have a part, "speaking the truth in love" and growing up into Jesus, the Head.[479]

---

477 Ephesians 4:12
478 Ephesians 4:13
479 Ephesians 4:15

"From Him the whole body, joined and held together by every supporting ligament, grows and builds itself up in love, as each part does its work."[480]

Love is the center; the motive. Love by Jesus for all present; love for Jesus by all present; love for each other by all present; love by all present for those not present: family, church family, lost friends and neighbors.

All present are being connected to Jesus and all are learning to respond to Jesus in what they speak in love to the others of the group. All are connected to Jesus, and all are connected to each other by Jesus. Each part is doing its work. The Body of Christ is functioning. Jesus is increasingly being allowed to actually speak to and through His Body.

We are all very glad that Paul was inspired to write *"aim for perfection."[481]*

TIME IN

Hal: "This is great. We've got to 'sprint to the finish' of our meeting. Is anyone thinking of a person at work or school who is not following Jesus, and the Lord is wanting you to care specifically about that person?"

Alivia: "Oh, yes. It is a person with whom I work. She is a really good person. Some of you know her. She is very antagonistic toward 'organized religion.'"

Hal: "Of your pre-Christian friends, is she the closest or the furthest or somewhere in the middle in becoming a Christ-follower?"

Alivia: "Probably 3/4ths of the way toward being the furthest away."

---

480 Ephesians 4:16
481 2 Corinthians 13:11

Maddie: "Do you think the Lord wants you to try to connect more with her or with those who are closer to becoming Jesus' disciples?"

Alivia: "I hadn't thought about that. Just aware that she is right next to me all day and needs help."

Addie: "What kind of help?"

Alivia: "Well, I was thinking of 'spiritual help,' but now that you mention it, she is having a terrible time with her teen age sons."

Maddie: "Would she talk about the challenge with her sons if you sensitively asked her?"

Alivia: "Sure. She already has."

Hal: "Is anyone sensing anything from the Lord?"

TIME OUT
Note again: the facilitator's task is to sensitively yet persistently keep the group aware that the Holy Spirit is present and we need to keep sensitive to Him by testing our thoughts and words for His influence. The church gathered does not intend to forget about Jesus being present to listen and speak, but we often do.

TIME IN
Alivia: "Yes. I think Jesus wants me to pray for my friend, and figure out good ways to listen to her tell me about her kids. I really need to be her friend."

Hal: "Anything any of us can do to help? We certainly will pray. Right, group?"

Alivia: "Nothing more so far. You have all helped me to realize that the Lord is calling me to get with my friend very intentionally to simply care for her by listening. I realize that the Lord will help me if I need to say or do something beyond that."[482]

Hal: "Everyone OK with that? (Pause) "Alivia, it sounds like Jesus threw the ball to you, and you saw it caught it. Now all you have to do is run with it."

TIME OUT

At the time of this writing, "Tebowmania" was in full swing. Tim Tebow has to be one of the greatest young Christ-followers of our time. And as a professional football player, he is an absolutely tremendous runner. The problem is that he is a quarterback, and NFL quarterbacks are expected to be tremendous passers, not runners.

During a meeting one night, I somewhat flippantly compared Jesus and Tim Tebow … as football players. "Jesus isn't like Tim Tebow." A few of the males in attendance perked up. "Tim loves to run the ball, but he's not as good at throwing it. Jesus is different. Of course, He could run the ball, and who could stop Him? He would score any and every time He wanted. And, to be sure, anytime He knows that in the big picture it is better for Him to smash through the enemy's line, He can do it. But He prefers not to run.

"Most of the time He prefers to pass, that is, to throw the ball to one of His receivers. Now, if the receiver is where he is supposed to be, and watching, and catches the pass, and runs with it, the team makes progress. But if the receiver is insensitive to Jesus, doesn't see the ball coming, or sees it but doesn't catch it, or even catches it but doesn't run with it, the team makes marginal progress or actually loses ground, for an opportunity was lost and that gets the team closer to punting."

---

482 Matthew 10:19-20

Of course, I was talking about the Holy Spirit calling the play in the huddle, thus telling us where to go, and then getting us what we need to make the play. I was seeking to make the very important point that we must hear (in the huddle), run the called pattern (go to where the Holy Spirit told us to go and the way He told us to go in the huddle), watch for and catch the opportunity the Holy Spirit throws to us, and run with everything we have which He has provided for us.

> "We proclaim Him, admonishing and teaching everyone with all wisdom, so that we may present everyone perfect in Christ. To this end I labor, struggling with all His energy, which so powerfully works in me."[483]

This meeting is the huddle before we go into the game, which is really a war for the heart of every person. Winning this war is worthy of our laboring intensively, with all the energy Jesus graciously gives us.

TIME IN

Hudson: "As you care about him, I know the Lord will open a way for you to give a reason for the hope that is in you."[484]

Hal: "Let's pray now. Someone be sure to pray for every person who has sensed the Lord's call to ministry, including those of us who have not made any "out loud" commitments to the group."

Several of the group members pray with faith in God to empower everyone's specific commitments to love others. Meeting adjourned. Good meeting.

Based on John 21, the Spirit of Jesus might have brought the following question to someone's mind in the above described meeting:

---

483 Colossians 1:28-29
484 1 Peter 3:15

Jesus: "Who do I call to care for and feed My sheep?" He might add, "The perfect? The mature? Was Peter perfect or mature?"

We can fairly easily spot the answer.

Someone in our group could say, "Lord Jesus, it looks like anyone who loves You in the same way that Peter did. And he had struggled and even choked in responding to Your questions."

Jesus might say: "I do not call the perfected. I perfect the called. Go! Feed and care for My sheep."

> "He who began a good work in you will carry it on to completion until the day of Christ Jesus."[485]

> "May God Himself, the God of peace, sanctify you through and through. May your whole spirit, soul and body be kept blameless at the coming of our Lord Jesus Christ. The One who calls you is faithful and He will do it."[486]

> "Aim for perfection!"[487]

If we want to see more Christlikeness in the church, we will need to practice more "face to face" time with Jesus, being discipled by His Word, Spirit, and Body. By this process, we can equip the saints for being discipled by Him on their own.[488] This can happen in meetings like those described above.

Do we want our families to experience the blessings of knowing and following Jesus together? Of being more like God intended when He ordained families? More love, peace, and joy as families live and work

---

485 Philippians 1:6
486 1 Thessalonians 5:23-24
487 2 Corinthians 13:11
488 John 15:1-9, John 17:17, Luke 10:38-42, 2 Peter 1:3, Romans 12:2

together, doing meaningful tasks and simultaneously being trained spiritually? Then we will need to disciple and equip the husbands and wives, the fathers and mothers, to caringly and wisely disciple their families. This can happen in meetings like those described above.

Do we want to see non-Christians become Christ-followers? Then we will have to disciple and equip the church to pray for, love, listen to, and lead one or two or three very specific lost persons toward Jesus. This can happen in meetings like those described above.

Do we want to see our church be discipled by Jesus and mature toward the fullness of Christ? We could determine to give priority, quality, and quantities of time to sit in Jesus' presence, responding to His questions, like …

- "Who do you say that I am?"

- "Do you understand what I have done for you?"

- "Do you listen to Me?"

- "Do you truly love Me?"

- "Do you believe Me?"

Is there a "one-size-fits-all" way to make disciples? Obviously, no. Can we learn some concepts and principles, even specific methods, from the Chief Shepherd (Disciplemaker)? It makes sense to look hard, or at least consider, His processes for making disciples. Are you being discipled? Are you making disciples? Are they ready to "feed" and "care for" Jesus' sheep? Truly loving Jesus is the first test of readiness.

FEEDING AND CARING FOR JESUS' SHEEP

So, because we DO truly love Jesus, and both He and we know it, Jesus invites us to care for and feed His sheep. Where do we start? Who are His sheep in our world? Right where we live?

The first of _His_ sheep in _my_ world is … surprise, surprise … me. This could be, but need not be, a selfish consideration. It is JESUS desire that I be cared for and fed, precisely because _HE_ cares for me. When I see to it that He, Jesus, is discipling me, because that is what He wants, I am not primarily being selfish, I am choosing to do what _JESUS WANTS_.[489] Because He loves me, He deeply desires to disciple me … to care for and feed me. He knows and wants what is best for me, and knows that being discipled by Him is what is best for me. He knows my desperate need to be well-discipled, and desires to meet that need. Because He loves me, He also wants me to receive benefits throughout eternity for caring for and feeding others, which I cannot do if I am inadequately cared for and fed. Of course, He cares equally for others, and because He wants them to also be cared for and fed, He delights in caring for me, knowing that will empower and equip me to better serve both Him and others He loves. Win for me, win for others, win for Him. To the degree that I am cared for and fed by Him, I am useful to Him in caring for and feeding others. Because I do love Jesus, I choose what He wants, which begins with letting Him disciple me for His purposes.

PRIORITY ONE: BE DISCIPLED BY JESUS

So, because I love Jesus, I will see to it that His sheep are cared for and fed. I am one of His sheep. Of all of Jesus' sheep on the planet, I have most control over, thus responsibility for, this one … me. Because of love for Jesus, and being responsible for my own actions, my first

---

489 To be sure, I win. Being discipled by Jesus is in my best interests, both now and eternally. In this case, wanting what Jesus wants, and what is best for everyone involved, is logically and probably theologically the one circumstance when "living for self" is actually righteous and holy and God-ordained. Jesus wants us to be like Him (selfless), but when what we want is truly what He wants and truly godly, wanting what we want is probably holy.

priority in serving Jesus is to put myself in a position to be discipled (cared for and fed) by His Word, His Spirit, and His Body.

Jesus: "If you love Me, do what I want for you, which is to sit at My feet, which is the best thing for you,[490] letting Me disciple you. It will not only be best for you, but to the degree that I disciple you, you will be better able to do what I WANT for others, which is that you care for and feed them (disciple them). You serve Me, you serve others, and you serve yourself when you see to it that, as one of My sheep, you are cared for and fed by My Word, My Spirit, and My Body. Come to Me.[491] Draw near to Me."[492]

So after Jesus clarifies that we love Him, He might want to press the issues that chapters one through six of this book address: "For My sake, and yours, and everyone's sake, when and how will you let Me disciple you? How will you let Me disciple you through a mature discipler or a small cadre of My followers? How are you going to let Me disciple you – just the two of us – this week? This day?"

In the presence of Jesus and a few of His disciples, we all need to regularly answer this question.

PRIORITY TWO: DISCIPLE MY FAMILY

"Do you love Me? Care for and feed your family with eternal food."

Jesus discipled twelve young men by inviting them into close and lengthy relationship with Him. They lived together like family. No, they were family. They ate, traveled, walked, and talked as a family. They worked and played as family; they disagreed and misunderstood and resolved conflicts as family. Jesus saw to it that His disciples watched Him pray, work, and relate. They heard Him interpret His work and

---

490 Luke 10:38-42
491 Matthew 11:28-29
492 James 4:8

words. He watched them. He gave them responsibilities. He coached them. He corrected and encouraged and inspired them. He did all this just like wise parents do, usually because they themselves have been parented well.

It is in the earliest years of life that the most important discipling occurs. Who knows exactly what the earliest years are ... up to age twelve? Nine? Five? Three? Who will see to it that your child's unenlightened dark heart, with all of its self-reliant and self-centered ideas and desires, will be identified and exposed and given an alternative called "The LIGHT of the world?" Who will see to it that the most formative time of life – the wet cement years – will be more about Jesus than what comes through the internet, the television, their little friends, and their own mind-wandering conclusions? Who will help the little children come to Jesus[493] by _listening_ to the perspectives they have come to that are not the perspectives of Jesus yet that shape how they interpret all other perspectives?

The greatest responsibility of the "provider" of any household is to provide FIRST[494] for the _eternal_ well-being of each household member. Or ... are we actually duped into functionally believing that there really is no Creator or Savior or eternity and it's all about eating and drinking and being merry?[495] Ten thousand years from now, what will matter to today's four year old?

When Jesus meets with a little band of His contemporary disciples, having helped us clarify that we do love Him, He will then direct us to feed and care for a very specific little group of His sheep... our family.[496]

---

493 Matthew 19:14, Mark 10:14, Luke 18:16
494 Matthew 6:33
495 Luke 12:19
496 My book, "If Jesus Were A Parent," describes discipling our children as much as possible like Jesus discipled His mostly teen-age disciples.

PRIORITY THREE: DISCIPLE MY CHURCH

Jesus commands His followers to "make disciples," which means that every baptized person is to be taught to obey _everything_ He commanded.[497] For many reasons, being discipled to obey everything Jesus commanded is occurring in precious few western churches. Every Christ-follower is to be fed and cared for until he or she has matured in obeying everything Jesus commanded. This includes His command to make disciples. Each of us as Christ-followers must make holy resolve to secure the help we need until we are intentionally, relationally, and strategically feeding and caring for a few of Jesus' sheep in our local church. In John 21, the lovers of Jesus are to feed and care for Jesus' sheep, that is, disciple them. In Matthew 28, all of Jesus' sheep are to be discipled until they are making disciples.

When Jesus meets with a little band of His contemporary disciples, having helped us clarify that we do love Him, He will then direct us to feed and care for another very specific little group of His sheep... a few Christ-followers who are willing to be discipled toward maturity and disciple-making.[498]

PRIORITY FOUR: DISCIPLE SOME LOST PERSONS

No one cares for lost sheep like Jesus does. Every Christ-follower who is being discipled by Jesus' Spirit, Word, and Body will logically, and ultimately compassionately, care for and feed lost sheep as Jesus did. Following prayer, the most effective evangelistic "tool" is to disciple a Christ-follower in Christlikeness, which includes doing what Jesus did ... caring for and feeding His lost sheep.

- _"For God did not send His Son into the world to condemn the world, but to save the world through Him."_[499]

---

497 Matthew 28:20
498 My book, "Walk with Me," gives four chapters to explaining why we must disciple the church, and the remaining nine chapters to demonstrating how this can be done, based on Matthew 28:18-20
499 John 3:17

- *"For the Son of Man came to seek and to save what was <u>lost</u>."[500]*

- *"But go and learn what this means:'I desire mercy, not sacrifice.' For I have not come to call the righteous, but <u>sinners</u>."[501]*

- *"I lay down my life for the sheep. I have <u>other</u> sheep that are not of this sheep pen. I must bring them also. They too will listen to My voice, and there shall be one flock and one Shepherd."[502]*

To disciple a "lost" person means to "fish for men."[503] It means to be a "friend of sinners." It means to "care for" lost sheep. It means to listen to, to understand, to value, to honor Jesus' lost sheep as He does. Wisdom "washes feet" before trying to "wash minds."[504] Almost always, we are to be Jesus' eyes, ears, mind, and hands before we are His voice. And be His voice we must, else we leave lost sheep more comfortable, still very lost, and not as inclined to be found.

- *"Why does your Teacher eat with tax collectors and 'sinners'?"[505]*

- *"The Son of Man came eating and drinking, and they say, 'Here is a glutton and a drunkard, a friend of tax collectors and "sinners."'[506]*

- *"While Jesus was having dinner at Levi's house, many tax collectors and "sinners" were eating with Him and His disciples, for there were many who followed Him. When the*

---

500 Luke 19:10
501 Matthew 9:13
502 John 10:15-16
503 Matthew 4:19
504 John 13:12-15
505 Matthew 9:11
506 Matthew 11:19

teachers of the law who were Pharisees saw Him eating with the "sinners" and tax collectors, they asked His disciples: "Why does He eat with tax collectors and 'sinners'?"[507]

- *"But the Pharisees and the teachers of the law muttered, "This Man welcomes sinners and eats with them."[508]*

When Jesus meets with a little band of His contemporary disciples, having helped us clarify that we do love Him, He will then direct us to feed and care for another very specific little group of His sheep... one or two very loved but very lost sheep we call neighbors or friends or work associates.

DISCIPLED TO PRACTICE THESE PRIORITIES
When we meet with Jesus and a few of His followers for Him to disciple us, we focus individually on each of the four above referenced priorities.

- We wait ... meditating on Jesus and what we know about Him ... even asking what He thinks or wants for those for whom we are praying. For example, we meditate with Jesus on our families. We ask Jesus to show us what He wants to do through us this week to care for and feed the eternal needs of each family member. We observe our thoughts, remembering the Holy Spirit might be giving us Jesus' thoughts.

- When someone shares something to which they think Jesus might be calling them, we seek to help them by discerning if they have truly heard the Spirit of Christ guiding them into this particular ministry as the Body of Christ. We ask questions to help clarify details, specifics, concerns.

---

507 Mark 2:15-16
508 Luke 15:2

- Having concluded that the group believes someone has clear direction for ministry from the Lord,[509] we agree to pray for that person as he or she goes into the week to care for and feed Jesus' sheep.

- We almost always ask if each person is willing to tell us the following week what Jesus specifically accomplished through them the preceding week.[510]

"The apostles gathered around Jesus and <u>reported</u> to Him all they had done and taught."[511]

"On arriving there, they gathered the church together and <u>reported</u> all that God had done through them and how He had opened the door of faith to the Gentiles."[512]

"Paul greeted them and <u>reported</u> in detail what God had done among the Gentiles through his ministry."[513]

Jesus said, "As long as it is day, <u>we</u> must do the work of Him who sent Me."[514] He invites and intends that His disciples love Him sufficiently to partner with Him in the mission of revealing Him to all His lost and found sheep.

Do you love Jesus? If so, is someone helping you to intentionally and specifically care for and feed a prioritized group of Jesus' lambs and sheep?

---

509 Matthew 10:5-20, Luke 9:1-6
510 Luke 9:10
511 Mark 6:30
512 Acts 14:27
513 Acts 21:19
514 John 9:4

CHAPTER 15

Do You Believe Me? (Part I)

FIFTH QUESTION

One of Jesus' special friends, Martha, was grieving the death of her brother Lazarus. She believed that Jesus could have healed her brother had He come before Lazarus died. In fact, she actually believed that even after Lazarus death God would give Jesus whatever He asked. When Jesus affirmed that Lazarus would raise again, Martha assumed Jesus meant at the general resurrection on the last day. Jesus' response was stunning. "Martha, the resurrection is not about a future time. It is not about a future event. It is about a Life-giver, namely, Me. I am the Resurrection. There is nothing so dead that I, the Resurrection, cannot resurrect to new life." Then He asked her this question, *"Do you believe this?"*[515] "This" refers to what Jesus had just said. Jesus was asking, "Martha, do you believe ME? It makes no difference how dead, how beaten, how battered any life or situation. I am the Resurrection and the Life, and I am more than able to bring back to life anything that is nearly or completely dead. Do you *believe* Me?"

On another day Jesus was walking on His journey. Two blind men saw Him. They cried out for help. Jesus asked them a question, *"Do you believe that I am able to do this?"*[516]

---

515 John 11:17-26
516 Matthew 9:28

Another day, a desperate father begged Jesus, "If You can do anything, take pity on us and help us." Jesus, apparently amused, responded, "If I can? That is not even close to the issue. Of course, I can. The issue is this: 'everything is possible for him who _believes_.'"[517]

Thomas admitted that he could not believe the disciples' report of a resurrected Jesus unless he himself saw Jesus. Jesus complied, and Thomas believed. Jesus summarized the eternal and infinite value God places on our believing. "… blessed are those who have not seen and yet have _believed_."[518]

Jesus' enemies drug Him to the phony trial before the crucifixion. "Are You the Christ?" they asked. Jesus identified the critical issue. "If I tell you, you will not believe Me."[519] Jesus did not need to ask if they believed.

Do I believe Jesus? Do you? Jesus asks every one of His contemporary disciples – not just once, but over and over and over and over – to honestly answer His question, "Do you believe this?" "Do you believe Me?" "You are not just saying you believe Me, are you?"

Why do we ask the question, "Do you believe Me?" at the conclusion of a meeting to be discipled by Jesus?

1. To honestly believe that Jesus is accomplishing His will in and through us.

2. To honestly believe that Jesus is accomplishing His will in our families, church, and friends.

3. To honestly believe that Jesus is meeting our temporal needs, or doing something better

---

517 Mark 9:22-23
518 John 20:29, cf. John 1:7, 12, 2:23, 3:15, 16, 18, 36, 5:24, 7:38, 12:44-46, Acts 13:39, 16:31, etc.
519 Luke 22:66-67, cf. John 9:36, 10:25, 38, 12:46

4. To leave the meeting experiencing Jesus' love, joy, and peace along with passion, purpose and plans for the future that come from honestly believing Jesus

The purpose of this chapter is to identify why and how we conclude the group discipling meeting as we do.

FIRST REASON: To boldly believe that Jesus is accomplishing His will in and through us.

In and through scripture Jesus identifies four key conditions for prayer to be answered. We have reason to boldly believe that Jesus is working through our prayer if we are meeting these conditions.

- Condition 1: the person or group praying must not _cherish_ _sin_ in his heart

  "If I had cherished sin in my heart, the Lord would not have listened; but God has surely listened and heard my voice in prayer."[520]

To cherish sin in my heart is to prefer and defer to my will over God's will. If the Holy Spirit has enlightened me about something I am doing that is not His will, or something I am not doing that is His will for me to do,[521] and if I am _unwilling_ to walk in His light, I am "cherishing" sin in my heart. When I know what My Lord wants, and am seeking to obey Him, but stumbling because I am weak, I am not cherishing sin in my heart. But when I know what God wants, and am not seeking to obey, I am resisting My King by cherishing my will over His. Jesus is essentially saying, "Look, because I love you, I have spoken to you about something in your life that needs to change. But you are ignoring Me. It would not be good for you for Me to reward

520 Psalm 66:18-19
521 James 4:17

your ignoring of Me and My will by giving you what you are asking for. When you take seriously what I have already spoken about to you, I will be responding to the issue about which you are raising with Me in prayer."

Conversely, if *"our hearts do not condemn us,"* that is, if we are not aware of any area of unwillingness or conflict with Jesus, then we have reason to be confident in prayer. Because we are resolved to obey whatever our King has commanded, and because we are resolved to please Him, He who sees our heart resolve is ready to respond to what we ask.

> *"Dear friends, if our hearts do not condemn us, we have confidence before God and receive from Him anything we ask, because we obey His commands and do what pleases Him."*[522]

- Condition 2: the person or group praying must face and turn from _wrong motives_

    "You do not have, because you do not ask God. When you ask, you do not receive, because you ask with _wrong motives_, that you may spend what you get on your pleasures."[523]

One of the reasons that Jesus died was to save us from wrong motives. He does not want to give positive reinforcement to our wrong motives by answering wrongly motivated prayers. Therefore, if we are to boldly believe God to answer our prayer, we must honestly evaluate our deepest reasons for asking to assure that our motives for asking are right, not wrong.

A right motive wants what God wants, which is the _best_ for others

---

522 1 John 3:21-22
523 James 4:3-4

and for self. Jesus' motives were to please His Father, and He died to make us like Him.[524]

> "By Myself I can do nothing; I judge only as I hear, and My judgment is just, for I seek not to please Myself but Him who sent Me."[525]

> "The One who sent Me is with Me; He has not left Me alone, for I always do what pleases Him."[526]

Like all of us, Jesus was severely tempted to drift into pleasing Himself, but He would not! His single motive was to please His Father.[527]

But we often come to Jesus naively praying with selfish motives. We do not realize that His great love for us requires that He do what is best for us, which is not to reinforce the very self-centeredness, the God-indifference, from which God wants to deliver us. He died to destroy our independent selfishness. He prefers to expose and cleanse selfishness than to give positive reinforcement to our wrongly motivated, selfish prayer requests.

Our good and wise King actually withholds answer to prayer in order to help us ask, "Why?" Then, motivated by His own love for us, He helps us to see our wrong motives, and to turn our wrongly-motivated prayer appeals to righteously motivated, bold beliefs!

- Condition 3: the person (or group) praying must pray *in Jesus' name* and ask *according to His will.*

Most Christian prayers are concluded with the words, "In Jesus' name we pray. Amen." Unfortunately, far too many of those prayers were

---

524 Ephesians 5:25-26
525 John 5:30
526 John 8:29
527 Hebrews 4:15

neither carefully considered nor crafted to truly be "in Jesus' name." Tacking the phrase, "in Jesus' name" onto the end of our prayers in no way guarantees that the prayer actually is in Jesus' name.

Note how many times Jesus emphatically connects praying "in His name" with answer to prayer:

> "Whatever you ask *in My name*, that will I do, so that the Father may be glorified in the Son. If you ask Me anything *in My name*, I will do it."[528]

> "... the Father will give you whatever you ask *in My name*."[529]

> "I tell you the truth, My Father will give you whatever you ask *in My name*. Until now you have not asked for anything *in My name*. Ask and you will receive, and your joy will be complete. In that day you will ask *in My name*."[530]

What does it mean to ask in Jesus' name? Simply this: Jesus is King of His Kingdom. We are His representatives wherever we are. We represent Him by re-presenting Him, that is, we present Him again. We thus must know Him so well that we know what He would ask, as if He Himself were here and He were asking. We ask "in His name."

His offer to us to ask for anything, so long as it is what He would ask, is one of His ways of doing what is best for us. Why? To ask what He would ask requires that we know Him, which is the very best thing for us. He uses the promise to answer our prayers as a means to draw us to know Him by requiring that we be in agreement with Him in our asking.

---

528 John 14:13-14, emphasis added
529 John 15:16, emphasis added
530 John 16:23-26, emphasis added

Writing through John, Jesus makes the same promise to answer prayer if we pray according to His will.

> *"This is the confidence we have in approaching God: that if we ask anything <u>according to His will</u>, He hears us. And if we know that He hears us—whatever we ask—we know that we have what we asked of Him."*[531]

Praying in Jesus' name and asking according to His will are one and the same. To ask "in Jesus' name" is to find out and know what He wants. To pray "in Jesus' name" is to pray according to His will. They are the same.

Why has Jesus made these dramatic promises to give us of whatever we ask if we ask "in His name" and according to "His will?"

First, because Jesus loves us, He wants what is the absolute best for us, and the absolute best is to know Him. To pray "in His name" requires that I know Him. We cannot pray "in His name" and according to "His will" without knowing Him well enough to know what He is thinking and wanting about that which we are praying. Thus, we must know Jesus so well that to pray effectively, we know what it is He would ask, and thus what it is that He wants to ask through us, His continuing Body on the planet.

Second, because Jesus loves everyone on the planet, He wants His will to be done on earth, just as it is in Heaven.[532] He commissions His disciples to be His vice-regents and ambassadors to establish His Kingdom on earth. How? First, before we march into His battle to serve with our hands and voices, we fall on our knees to release His power by praying in His name, which is praying according to His

---

531 1 John 5:14-15, emphasis added
532 Matthew 6:10

will. Then, *in His name,* He sends us to welcome little children,[533] to meet together,[534] do miracles,[535] give cups of cold water,[536] drive out demons,[537] be chosen instruments,[538] even suffer.[539] But before we march, we kneel.[540]

- Condition 4: the person or group must truly *believe* that Jesus will answer the prayer.

  o *"If you believe, you will receive whatever you ask for in prayer."*[541]

  o *"Therefore I tell you, whatever you ask for in prayer, believe that you have received it, and it will be yours."*[542]

  o *"Some men brought to him a paralytic, lying on a mat. When Jesus saw their faith, he said to the paralytic, "Take heart, son; your sins are forgiven."*[543]

  o *"Then Jesus told him, "Because you have seen Me, you have believed; blessed are those who have not seen and yet have believed."*[544]

  o *"Then Jesus said to the centurion, "Go! It will be done just as you believed it would." And his servant was healed at that very hour."*[545]

---

533 Matthew 18:5, Luke 9:48
534 Matthew 18:20
535 Mark 9:39
536 Mark 9:41
537 Mark 16:17
538 Acts 9:15
539 Acts 21:13
540 2 Chronicles 7:14, 20:18
541 Matthew 21:22
542 Mark 11:24
543 Matthew 9:2
544 John 20:29
545 Matthew 8:13

o   "'If you can?' said Jesus. 'Everything is possible for him who _believes_.'"[546]

Jesus looks us in the eye and asks, "Do you believe Me?" He understands how easy it is for us to say we believe without even recognizing our unbelief.[547] If fear, or worry, or anxiety, or guilt, or shame, or envy, or jealousy, or dozens of other unbelief-based soul maladies govern us, we are deceived about our level of faith.

"... everything that does not come from faith is sin."[548]

The essence of sin is ignoring or leaving God out. When we include a sufficiently accurate understanding of God in our calculations, believing Him is the result.

Because He so loves us, and because believing Him is so good for us on every count, Jesus experienced some of His greatest frustration with unbelief.

"O unbelieving generation," Jesus replied, "how long shall I stay with you? How long shall I put up with you? Bring the boy to Me."[549]

The biblical stories of victory through believing our King flood the Scripture. The promises for believing capture the hope and imagination of any reader. The requirements to believe and warnings against unbelief send terrifying chills up and down the backbone.

"Believe!" "Have faith!" "Trust!" "Be confident!" At any cost, this eternity and temporal life-saving response to God's word called "believe Me" must be established and nurtured.

---

546 Mark 9:23
547 Mark 9:24
548 Romans 14:23
549 Mark 9:19

Practical note: the first four questions described in previous chapters for use in a small gatherings of Jesus' disciples is intentionally designed to lead to the establishment and development of believing Jesus … trusting Him … having faith and bold confidence in Him.

The meeting is to be all about Jesus. Faith comes by hearing and seeing Jesus. Every question draws those answering to grow in knowing Jesus. This leads to both greater faith in Jesus and deeper love for Him. Faith and love are the key components to answered prayer.[550]

- *"Who do you say that I am?"*

    This question focuses on who Jesus is. In other words, "Do you know Me?" The ensuing discussion about Jesus creates faith and belief in Him. Directly answering Jesus' question, speaking to Him while "staring into His eyes," creates and strengthens belief in Him like few devotional experiences. Faith comes by hearing.

    Further, the better we know Jesus, the more we love Him, and loving Jesus draws us to desire, discover, and do His will. This equates to living "in His name," as His ambassador and representative. The prayer of those living "in His name" is highly effective.

- *"Do you understand what I have done for you?"*

    This question focuses on what Jesus does. In other words, "Do you see My activity, and do you know My motive?" As we respond to Jesus' question by looking back at all the good things He has done for us and others, and what He has said to us in our times alone with Him and the rest of the time, and

---

550 Love leads us to satisfy 4 keys to answered prayer; faith itself is a major key to answered prayer

all that He has done through us for others, we are thrilled, often shocked with delight. We "see" Him serving – washing feet, including ours. He washes our minds. He guides us and we see Him empowering us as we serve – washing others' feet and, sooner or later, their minds. If a picture is worth a thousand words, and if faith comes by hearing, then our seeing what Jesus is doing creates a thousand fold increases in our faith. Since faith does come by hearing, how much more does faith come by seeing?[551]

Further, as we "watch" Jesus serve by observing all the good He is doing, our love for Him grows exponentially (a thousand fold) motivating us to live for Him, thus fulfilling the conditions for effective prayer as stated above.

- *"Do you listen to Me?"*

This question focuses on what Jesus says. Jesus now talks to us directly through Scripture. As long as we listen well, not adding to, nor twisting, nor overlooking the plain text, we now hear Jesus in His own words speaking directly to us. This is the ultimate basis for belief. Faith does come by hearing, and faith is a necessary condition for effective prayer.

- *"Do you truly love Me more than these?"*

This question focuses on what Jesus wants. Jesus, knowing that we love Him (at varying levels to be sure), now guides us to follow Him into our shared future. Based upon what we know about Him and His Word, He helps us discern how we are to represent Him, that is, to know what His will is for our lives. He helps us work through our four priorities: being discipled by Him, discipling our families, discipling a few in

---

551 John 20:29

our church, and discipling a few lost neighbors. Because we are seeking to find His will, and because we know that He answers prayers that are according to His will,[552] our faith in Him to answer our prayers to do His will is multiplied.

Further, as we honestly answer His probing question regarding our love for Him, we come back to those very realities that generated love in the first place, and love is renewed or increased.

- "Do you believe Me?"

This final question focuses on Jesus' goodness and power to accomplish what He knows is best. Most importantly, it raises the issue of our true knowing of Jesus and our certainty of His preferred future being actualized.

  o   We looked at who Jesus is; we believed anew.

  o   We looked at what Jesus has done; faith grows.

  o   We listened to what Jesus is saying; confidence increases.

  o   We carefully discerned what Jesus wants, knowing He answers prayer according to His will, and assurance is established

- So we must answer: "Do you believe Me?"

Answer: "Yes, Lord. We look into our own hearts, and we realize that we truly do believe You, we trust You; we have faith and confidence in You."

---

552 1 John 5:13-14

Jesus might say: "Of course you do. You have been with Me and letting Me disciple you. Now ... go in the strength and power of My name."

We conclude this section with a powerful promise:

"The effective, fervent prayer of a righteous man avails much."[553]

We need to know and boldly believe that our prayers are "effective." By testing our prayers for the above referenced conditions, we can boldly believe and know that we are meaningfully and powerfully partnering with Jesus through our Kingdom prayers.

SECOND REASON: To honestly believe that Jesus is accomplishing His will in our families, church, and friends.

Jesus' little bands of believers that gather are to help each other, at great cost if need be, to "believe in the One the Father has sent." God works, and we work, to solidify and strengthen our knowing of Jesus that leads to authentically believing Him.

"The work of God is this: to believe in the One He has sent."[554]

Paul recognizes that faith is a battle, a fight.

"Fight the good fight of the faith."[555]

"I have fought the good fight, I have finished the race, I have kept the faith.[556]

---

553 James 5:16, NKJV
554 John 6:29
555 1 Timothy 6:12
556 2 Timothy 4:7

In our meeting, we "work" long to believe and we "fight" hard for faith for our own Kingdom life and godliness.[557]

All that has happened to strengthen our faith in Jesus can now be applied to intercessory prayer for others. Now we are postured to ask boldly and believe greatly for our families, our church family, and our lost friends and neighbors. Where this magnificent ministry of intercession is modeled and multiplied around the world, Jesus' Kingdom has come in great measure to earth. Where the church does not intercede, much activity happens, but little Kingdom advancement occurs.

Intercession is our partnering in prayer with Jesus for His highest and best for our family, church family, and lost friends.[558] It needs to be the first and foundational component of our intentional discipling of others. It is enabling Jesus' influence to be released into their lives. Like the air force preparing the way for the armed ground troops, our intercession releases the power of the Holy Spirit which then prepares the way for our ministry of listening and lovingly serving. This eventually opens the doors for us to engage our family and friends in on-going conversations about Jesus, and His victory for them, through our discipling ministry.[559] It all starts with intercession.

The third and fourth reasons to carefully respond to Jesus' question, "Do you believe Me?" will be answered at the end of the next chapter. Please proceed to observe our little band of disciples being coached and guided by Jesus' Word, Spirit, and Body as they respond to Jesus' last question.

---

557 2 Peter 1:3
558 Hebrews 7:25
559 We are guided and equipped for this ministry as we respond to Jesus' fourth question earlier in the meeting.

CHAPTER 16

Do You Believe Me? (Part II)

FIFTH QUESTION (CONT.)

Welcome back to our little band of disciples who are still meeting together to be discipled by Jesus. Join us as we respond to Jesus' last question, "Do you believe Me?"

Hal: "I love trying to imagine how pleased Jesus is to hear you tell Him again of your love and how you intend to 'feed and care for His sheep.' Because we love Jesus, and are committed to feeding and caring for His little ones, I must remind us that we are in a horrific battle and will be resisted as we seek to make specific, intentional Kingdom advances.

"Let's move on to the culmination of all our meeting by answering Jesus' last question, "Do you believe Me?' He promises to empower us to do what He has called us to do.[560] Most of you have made specific commitments to be with Jesus, to be like Him, and to "wash others' feet" this week. Do you believe Jesus will empower you?"

Dawson: "My pattern of reacting negatively to my son is deep and long. I must have Jesus' power if I am to actually listen without interrupting or telling him what he needs to do."

---

560 1 Thessalonians 5:24

Hal: "So ... do you believe Jesus will empower you?"

Dawson: "I guess if I am honest I am having a hard time believing."

Amy: "Jesus loves your honesty. I actually believe that Jesus is going to help you. I will be praying for you. What night did you say you are going to be with your son?"

Dawson: "I hope we can go out after his game on Thursday night."

Amy: "I will be praying for you this Thursday night."

Hal: "Amy, will you pray now?"

Amy: "Sure. Lord Jesus, Dawson is not trying to do this on his own. He and we all waited on You to seek Your will for how he could serve his son this week. We agreed with Dawson's sense that You guided him to ask his son to go out after his game, and work primarily on valuing and listening to him. I truly believe that You will remind Dawson to listen much and guard carefully what he says.[561] I thank You ... I praise You for empowering Daws. I believe You to give him special grace to do this good work.[562] You obviously want what he is seeking to do, and we know that since You are for us, we can more than conquer.[563] I see Daws being victorious in this meeting. Victory will be loving and valuing and caring and listening to his son. Thank You for this victory."

TIME OUT

Time will always feel like "the enemy" as you are meeting to be discipled by Jesus. Even in a very small group of 4 or 5, any one of the five questions could easily expand into a very meaningful 90 minutes.

---

561 James 1:19
562 2 Corinthians 9:8
563 Romans 8:31, 37

The goal cannot be to answer all 5 questions. The goal is to recognize and respond to the presence of Jesus. If all that is accomplished is interacting and answering His question, "Who do you say that I am?" ... and if several actually "see" and have a real encounter with Jesus, would it be a good meeting? Of course.

Would it be wonderful to have 90 minutes to simply intercede for the eternal and temporal needs represented in the group? Absolutely.[564] In the meeting from which we just took a time out, Amy's prayer of faith released the Holy Spirit to powerfully work in Dawson and his son. Kingdom work! It also served to at least encourage Dawson, and probably strengthened his faith for victory. Kingdom work! Priceless.

Jesus' first disciples were confronted by each of these five questions. Each is very important, nearly essential, in growing as His disciple. Which question do we not need to answer? To not stare at Jesus and respond to whom He is? To not recognize and rejoice in what He is doing? To not listen to what He is saying? To not evaluate our love for Him or know what He wants to do through us? To not evaluate our believing Him or establish belief for victory in our lives and others?

Until most of us are more desperate for Jesus' Kingdom on earth as it is in Heaven, we will struggle with giving enough time together to be better discipled by Jesus. But we must do the best we can with what we have.

In light of the time crunch for each meeting, the functional goal must be to cover well all five questions, but over _MANY_ meetings. Through this repetition, Jesus' disciples present are being equipped to answer His questions in private and to then help others with the same questions. Given many months or even years together, we can work many times on all five questions. Again, the goal of each meeting is _NOT_ to get through the five questions, but to have an

---

564 A response to the "time" tension for prayer is suggested in Reason 3 below

authentic encounter with the Living God. What does not get done this week can be worked on next week. If you only get through the first two questions in this week's meeting, briefly review the first two and major on the last three questions the next week. The intention is to have all of Jesus' disciples in the group being exposed to and learning to honestly answer all five questions. The facilitator needs to see that, over the long haul, plenty of time is given to respond to each question.

TIME IN

Hal: "Thank you, Amy. And Dawson. Jesus is here, and He again is asking, 'Do you believe I will make victory possible in what I have called you to do this week?'"

Phoebe: "I am trying to choose to believe, but all I can see is that whole classroom of unruly, undisciplined kids. I so want to remain poised and sensitive. And I don't want to blow my chance to really help a few by blowing up in front of everyone. Do you mind if I just talk to Jesus now?"

Hal: "That's why we are here. Go for it."

Phoebe: "Jesus, I hate getting so upset. I know I don't 'blow up' outwardly but I also know the kids see and feel my frustration with them ... and anger. I am not sure if I believe You will give me enough grace to be gentle and still manage the whole classroom. I thought I had faith when I started talking to You, but right now I feel almost hopeless. I don't even want to go back into the classroom Monday ..."

Addie: "Phoebe? Forgive me for jumping in. I think the Holy Spirit just whispered a verse to me. Could I read it to you?"

Phoebe: "Sure."

Addie: "This verse has turned my life around. I will just read it and see if the Lord says anything to you.

> *"His divine power has given us everything we need for life and godliness through our knowledge of Him who called us by His own glory and goodness. Through these He has given us his very great and precious promises, so that through them you may participate in the divine nature and escape the corruption in the world caused by evil desires."*[565]

Phoebe: "I loved the 'everything we need for godliness' part. But it always comes back to knowing Jesus and His promises."

Addie: "You sound a little bewildered …"

Phoebe: "I am just so tired. I KNOW I need more 'knowledge of Jesus and His promises.' It is just so hard to have good times with Him."

Hal: "Addie, would you pray for Phoebe now?"

Addie: "Lord, I know You want to help Phoebe. I absolutely believe that You will help her. We all see how she is making good progress in caring for these little children who come from such difficult homes. I ask You now to reveal to Phoebe Your delight in her progress. In fact, I ask You to show her how You delight in her. Let her see Your smile as You look at her. I believe You want to do this, and will. I know that when she again sees Your delight in her, she will be renewed and strengthened. Thank You for blessing her with a new touch from You. Thank You for showing her Your heart for her. I am confident You will help her see Your heart for her without her having to struggle to see You or know You. Thank You for giving her everything she needs for godliness this week because You are giving her the knowledge of Your delight in her and what she is being in the classroom. Thank

565 2 Peter 1:3-4

You for giving her such peace and joy that she will be able to tell us next week of the way You answered all our prayers for her. Thank You. Thank You."

Phoebe: (Tears are coming down her cheeks.) "Wow. I think I actually believe Jesus is going to help me. This is crazy."

David: "Crazy love? Did you sense Jesus revealing how He delights in you?"

Phoebe: "I did. It just hit me …"

David: "It … or … He?"

Phoebe: "Got it! Thank you. Jesus, thank _You_ for gently assuring me, yet again, that You are with me, that You truly delight in me, and You have helped me to make progress. I think I actually believe we are going to do well this week in the classroom."

Group: Spontaneous applause.

Hal: "We are on holy ground. And as always, the clock spins. We said we would quit at 8:30. We have one minute. Is there anyone here who actually believes Jesus is going to help us all be truly set apart for Him this week? Live our priorities? 'Washing feet and minds?'"

TIME OUT

The clock is not to be Lord, but we do have to be sensitive to the long haul. We can occasionally go past the agreed upon time to finish, but if we consistently do so, soon people with baby-sitting challenges and early morning alarms for work will find it harder and harder to keep coming. As always, being sensitive to the Spirit is the key. Someday – maybe soon – we will be hungry or desperate enough for Jesus that we will not have to live with such time constraints.

TIME IN

Debbi: "Oh Lord Jesus. I do believe You are wonderfully at work to empower us all to grow in sensitivity to You, to prioritize more time to be discipled by You. I really believe You will remind us to serve and honor each of our family members this week. I especially want to pray for Huds as he has committed to writing a letter to seek reconciliation with his brother. I believe You will help him write the very words You know will be most Kingdom effective. And I believe You will keep us sensitive to each other as a group, and make us all salt and light in our schools and workplaces this week. I believe You will do more than we have imagined, and look forward to hearing about it next week. I do pray all this, truly believing that it is in Your name, because I believe it to be close to Your will and what You would pray. Again, thank You for the victory that is ours as we are Yours this week. Amen."

So ended that gathering of Jesus' contemporary disciples to be intentionally discipled by His Word, Spirit, and Body.

We now return to the third and fourth reasons that we work so hard on Jesus' 5th question.

THIRD REASON: To honestly believe that Jesus is meeting our _temporal_ needs.

I usually finish our meetings to be discipled by Jesus with very particular prayers. These prayers are for this coming week's _discipling_ ministries by group members … intentional times and ways to listen to Jesus and others, which leads to lovingly serving and/or toward meaningful conversations. These disciples of Jesus have just discerned and committed to God's specific will for them regarding their time with Jesus, and the discipling of their families, church, and a couple friends. Thus, these prayers are for _eternal_ needs, not immediate _temporal_ needs.

Praying for our needs, both temporal and eternal, is essential to releasing God's special grace into our lives.

What follows will almost certainly be misunderstood. Even when understood, it will probably be greatly disagreed with, with a plethora of Bible verses to support the disagreement. It is offered as a possible help to the meeting, not to pick a fight. It comes from years of not having enough time in discipling meetings to "pray effectively" for ALL the needs represented, both eternal and temporal.

One of Jesus' most prominent promises to all of us is underlined in the passage below:

> *"So do not worry, saying, 'What shall we eat?' or 'What shall we drink?' or 'What shall we wear?' For the pagans run after all these things, and your heavenly Father knows that you need them. But seek first His kingdom and His righteousness, and all these things will be given to you as well. Therefore do not worry about tomorrow, for tomorrow will worry about itself. Each day has enough trouble of its own."*[566]

Jesus clearly promises that if we will seek first His Kingdom (His will, His reign, His government, His rule) which includes His righteousness (His goodness, His holiness, being and doing what is righteous in every part of our lives) that He would see to it that our temporal needs would be met. He says, "If you give yourself to finding and following My will in all aspects of your life, I will care for your temporal needs."[567]

One day a thought came to mind. You may judge if the thought was my own or from the Lord.

---

566 Matthew 6:32-34
567 Needs and desires must not be confused. "I need the ketchup" is a false statement. I may desire and would enjoy ketchup on my hamburger, but I do not NEED it. Western, affluent culture is often deceived about what is a real need.

I routinely noticed that when we were able to gather a few Christians into a little group to dialogue about and with Jesus, that it was hard to lead us into _effective_ prayer, as described above.

When we began to pray, the prayer time was almost entirely given over to _first_, telling about the TEMPORAL problems being faced (real, genuine needs for healing, finance, recovery from abuse, addictions, broken relationships, etc.) These problems were and are heart wrenching. The time for meeting together would be moving by quickly. The pained persons telling their painful story, or someone else's, could not help but explain more and more of the story … leaving less and less time for prayer. Then, _secondly_, others would compassionately empathize, affirm, and encourage. _Finally_, with time having run out, one of us would quickly ask God to help alleviate the pain and suffering that had been revealed. Very little time was available to pray "_effectively_."

The experience repeated itself week after week, year after year. Many things were done to attempt to balance the "prayer time." We sought to balance real and painfully felt temporal needs with prayer for Kingdom, eternal needs.[568] Though never openly said, it was clearly understood that to "push" for prayer about eternal, Kingdom, and righteousness issues[569] was somewhat "heartless" in contrast with these imminent, pressing, painful "temporal" issues.

So … back to "the thought" I had one day. It was simply this. Certainly Matthew 6:33 applies to seeking first the Kingdom and righteousness of God in all of life's activities, with the promise that our Father will provide for our temporal needs.

Therefore, the promise could reasonably be applied to the precious little time we give to prayer. If during our time for prayer, we prayed

568 To be sure, healing the sick is a Kingdom issue and need. The issue is decreasing prayer for temporary comfort if necessary to increase prayer for eternal character
569 Essentially, being discipled and making disciples in our family, church, and world

first and pre-eminently about God's Kingdom and His righteousness, then, even if we had no time in the meeting left to pray for each other's temporal concerns, Jesus has promised that "all these other things would be given us as well."[570]

The point is this: in the typical prayer meetings where most of the prayer is targeted toward the "other things," about all that gets prayed for are the other things. Our prayer of faith gives God permission to increase His influence primarily in things that are not eternal.[571]

But when in prayer we seek first His Kingdom and His righteousness, that is, we wrestle to find out God's will concerning His reign and holiness being established in lives, and we wrestle to actually believe that He will accomplish this, then not only is God "freed" to work in the eternal dimensions being prayed for, but He promises to influence the temporal dimensions every bit as much or more than if we had spent all our time praying only for the temporal.

Thus, we get BOTH eternal blessing and temporal blessing, even though we gave little or no time to praying for the temporal.

The purpose of the prayer time is to release God's healing and creative power, not to be *primarily* a horizontal "support group" for legitimately hurting people to feel loved by other people. Support from the Body is good and required. We must be committed to working hard to facilitate it.

> *"Carry each other's burdens, and in this way you will fulfill the law of Christ."*[572]

---

570 Matthew 6:33
571 The principle of intercession: In light of making us for loving relationship, God gives us free will. He is willing to influence us to the extent that His love and wisdom allow without violating our free will / personhood. But He provides a vehicle to increase His influence: prayer. When we ask and believe Him to work in accordance with His will, we give Him permission to increase His influence beyond the limits He self imposes. This is the privilege of intercession: partnering with God to increase the probability of free individuals choosing to respond to His Kingdom and righteousness.
572 Galatians 6:2

But if there has to be a trade-off, which is better: to release God's power into both eternal and temporal needs or only into temporal needs?

I encourage you to think with the Lord (pray), and take all this or leave it. I happen to believe the above stated idea results in better stewardship of our precious little time together to be discipled by Jesus. It could well be that Matthew 6:33 could be applied to prioritizing our time of intercession to seeking FIRST what is on His heart in His kingdom and His righteousness, and as we first take those things to His throne in prayer that He will add "all these things" (food, money, health, etc.) unto us, even if we run out of time to pray for them.

Thus, the third reason to answer Jesus' question, "Do you believe Me?" is to release Jesus' power to bring about His reign and righteousness, while simultaneously establishing bold belief that the real temporal needs of all present (and the loved ones of those present) will be addressed by God in the same way as if they had been prayed for specifically. This is based on the promise of Matthew 6:33.[573]

In light of this perspective, I often conclude our times of being discipled by Jesus together in this way: "Lord, we praise and honor You for working powerfully in all the ways we have identified to be Your will as we seek to be discipled by You this week and to make disciples at home, in our church, and with one or two lost friends. It is now time to leave and we have not addressed many, many temporal needs for physical help, financial help, and other painful challenges. However, You promised that if we would seek first Your Kingdom and righteousness, which we have spent the entire meeting doing, that You would equally care for our temporal needs as well. I believe You to do this, just as much as if we had spent our entire evening talking

---

573 It is clearly ideal to pray for ALL the needs represented, both temporal and eternal. The problem is that to do so takes time from the other equally ideal issues of the meeting. There are so many important things to be done in the time with Jesus that sometimes we are pressed into prioritizing what is best.

and praying about these temporary concerns. Thank You! We thank You. We go from here boldly confident in Your care for every part of our lives. And we believe we are agreeing in Jesus name. Amen?" Amen!!!

FOURTH REASON: To leave the meeting experiencing love, joy, and peace along with passion, purpose and plans for the future that come from honestly believing Jesus.

Jesus wants us to leave our "formal"[574] time with Him filled with bold confidence in Him.

When a life altering loss gives a disciple of Jesus much reason for sadness, yet that disciple believes Jesus to be at work in all things to bring good for those who love Him,[575] resulting in joy,[576] our Lord dances with delight. He is pleased when we are peacefully experiencing His rest in the eye of a storm, while enduring a fearful storm on life's sea. When hatred, hostility and harm penetrate our souls and bodies, yet we love our enemies with His love, He rejoices at our progress in Him and in becoming like Him.

Here is the good news: the truth about our Triune God's great love for us, His supreme wisdom, and His infinite power can be dominatingly clear to us. His great love, supreme wisdom, and infinite power can be so experientially real to us that we walk on the water of life's mental, emotional, and even physical pain.

This pain is not unreasonable; it is created by very tangible forces in our life. In spite of those real forces, through believing Jesus, we can have a clear vision of a condition superior than what our eyes and

---

574 Formal discipling times: intentional times of meeting with Jesus being the single objective; usually involves a specific time and place with a specific process to be discipled by Jesus. Informal: all the rest of our lives when we are not formally meeting with Jesus but are growing in being sensitive to Him for "informal" discipling
575 Romans 8:28
576 John 17:13, Romans 15:13

ears tell us about our present experience, or the experience of others. It can be as simple as a profound awareness of our good Shepherd, or our Bread of Life, or our Lamb that takes away the sin of the world.

> *The truth about Jesus and His preferred future can be so clear and so real that what we see by faith is actually more real to us than what our eyes, ears, and memories bring to our minds.*

Truly believing King Jesus enables us as Jesus' disciples to experience tangible *internal* victory … righteousness, peace, joy, love … in the midst of life's storms. Others see our victory and ask for a reason for our hope.[577]

The above referenced love, joy, and peace are truly the fruit of BELIEVING Jesus.[578] As long as sadness from painful circumstances remains, believing Jesus has not yet reached its full potential. As long as the fear of difficult circumstances persists, our faith has not yet accomplished all that Jesus desires it to do. As long as resentment or hatred or unforgiveness persist, confidence in God's love and truth are not yet playing their optimum role. As long as shame and guilt from our past failures haunt us, something is painfully and needlessly missing in our believing Jesus. As long as dependence on others for approval and value persists, Jesus' aches for us to know and agree with what He thinks about us. "Do you believe Me?"

This must not be construed in a way that creates guilt or discouragement or defensiveness for anyone struggling with sadness, fear, unforgiveness, or shame, etc. It is intended as a hope-filled proclamation for authentic emotional victory through fully BELIEVING all that Jesus is and does. The Truth believed does set us free.

This faith that enables internal victory in the storm simultaneously gives

---

577 1 Peter 3:15
578 Acts 16:31-34, Romans 15;13, Galatians 5:22, 1 Peter 1:8

Jesus the permission He requires to stop the storm, or do something better. Truly believing enables internal victory until Jesus provides external victory. Those who believe endure the storm victoriously until their Master, through their faith, calms the storm. Faith that He will becomes assurance that He has.

Through thus believing Jesus, we are empowered to walk from our meetings with Him filled with His peace, joy and love that the world longs to experience. It is not "put on" or fake. It is deep, authentic, and real. It is what Jesus wants for us: "Do you believe Me?" This inner vision and delight is able to persist throughout the day, through every experience, every relationship, and every thought that wars against the truth.

The truth is that Truth Himself is for us, and if He be for us, who can be against us?[579] The challenge is to keep answering the all-important question, "Do you believe Me?" with the bold assurance,

> *I am able to do immeasurably more than all you ask or imagine, according to My power that is at work within you!* [580]

"Do you believe Me?"

-

---

579 Romans 8:31
580 Ephesians 3:20

Conclusion

Jesus came and was discipled by His Father more than any person has ever been discipled by anyone. He spent volumes of time in dialogue with His Father. This quality and quantity of time with His Father empowered Jesus to do nothing apart from His Father's will, say nothing apart from His Father's will, and make no judgments on His own without His Father. He was unquestionably the most discipled Person ever.

Then, Jesus invited 12 young men to similarly spend quantity and quality time with Him. This is how He discipled them.

Then, He commanded that they propagate His world transforming mission by doing for others what He had done for them, that is, amidst all their other responsibilities, that they also adopt a few to spend quantity and quality time with, discipling them until their disciples were obeying everything Jesus commanded. This would include Jesus' great commission command: "Make disciples." So every baptized person is to be discipled until they are obeying all Jesus commanded, including making disciples.

Had Christ-followers throughout the centuries somehow included the above "multiplication of disciplemakers" process in their church life, the church would have multiplied Christlikeness instead of adding nominality. World history would have been dramatically different.

However, it is not too late. What has been written is in no way intended to be yet another simplistic "programmatic" approach to facilitating small groups. It is intended to be a helpful process for those who, themselves being discipled by Jesus' Spirit, Word, and Body, are thus equipped to obediently and intentionally adopt a few others to facilitate their being discipled by Jesus as long as necessary for these disciples to mature to the point of adopting their own set of disciples. It is built on this idea: for me to be Jesus' disciple, I must spend great quantities and quality of time with Him, by His Spirit, through His Word and Body ...

- knowing who He is: "Who do you say that I am?"

- watching what He is doing: "Do you understand what I have done for you?"

- listening to what He is saying: "Are you listening to Me?"

- doing what He wants: "Do you truly love Me more than these? Care for and feed My sheep."

- believing what He has promised: "Do you believe Me?"

When I know how to meet with Jesus for Him to disciple me somewhat in this fashion, then I can invite a few others into my time to be discipled by Jesus, and I can facilitate their being discipled by Jesus.

When they are growing in trusting, loving, and serving Jesus through being discipled by Him, then I can coach and help them in adopting a few prayerfully chosen persons to coach them in being discipled by Jesus as I have coached my few to be discipled by Jesus.

Then, because it is in their DNA as normal Christianity, they will help those they have adopted to adopt others to help be discipled by Jesus. And on and on goes the multiplication of being and making disciples and disciplemakers.

Why do this? Because it is the fastest way to help the entire world be discipled? I believe it to be so, but that is not my primary motivation.

I must do this because one day I will stand before Jesus, and I will give an account of my stewardship of the life He gave to me to manage for Him.

Jesus thought the priority things, the most important things, in His earthly life were to be discipled by His Father and to make disciples. Do you think He knew what He was doing? I am willing to "risk" all that He did, that is, I have faith in Him!

Jesus commanded His disciples to do for others exactly what He did for them. I wonder if He knew what He was saying. I am willing to assume that He did.

Above all, I am compelled to make disciples because I love Jesus, and He commanded His disciples to make disciples. If I love Him, I will obey Him.[581]

What will most inhibit our being discipled by Jesus together?

EVIL INFLUENCE

One of the most agreed upon experiences of Christians is that whenever we make plans to spend time with Jesus, we go through serious struggles to keep our commitments. The general conclusion is that the demonic enemies of our souls fight most and hardest when they see us seeking to be with Jesus. Beware and resist with truth, faith and tenacity.[582]

---

581 John 14:15
582 1 Peter 5:8-9

BOREDOM

The single greatest reason we get bored in being discipled by Jesus is that we forget that "God is among us." To prevent meaninglessness and boredom, intentionally and intensively keep focused on the real presence of Jesus.[583]

PEOPLE PRESSURE

People will not understand us taking time from them or their desires or even our using our time in ways that do not agree with their priorities. They will pressure us to do things for or with them, or good things for others, or for the church, or even for ourselves. We must be clearly persuaded that Jesus has said, "Come to Me. Learn of Me."[584] We must act on our persuasion.

TIME – PERSONAL PRIORITIES WHICH REVEAL OUR FAITH AND LOVE

The final battle is in our own minds and wills. Are we smart enough to realize what the very best thing is for us? Do we believe Jesus has called us to be with Him? If we believe that He has, do we believe His promise that if we would seek first His Kingdom and will that He will take care of all the other things we need to do? Do we love Him enough to do what He wants, which is to disciple us, even when we want something not so eternally valuable?

I plead with you to pray about living the remainder of your life with your first two priorities being this:

1) being discipled by Jesus

2) helping a few others (family, very small group of Christians, one or two lost persons) to become His disciples and be discipled by Him until they are also helping others to be discipled by Jesus.

---

583 Matthew 18:20, 28:20, Isaiah 41:10, etc.
584 Matthew 11:28-29

One final question: will you think clearly enough to choose to resist evil influence, excuses, people pressure, and even your own needs and desires, in order to spend time with Jesus? If you will, not only will Jesus wonderfully disciple you, but He will equip you to help others be discipled by Him, just as you have been discipled by Him.

Further Help for Disciplers

WHY ASK QUESTIONS?

- Asking questions of our disciples is necessary for them to mature in articulating the truth. Most sincere Christians have far too little experience in talking about Jesus and His Kingdom issues. They can hardly speak the language. If they cannot articulate the truth in a caring environment, they are very unlikely to be able to remember and tell themselves the truth in the dark, even hostile environment they live in all week. The point of "small groups" is _not_ primarily for the facilitator to teach – that can be done for 100's and 1000's far more efficiently. "Small" allows for group members to be able to articulate the truth. It is a safe place for the disciple to clarify and practice articulating the truth.

- Asking questions empowers less mature persons to wrestle for the answer, rather than forever remaining the "child" who is spoon fed by the "parent," thus retaining dependency on the "parent" instead of maturing to spiritual adulthood.

- Asking questions reveals to the one being asked his/her level of maturity in thought, articulation, commitment, and application. They realize their specific area of need. This testing and accountability are generally missing yet most necessary components of church life.

- Asking questions as a significant method of discipling equips those being listened to for discipling others, for this is how they were discipled, thus this is how they can and will disciple.

- Asking questions can and must reveal loving care for those being listened to, and allows the discipler to truly know the disciple. The good shepherd knows his sheep. Note: if asking questions is merely a method without genuine care, the facilitator has a problem with loving as our Lord expects. We ask and listen because we truly care and want to know and understand people.[585]

- Asking and listening models a greatly needed life skill for all of Jesus' disciples present

- Asking in order to truly listen is commanded of Jesus' followers[586]

- Jesus asked His disciples many, many questions. *"Learn from Me."*[587]

- Jesus asked questions strategically. *"When Jesus looked up and saw a great crowd coming toward Him, He said to Philip, "Where shall we buy bread for these people to eat?"* <u>*He asked this only to test him,*</u> *for He already had in mind what He was going to do."*[588]

---

585 John 10:14
586 James 1:19
587 Matthew 11:28-29
588 John 6:5-6, emphasis added

QUESTIONS WE ASK

The five core questions from chapters 7-16 of this book provide a helpful core framework for helping persons be discipled by Jesus, both in groups and alone, and then to help others through the same core framework.

These questions are based on the reality that Jesus promises to be present by His Spirit when two or three gather in His name[589] and that it is better for His Spirit to dwell in us than that He be physically one of several among us.[590]

These questions take very seriously Jesus' promises that His Spirit is present to counsel us, guide us, teach us, remind us of all He said, tell us the truth, testify of Him, convict of sin, of righteousness, of judgment, guide us into all truth, tell us what is to come, make known to us what He is in Him – what He currently is thinking and wanting.[591]

These questions help us keep the meeting meaningfully "alive," for they keep all present well aware of Jesus' very real presence.

Examples of questions that lead to sensitivity to the Holy Spirit:

- "What thoughts are going through your mind? Are they 'good?' Might they be from the Holy Spirit?"

    o We must increase sensitivity to the reality that the Holy Spirit is actually speaking to us

    o As the meeting goes along, all are regularly invited to examine and consider articulating good thoughts in order

589 Matthew 18:20
590 John 16:7
591 John 14:16-17, 15:26, 16:7-15. Cf. 1 Corinthians 2:10, 16

for the group to consider if the thoughts are from the Holy Spirit

- o The group plays a serious role in evaluating if the thoughts shared seem to be from the Holy Spirit, thus providing a safe place to practice listening for and articulating the teaching, reminding, etc. of the Holy Spirit

- o We are practicing and learning how to bring more and more of our thoughts captive into obedience to Christ

- "Can we be certain your thought is from the Holy Spirit?"

- o Prerequisite: humility of all involved

- o When someone says, "God told me ..." that person is carefully questioned to clarify and articulate rationale for strong statement. Gradually, humility replaces dogmatism.

- "What do you think Jesus is thinking and feeling about what we are saying to Him?" ... or ... "Jesus, what are You thinking and feeling about what we are saying about You? To You?" (Good to occasionally ask after answering, "Who do we say Jesus is?") We routinely try to "imagine" what those we are with are thinking, and that helps us relate better to them. Jesus said the Holy Spirit would empower us to know what He is thinking (John 16:14). It is very good to invest time attempting to discern what Jesus might be thinking. It helps us "know" Him.

- "Is anyone willing to share what you think Jesus might be thinking or might even want to say to Bill?"

- o We work hard at keeping the focus on the real presence of Jesus who, by His Spirit, may speak

- We are here to recognize the presence of Jesus, who is always with us but much of the time quenched because we have not learned to be sensitive to Him. Thus, we practice being aware of His presence in these meetings.

- We ask questions about Jesus thoughts, emotions, desires, attitudes, motives, even words in response to our words, mostly to grow in knowing Him and learning to represent Him more accurately

- "Jesus, who do You say that we are?"

  - To articulate Jesus' most important Scripture-revealed thoughts about us

  - To practice articulating truth of Jesus to ourselves and others

  - To again keep our focus on the real presence of Jesus, who speaks by His Spirit

- "Assuming that what 'Alivia' said she thought Jesus might say to you is in fact from Him to you, would you like to say something back to Jesus?"

  - Create dialogue with Jesus

  - The full intention of the meeting is to be discipled by Jesus. In this context, He disciples us by speaking by His Spirit through His Word and Body. It is the responsibility of the facilitator to secure quality dialogue between Jesus and His disciples who have gathered.

- "What do you think Jesus thinks about you right now?" "What is your response to Him?"

  o This is important after a group member shares some behavior, either good or bad.

  o To keep all alert that the Spirit of Jesus may speak

  o Jesus is right now thinking about this particular person's value to Him and His behaviors, whether good or bad

  o To establish the truth of Jesus' love regardless of our success or failure.

  o To learn to dialogue with Jesus in groups and alone

- "What do you think Jesus thinks about the issue we are discussing?"

- "What are you thinking? Do you think that thought is from the Holy Spirit?" (Our thoughts? Could they be Jesus thoughts?)

- "Jesus, what are You thinking and feeling about what we are saying about You?" (Jesus thought's about our words)

- "Does anyone have something you think Jesus wants to say to Dawson?" Madison shares what she thinks to be Jesus' words for Dawson. "Group, do you think what Madison said to Dawson is actually from Jesus?"

  o Group needs to confirm or question if the message is from Spirit.

- We want to develop skills in listening for what Jesus might say to us through what others say.

- Our words _might_ be Jesus' words. We want to learn to consider the possibility. Our words, if we are following Jesus, are to be His Words[592]

- To learn to (humbly) speak our perception of Jesus' words to others

- To learn to test / discern the voice of the Spirit

- We want to keep the focus on the real presence of Jesus who, by His Spirit, may be speaking.

- "Dawson, do you think that what Madison just said is from Jesus? If so, would you like to say anything to Jesus in light of what we think He just said to you through Madison?"

- "What do you think Jesus thinks right now about Ellie?"

- "What do you think Jesus wants to say to Ellie right now?"

- "What do you think Jesus thinks right now about Ellie?

  - Jesus has thoughts about others; He may speak them for group member to say to others.

  - Group agree? "What do you think Jesus would say to her right now?"

- "What do you think Jesus thinks about this issue we are discussing?"

---

592 1 John 2:6 with John 8:28-29

- "Will you stare into Jesus' eyes and tell Him what you want to say to the person who is criticizing you?" Then ask Him what He wants you to say.

- "Alivia thinks Jesus wants her to get up at 5:00 every morning to be with Him. Do you agree or think that might be her own idea? If it is her own idea, do you think Jesus agrees with her?"

Overall, keep aware of the presence of Jesus and keep encouraging group members to bring their thoughts into the open in case it might be Jesus, to bring their thoughts to Jesus, to speak to Jesus (not a distant or impersonal force), and to listen for Jesus through the Scripture and through others. We are touched and changed by awareness of Jesus, and dialogue with Him.

LENGTH OF MEETING

90 minutes is generally best over the long haul. There is almost always too much to cover during a meeting. Remember, the goal is not to get through all the questions. The goal is to be discipled by Jesus, that is, to see and hear and respond to Him. What you do not cover this week, start with next week. Over the long haul, seek to work on each of the five questions about the same amount of time.

GROUP MEETING TRAINS FOR PERSONAL MEETING

Keep in mind that in facilitating the group meeting, you are training attendees to do on their own what you do as a group together. Speak regularly about this. You want them to be discipled by Jesus in the group so that they learn how to "sit at His feet" on their own. Encourage them to do a little bit well, and keep coming back tomorrow. "Well" means focus on and experience Jesus' presence with them. A consistent, brief time with Jesus is very helpful, and will grow naturally into lengthier meetings. Better to do a little and keep at it than to try to do a lot and give up in discouragement.

GROUP MEETING TRAINS TO COACH OTHERS IN BEING DISCIPLED BY JESUS

As group attendees are growing in being discipled by Jesus, both in the group you are facilitating and then by themselves with Jesus, keep reminding them that what they are watching you do they can learn to do with one of their children, or all their family, or others, both Christian and pre-Christians.

COACHING POTENTIAL DISCIPLEMAKERS

Watch for group member who are making good progress as Jesus' disciple. "Good progress" means he/she fairly consistently reports spending time alone being discipled by Jesus and reports growth in serving his family, church, and lost people. This level of seriousness as Jesus' disciple alerts you that he may be one Jesus may want you to further invest in (disciple). Invite him to facilitate part or your entire group meeting with Jesus. Watch. Take mental or actual notes (as inconspicuously as possible). After the meeting (or another time), coach by asking questions about what he did and why. You are helping him to help others be discipled by Jesus.

Another option for this disciple is to meet privately and have him lead you in the meeting. You can role play being the kind of person(s) who come to meetings to be discipled by Jesus. In that setting you can stop and talk about issues as they arise. It is a good way to equip him to disciple others. The primary downside (other than requiring more time) is if you prematurely select someone who says he wants help but ends up being unwilling to "jump out of the boat" to actually lead others to meet with him. Select prayerfully.[593] Put time limits on the process. "Let's meet for the next 13 weeks with the plan that at that time we will invite others to come to our meeting." The "best" others could be his wife and/or other family members.

CORE CONVICTIONS ABOUT BEING DISCIPLED BY JESUS
- Jesus gave volumes of time to being discipled by His Father[594]

---

593 Mark 3:14
594 Luke 3:22, 4:42, 5:16, 6:12, 9:18, 11:1, etc.

- Jesus so loves us that He painfully longs to disciple us for our sake

- Jesus is infinitely worthy of "our" time and deserves much more of our attention

- Jesus is actually present, is watching and listening, and values being included

- Jesus has the best "opinion" about our thoughts, desires, and circumstances, and He will share it if we need to know and if we will with faith ask Him to reveal His Truth[595]

- Jesus seldom forces His Truth in and through us; we must say "no" to all rivals for our thoughts,[596] and doggedly bring our thoughts to Him[597]

- We need coaching until we are obeying everything Jesus commanded, including making disciples

- Jesus wants to turn the world upside down through our being with Him[598]

- Jesus likes our company and is blessed by "hanging out" with us

- *"No person can do a great and enduring work for God who is not a person of prayer, and no person can be a person of prayer who does not give much time to praying." E.M. Bounds*

- *"Many Christians backslide...They are unable to stand against the temptations of the world, or of their old nature. They strive*

---

595 James 1:5-6, John 14:26, 16:13-15
596 Titus 2:11-12
597 Proverb 3:5-6, 2 Corinthians 10:5
598 Acts 4:13, Mark 3:14

to do their best to fight against sin, and to serve God, but they have no strength. They have never really grasped the secret: The Lord Jesus will every day from heaven continue His work in me. But on one condition—the soul must give Him time each day to impart His love and his grace. Time alone with the Lord Jesus each day is the indispensable condition of growth and power." Andrew Murray

CORE CONVICTIONS ABOUT BEING DISCIPLED BY JESUS IN A GROUP

- Without the group, we are prone to forget or give up on Jesus' narrow way

- Without the group, we miss making specific ministry commitments, prayer for ministry, and accountability

- Without the group, we miss the regular encouragement we need[599]

- Without the group, we miss the practice of listening and responding to the Holy Spirit

- Without the group, we have inadequate objectivity and discernment

- Without the group, we miss the coaching we need and learning to coach

- Without the group, we do not learn to experience Jesus' presence in others[600]

- Encourage one another daily[601]

---

599 Hebrews 3:12-13, 10:25
600 Matthew 18:20
601 Hebrews 3:12-13

FURTHER HELPFUL HINTS IN FACILITATING

- When someone says, "Jesus is a Friend," don't just stop there. Go deeper and invite person who spoke, and rest of group, talk about Jesus as a friend from scripture and from life experience ... then talk to Jesus about His being our Friend; sometimes imagine what Jesus is thinking, even saying, to us. Learn how to take what anyone says to deeper and deeper levels ... asking group to unpack what is being said

- When one person talks on and on and on ... and on , say, "Just a second ... what do the rest of you think about what he is saying?"

- Guard against group members counseling, including you as the facilitator: no one is allowed to give advice or teach without securing permission ... all must be encouraged to develop the skills of asking questions. The key concept: when I have counsel I feel compelled to give, I can think of what I want to say, and then ask an open-ended question about what I want to say to the person I want to counsel. This allows the Holy Spirit to speak, the person to think, to not feel "lectured," to learn to articulate, etc. It helps the question-askers develop leadership skills. Both the question asker and the question recipient are helped to mature through this process.

- When one person actually talks to or hears or dialogues with the Lord (either in praise, or thankful observing of Jesus' work, or dialoguing with Jesus through His Word, etc.,) the group can move on to next question because all have either experienced or observed, and thus somewhat vicariously experienced, connecting with the Lord. The point: everyone does not need to personally interact on every question.

- Keep coming back to the Person of Jesus … avoid the trap of talking about ideas or concepts or about behaviors or people … Jesus still says, "Come to Me."

- Facial expressions, eye contact, and hand motions are powerful influencers

Listen to this report from a volunteer youth pastor who spent one week being discipled by Jesus and learning to help others be similarly discipled:

"I just had to share more of what Jesus is doing here. Short version......A couple of girls in their late teens started attending our morning meetings a few weeks ago. They are not from our church and heard about the morning Discipleship time from other teens. Yesterday we had an especially moving meeting. One of the girls went home and told her mom about the meetings. Mom has been praying for God to provide a "program" for the college students in their church. This morning mom came to our meeting and she thinks that Jesus is asking her to lead the Discipled by Jesus meeting at their church for the college students. What a joyous time!!!

Also this morning, the wife of a Pastor from a non-denominational church that is 45 miles away came to meet with us. She had heard about the meeting from a teacher at her son's school.

Then.....A woman in OUR church came to me this morning and asked if I would help her begin facilitating a new Sunday School class that she has titled "Walking with Jesus and John". She thinks Jesus has asked her to start a Discipled by Jesus Sunday School class. That is huge for our church.

It is so exciting when we remove ourselves and make room for Jesus."

One Name of Jesus for Every Day of the Month

The reader is encouraged to discover and meditate on the names of Jesus. Listed below is a one name for every day of the month.

1. Advocate ("One called alongside to help", Intercessor)...I Jn. 2:1; Heb.8:24, 25

2. Alpha and Omega (Beginning and End)...Rev. 1:8; 21:6; 22:13

3. Anointed One...Isa.61:1; Lk.4:18

4. Beloved Son...Mt.12:18; Mk.1:11

5. Bread of life...Jn. 6:35, 48, 51

6. Bridegroom...Isa. 62:5; Hos. 2:19, 20; Eph. 5:25-30; Rev.19:9

7. Chief Cornerstone...Ps.118:22; Mt.21:42; Mk.12:10,11; Lk.20:17; Acts 4:11; Eph. 2:20; I Pet. 2:6-8

8. Christ...Mt.16:16-18; Jn. 7:26, 41

9. Creator...Gen.1:1; Jn. 1:2,3; I Jn. 1:1-3

10. Deliverer ...Ps. 18:2; Isa. 59:20; Rom. 11:26

11. Emmanuel/Immanuel ("God with us")...Isa. 7:14; Matt.1:23

12. Faithful and True...II Tim.2:13; Heb.3:2,6;10:23; Rev. 19:11

13. Good Shepherd...Ps.23; Isa. 40:11; 50:4; Jer.31:10; Eze.34:12,14,23,31; Mic.5:4; Jn. 10:11,14-16

14. Great I AM ...Ex. 3:14; Jn. 8:58

15. Holy One...Lev.11:44; Isa. 6:3; 30:15; Lk.4:34; Acts 3:14; I Pet. 1:16

16. Jealous ... 2 Cor. 11:2, John 21:15-17, Ex. 34:14, Dt. 4:24, 33:21, Josh. 24:19

17. Jesus...Mt. 1:21; Lk.1:31

18. King of Kings...Rev.17:14; 19:16

19. Lamb of God...Isa.53:7; Jn. 1:29; Acts 8:32; Rev. 5:12; 12:11

20. Light of the world...Ps. 27:1; Isa. 9:2; 49:6; 60:20; Mic. 7:8; Lk.2:32; Jn. 1:4,7,8; 8:12; 9:5; 12:35; Rev.21:23

21. Lion of the tribe of Judah...Rev. 5:5

22. Lord God Almighty...Rev. 1:8; 4:8; 21:22

23. Messiah (Christ, the great Deliverer of Israel)...Dan. 9:25,26; Jn. 1:41; 4:25

24. Most High God...Gen.14:18-20,22; Deut.32:8; Ps.9:2; 21:7; 82:6; 92:1; Lk.8:28; Heb.7:1

25. Only Begotten of the Father...Jn. 1:14,18; 3:16,18;Acts 13:33; Heb. 1:5; 5:5; 11:17; Rev. 1:5

26. Prince of Peace...Isa. 9:6;

27. Redeemer...Job 19:25; Ps.19:14;Isa.48:17; 49:7; 49:26; 59:20;60:16; Jer.50:34

28. Savior...Lk.2:11; Jn. 4:42; Acts 5:31; Eph. 5:23; Phil. 3:20; II Tim.1:10; Titus 1:4; 2:13; 3:6; II Pet. 1:1,11; II Pet.3:2,18; I Jn. 4:14

29. The Truth...Jn. 1:14; 8:32; 14:6

30. The Way...Jn. 14:6

31. The Word...Jn. 1:1,14; I Jn. 5:7; Rev. 19:13

CPSIA information can be obtained
at www.ICGtesting.com
Printed in the USA
FFOW05n2124131116